Contents

REIGN OF
FEAR

*Fiction and Film of
Stephen King (1982–1989)*

Edited by Don Herron

PAN BOOKS
London, Sydney and Auckland

First published in the United States 1988 by Underwood-Miller
First published in Great Britain 1991 by Pan Books Ltd.,
Cavaye Place, London SW10 9PG
9 8 7 6 5 4 3 2 1
© Tim Underwood and Chuck Miller 1988
ISBN 0 330 31347 9

Printed in England by Clays Ltd, St Ives plc

Part of 'Stephen King: The Limits of Fear' first appeared in
Knave, Vol. 19 No. 5, © Jo Fletcher 1987, and is reprinted by
permission.

'Digging It' by Whoopi Goldberg first appeared in the *Los Angeles
Times* and is reprinted here by permission of the author.

'Stephen King and the American Dream' by Burton Hatlen was
originally presented as a paper at the Maine Writers and
Publishers Alliance at the college of the Atlantic in Bar Harbor.

Portions of 'The King and His Minions' by Thomas M. Disch first
appeared in somewhat different form in *Twilight Zone*, and are
used by permission of the author.

Part of 'The Summation' by Don Herron first appeared in *Newsday*
under the title 'Ravening Beast Meets Losers', and is reprinted by
permission of the author.

REIGN OF
FEAR

Stephen King: The Limits of Fear

Interview with Stephen King by Jo Fletcher

Jo Fletcher: You write about fear, about putting ordinary people into extraordinary situations and watching the way they react. It permeates your work, but does it also play a major part in your real life?

Stephen King: Fear. Well, I will take you way past the stop sign, I will take you beyond the things you think you want to know about, right down into the very depths. I will touch your darkest phobias. You may *think* you want to know, but by the time you realize you don't – well, sorry buddy, but it's just too damn late . . . Deep down inside, most of us are afraid. I can still find fear – in fact, I can find more fear now than I used to. I'm afraid the world will blow itself up. I'm afraid of flying. I'm nervous when I don't know where my kids are and I'm still afraid of what's lurking under the bed. I write about fear. Other guys go to psychiatrists and pay a lot of dough to lie on an imitation leatherette couch and spout on about all their crazy terrors and weird ideas. Well, I get to do all that in my books and I get paid for it. It's sort of like expiation, if you will. It's a marketable obsession.

JF: Both your movie *Maximum Overdrive* and your latest novel IT have received pretty unenthusiastic reviews, even though the former is doing well in the provinces and IT hit the best-seller lists almost before it was published. Do you care about what the reviewers say? Does criticism bother you?

SK: Of course I care about reviews, and any writer or creative person who says he doesn't is a goddamned liar. And secondly, if they are really disregarding what the critics say, they are making a terrible mistake. Although the way the business is set up now—and it is a business; both criticism and creation have become *big* business—you have to take it with more of a grain of salt, because critics have a tendency to buy the celebrity syndrome, in the same way the public does. So you are evaluated on the basis of whatever your celebrity status seems to be. That's a bit like trying to get shortwave radio through an ionized atmosphere. It's ridiculous to have to deal with that, or to have a critic begin a review of a book or a film with "Stephen King, multi-zillionaire hack" or "horror writer," or whatever the label happens to be. It's stereotyping; it's a type of shorthand critics should be forbidden, and yet they are not. British literary critics are much less prone to it than Americans, but British film critics are much more prone to it.

The trade press reviews of IT over here in America were bad, but I think they were bad mostly because a lot of books review badly. I think at *Publishers Weekly* they jumped all the way up to $27 for a review. Now you can make $27 by reviewing THE BRAVE LITTLE TOASTER, which is 73 pages long, or you can make your $27 by being assigned IT, which is 1248 pages long, and it tends to put reviewers in a bad humor. But the trade reviews of IT really didn't make any sense. In one they said "King has written about seven stereotyped characters, in fact, each one is a type. There are two handicapped persons." Well, that makes sense, there is a stutterer and there is Eddie, who has asthma. And then you have a token woman, that's Beverly, and you have a token Jew, Stanley Uris, and you have a token fat kid, Ben, and a token black kid, Mike, and then they said there was a token gay or effeminate, and the only one left is Richie Tozier and Tozier has been married and there is this whole thing about his vasectomy that didn't work and if that's effeminism, I missed something somewhere. So it makes you wonder, did the reviewer read this book? Did he read the book I wrote? 'Cos the book I wrote was on what it's like to be a kid and what it's like to be a grownup and where the two meet. I thought that people would get off on that, and also on what it was like growing up in the '50s. So maybe they are reading the book they expect, the celebrity version or something. Maybe they are looking for a celebrity book; maybe they are looking for a bad book—I don't know. On the other hand, maybe I'm too close to it and maybe they're right.

JF: You are labeled a horror writer, and you are firmly placed on the horror shelves, and yet your best books work on many more levels. In a recent television interview, you stated very firmly that your next novel, MISERY, has no supernatural horror at all. Does this labeling bother you?

SK: You can call me anything you like, but I've always been a fairly subversive horror writer. I remember doing an interview about eight years ago, just after 'SALEM'S LOT, when the lady interviewing me said, "As a horror writer, do you think . . ." and then she stopped and kind of recalled it and said "Oh, do you mind?" It was as though she had said, "As a nigger, oh sorry, as a black . . ." And I said no, you can call me anything you like.

When people ask me if I am ever going to write anything else, well, I wrote THE DEAD ZONE, which is a love story, and I wrote THE STAND and FIRESTARTER and THE DEAD ZONE, which are all political novels, and THE GUNSLINGER, which is a high fantasy. To me a book is a book. Well, I get letters from 13 and 14-year-olds. Does that make me a children's novelist? Maybe, but that's fine.

JF: Do you write now to make money, or do you write because you have to?

SK: I didn't write EYES OF THE DRAGON with a view to publication, I wrote it for my daughter Naomi. Well, I have never offered anything for publication that I didn't feel warranted, but that is not to say that I never sat down to write something just on the chance that I might enjoy it. I think of writing as an act of communication with other people, as an act of getting in touch with them. And people seem to like what I do and I have always wanted to please other people. I was raised to please people. That was one of the things my mother taught me to do; that I was not to live life for myself is another way of putting it. That is not to say that my writing is a selfless act, because obviously it has made me very wealthy, not wealthy by the standards of the Vanderbilts. Vanderbilt himself, at the turn of the century, was heard to say that so-and-so, just because he'd become a millionaire, acted as though he were rich. I don't really think that any writer is going to become a Rockefeller or a Hughes, worth umpty umpty millions of dollars, but we are comfortable and that's nice.

But it's actually worth more to me, as a writer, when people write you a letter and say, "I stayed awake all night—you scared the shit out of me", or you get a letter from a woman who says, "My kid never read anything and now he's insatiable and he reads all your books; now he's even started to read some other things. Thank you." And your critical reward for that sort of reaction, to turning kids on that don't read, is to have *Time* magazine calling me the Master of Post-Literate Culture, which seems to me to be a little bit hard. But I guess I'll keep writing anyway.

And I should say that having this money means that I can go off and do other things if I want and that's great.

JF: One of the "other things" you have been involved with was the movie *Maximum Overdrive*, which you directed. Did you enjoy the experience?

SK: You know, Graham Greene, my favorite writer when he talks about writing, says a writer lives for 21 years, then spends the rest of his life writing about it. He said writers write books they can't find on library shelves. And that's why I made this picture: it was the kind of picture I'd go see, the kind I'd pay money for. It isn't the kind of picture like *The Big Chill* or *2001*, where people sit up all night and talk about it; it's just the sort of picture where you go see it and you say, yeah, that was good, that was fun.

In the cities, in New York, L.A., Washington, the critics lacerated it. I think a measure of my success at doing what I wanted to do was that the New York *Daily News* said they would give it zero stars, and furthermore, there was a bathroom scene that is vulgar beyond description, and I thought damn, I've succeeded! Once you get outside the big cities the reviews improved drastically, because I think people seemed to understand that what I was doing was in a spirit of fun.

JF: Did you enjoy the chance to direct your own movie, and is that something you would want to do again?

SK: Well, yes, I think I would do it again, but not for a long, long time. I mean really, I hated it—it was too much like real work. You're looking at a man who's been retired for ten years. I can't see myself doing it again until my children are all grown up. It took too much time. I was away, I wasn't a husband, I wasn't a father for a year. It would have been a little different if it had worked out the way we had foreseen. We thought that we would film the beginning of September, and the shoot would last through October and November and maybe the first two weeks of December, to make the movie on location in North Carolina, and to make it mostly outdoors. But we made it in the summer time and that was sheer insanity. Two of my three kids were at camp and for all of them to get down, my wife included, meant that they had to commute—which they did. I got a chance to come back once, for five days, which I did, but otherwise it was incumbent upon my wife to get in a private plane and shepherd the kids down so they could spend some time with their father. So it made things difficult for Tabby and it made it difficult for me, it made it difficult for the marriage and the kids and I just can't see going through that kind of thing again. Not under any circumstances while I have children that I can enjoy and a wife that I can enjoy. It would be one thing if she were a bitch and I wanted to get away, and it would be one thing if the kids were a bunch of spoiled rotten little monsters and I didn't like them, but the fact is I do and I like them better than the job. And I don't like having to work for a living. And that's what it is.

Y'know what? I discovered what a producer is. A producer is not only a man who funds pictures and puts packages together. He is the guy who directs from the comfort of his air-conditioned office, while you stand in the hot sun with sweat running down the crack of your ass and into your Keds.

I would spend the day out on set, then we would come back and Dino (De Laurentiis) would say, "Stephen, you comma-into-my-office." And he'd tell you what you were doing wrong and how to fix it and maybe you'd argue a little, and sometimes you'd win, but mostly he'd win. And nine times out of ten you'd realize at the end of it all that he'd been right. He is an honest man. He says what he's going to do and he stands by it.

JF: So what were the things that you enjoyed about making your own film?

SK: Blowing things up! No, really, it did have its highs. It was a pleasure to work with Emilio Estevez and Pat Hingle. And most of the people who worked for me and with me on the picture really put out. It was a pleasure to discover what actors could do, because my impression going in was that they spend about fifty percent of the time looking at their pretty faces in the mirror and about twenty-five percent on the West Coast screaming that their hairdressers were not there and so they couldn't do the part, and maybe about twenty-five percent of the time doing lines. So that was a real joy. Pat Hingle taught me much about directing, in a very gentle way. He was not going around saying, "Hey, you're wet behind the ears, I'm going to dry you off," it wasn't that way at all.

The first sequence of the movie features a bridge going up and there were two drawbridge keepers. One was a guy who was a fairly nice guy and the other was this woman who was like a dragon at the gate. The other guy would go as far as he could for us. I wanted to go up one day and do points of view shots for this dump truck driver at the top of this drawbridge. The bridge is counter-weighed and in reality you couldn't go up that far with a truck on it, but we asked the operator how high we could go up. And he asked how much the cameraman weighed, and how much I weighed, and how much the camera weighed, and then he said no problem, he'd take us up as high as we wanted. So the bridge goes up, very very slowly, and it's near the beginning of the shoot and I didn't understand that camera operators are suicidal—that's why they go to places like Viet Nam, and that's why sometimes they get killed. So we're going up and you can feel the machinery and some movement, but that sensation goes away very quickly because you get used to it. So I'm saying to the cameraman, like "How is it for you, darling?", you know, it's a bit like making love, and he says can we go a bit higher and I say sure. The only sensation I'm feeling, and like I'm getting off on this too, is feeling the weight shift from flat feet onto the balls of the feet and then onto the toes.

I don't know how much further he would have taken us, but finally I hear the continuity lady screaming "Stephen, for God-sakes, make him stop it, make it stop," and I hear a lot of other people yelling and screaming. And I looked around and we were up to about 57° and I felt this urge to just lie down and clutch at this grating. It was scary, but it was very exciting too. Oh, and I got to blow up a milk truck on my birthday—that was cool!

At the end of making the movie, Dino says to me, "Hey, Stephen, whenna-you-gonna make-a you next-a picture?" And I told him, "Dino, I think about the year 2000." But he said no, I'd want to do it again. He told me it's addictive, like cocaine. And he's right in lots of ways: there is an addictive quality to filmmaking and his simile is correct, it is not a benign addiction. But I can't see myself doing anything like this again, at least not until my family has all grown up. I want to be around to enjoy them while I can.

JF: You have fame, you have fortune, you have an ever-increasing row of books on the shelf: what ambitions do you have left?

SK: I don't have any long-term ambitions—stay alive, stay married, stay writing . . . I live day by day. I think perhaps I'm done writing about kids the way I have been doing, particularly in "The Body" and IT – in many ways the latter was an extension of what I'd been doing in the novella. One of the reasons I have written about kids so much is because I have my own, but they are growing up now, so my interest in childhood is fading.

You live your childhood twice if you have kids, once as you live it yourself and the second time as you raise your children and watch them. You get a kind of perspective on what your own childhood meant, what you went through. There is a need to finish being a child and I don't think that can be done until you have kids and they have finished with it completely.

At the same time, coincidentally, I think I am about done writing about monsters. It was like an orals exam: if I was going to say it, then I had to say everything I was going to say and screw the critics if they didn't like it. But I will listen to them, and if they don't like it, well, they won't have to face that sort of thing again.

Going back to Graham Greene again, the one time in my life I ever went against writers writing what they couldn't find on library shelves was when I wrote the fantasy for my daughter. She doesn't like horror stories and she had never read very much of my stuff and what she had read was because her mother sort of pushed her at it, like carrots, with the idea, well, this was a better way for her to know her father. And she did it, but not with much enthusiasm, so, I thought Goddamnit, if the mountain won't come to Mohammed...I knew that she liked fantasy, she had read some of the Conan comic books and Piers Anthony and stuff like that and in the end I really got into it. And I did her the courtesy of writing EYES OF THE DRAGON for myself too, because if you are writing just for someone else, you always write down.

JF: You obviously don't have much privacy any more: you are one of the highest profile writers around and I know you get mobbed at football games, or even when you're in the public lavatory. Is this making you more of a hermit?

SK: I'm still a fan at heart and one of the things which is real rough is not being able to go to a convention and go into the hucksters' room and look around, maybe pick up some copies of *Weird Tales* or other pulps without having people come up for autographs, or to talk about something they've written, or you've written. They're hitting on you all the time and you try to be polite and you try to talk to them but often you are just thinking to yourself "Why can't I be like these other people and just be allowed to browse?" You've become the browsee instead of the browser, kind of like a walking, talking book. But I haven't totally stopped going to conventions. I like to meet my peers, people like Peter Straub, Ramsey Campbell, Whitley Strieber. I like to sit around with these guys and shoot the shit and have a few beers.

So I haven't quit and I won't retreat from my own ideal, which is that I am no better and no worse than anyone else. I should be allowed to live a life which is not necessarily more private and not necessarily more public than anyone else's, but just simply a life.

I guess to me public life is when I leave this room and I walk down the street and someone I don't know just passes me and say, "Hi, Steve, loved your book," and walks on. That's just fine.

And I guess I am going to continue writing, but I think the public has got a bit of Stephen King overload at the moment, or will have by the time everything currently scheduled has come out, so I think it's about time to shut up for a while.

REIGN OF
FEAR

FOREWORD

by Dennis Etchison

Much has been written about Stephen King. This is not surprising, considering his phenomenal popularity. What is surprising, and disappointing, is the tenor of most of the articles, reviews and critical studies – thousands of pages by now, in length equalling or surpassing their subject's own prodigious output. Indeed they constitute a new publishing category, and their numbers multiply as restlessly as the closet coathangers in Avram Davidson's amusing and frightening "Or All the Seas With Oysters."

Less amusing, and too sad to be frightening, except possibly to King, is the naked profiteering that all-too-often motivates such ventures, not to mention the faint air of dishonor that accrues to their participants, who have jumped on the bandwagon in hopes, I suppose, that a bit of the glory will rub off on them. Some are attempts to connect the dots, explicating King's works in the style of good, gray senior English papers; others are recountings of personal inspiration upon first reading the Master, told as solemnly as parables of religious epiphany, as if the disciple were the focus of reader interest; still others are blatantly fawning puff-pieces masquerading as anecdotal histories of association and imagined friendship, rather in the manner of those Guest of Honor homages printed in science fiction convention program booklets. But to a greater or lesser degree almost all are embarrassments, lacking any real insight, original thinking, or dignity.

The present volume aims to remedy this sorry situation.

Over the past several years we have learned a great deal about this celebrated author. (The most interesting and illuminating material has come from Douglas Winter, Tim Underwood and Chuck Miller, and from King himself by way of his own refreshingly forthright interviews and essays.) We have seen the fanboy publications track each new film adaptation as obsessively as the compilers of pop charts in *Rolling Stone*. We have been lectured to about his place in "the field" and the value of his contribution to a literary tradition—curious both for the presumptions made about his purposes and the ultimate limitations to his career that such a parochial view implies; this sort of thing reminds me of nothing so much as a premature summary of a life in process, as though a priest were too busy delivering a eulogy to notice the dearly departed still very much alive and kicking.

Better, perhaps, to recall the words of André Gide, who implored: "Please do not understand me too quickly."

Too little, I think, has been said about the books and stories as artifacts or epiphenomenal accompaniments of a life, about the body of work as an expression of the man and his values, which are inseparable.

> Your fiction is an outgrowth of what you live, the same way that if, you know, what you piss... I mean if you've been eating certain things your pee turns yellow, and if you haven't been it's white or whatever it happens to be. *What comes out of your fiction is what you live.*

This is King speaking, from a taped conversation in 1979, when I met with him—and here I myself must risk appearing to play the game of fame by association—prior to my efforts at turning "The Mist" into a movie. (The film was never made, but the script was in turn adapted for radio by ZBS Media, who broadcast a 90-minute dramatization that was later released on audio cassette.) It had been our agent's idea, and with CARRIE already a resounding success at the box office and THE SHINING in production, it might have been possible to negotiate an expensive screen version of this short novel. Instead King imagined it in the style of those modest AIP flicks from the 1950s, or as close to the low-budget Roger Corman model as we could come twenty years later. We wouldn't need millions of dollars. Shoot it in a real market, he said; cut the Walker, if necessary, a six-legged behemoth so tall we never see the top of him. All we need for the lobster creature is a couple of claws. Substitute fog and suggestion for most of the special effects. Make it in sharp, glossy black-and-white — in other words, cheap — and focus on the relationships.

Money wasn't the point.

Neither were the scary monsters, which is not something you would expect to hear from an alleged horror writer.

No, his concern was the people. Like Brent Norton and Bud Brown and Mrs. Carmody and Mrs. Turman and even the bagboy. Or Ollie Weeks, who once won some money in the state lottery and bought a star-sapphire ring for himself because he didn't have a girlfriend to give one to. Or the protagonist, David Drayton, who so loves his son that he is willing to let go of everything, *including his wife*, to ensure the boy's survival. (This is not an easy plot solution. It is an example of the difficult choices a man must make under pressure. For some reason such authentic demonstrations of character are nearly always left out of the films made by others from King's works; they are present in "Children of the Corn," in the original story and in King's script, which is not the one that was finally shot, though I did retain them when asked to revise his final draft; and they are powerfully present in "The Monkey," shining through even, I hope, in the heavily-compressed radio play I must take the blame for. . . . One wonders whether there is room for action as a manifestation of character, which is the embodiment of moral values, anywhere in today's Hollywood.)

For me, King's ultimate selflessness is nowhere more apparent than in his attitude toward the rack-sized edition of DANSE MACABRE. The Everest House and Berkley trade printings

were successful enough to go directly into mass-market paperback when the time came with no further revision. But King
had accumulated a pile of letters taking him to task for certain
factual oversights or technical errors. Though he did not have
to bother, he carefully saved these letters and, because he was
snowed under with another project as the reprint was being
prepared, it fell to me to follow up on each and every one, and to
give credit in the text for the help he had received from his
readers, thanking them by name whenever possible.

Writers get letters. King gets a great many, not only because
his readers number in the millions but because of the special
relationship with them that he has engendered. I came away
from the DANSE MACABRE correspondence deeply touched.
The majority of these were not your usual fan letters. They were
personal communications of the kind most of us will see in our
lifetimes only from caring friends. They responded to his book
as if he had been writing directly to each of them.

I suspect that the level of intimacy King has with his readers
is unique among modern novelists. I wish it were the result of a
trick that the rest of us could learn, because this kind of connection is the goal of every artist, even more than the satisfaction of self-expression, which is pointless unless another
human consciousness is involved. It is proof of what can be
accomplished if you have kept faith with your audience.

King's audience trusts him, for reasons beyond the colloquial accessibility of his narrative voice, beyond the verisimilitude of his characters, beyond even the shrewdness that informs his most intense passages, when he is at one with his
prose, as in "The Woman in the Room" or the following from
THE STAND:

> He hammered along, arms swinging by his sides. He was known,
> well known, along the highways in hiding that are traveled by the
> poor and the mad, by the professional revolutionaries and by those
> who have been taught to hate so well that their hate shows on their
> faces like harelips and they are unwelcome except by others like
> them, who welcome them to cheap rooms with slogans and posters
> on the walls, to basements where lengths of sawed-off pipe are held
> in padded vises while they are stuffed with high explosives, to back

rooms where lunatic plans are laid: to kill a cabinet member, to kidnap the child of a visiting dignitary, or to break into a boardroom meeting of Standard Oil with grenades and machine guns and murder in the name of the people. He was known there, and even the maddest of them could only look at his dark and grinning face at an oblique angle. The women he took to bed with him, even if they had reduced intercourse to something as casual as getting a snack from the refrigerator, accepted him with a stiffening of the body, a turning away of the countenance. Sometimes they accepted him with tears. They took him the way they might take a ram with golden eyes or a black dog—and when it was done they were *cold*, so *cold*, it seemed impossible they could ever be warm again. When he walked into a meeting the hysterical babble ceased. . . . For a moment there would be dead silence and they would start to turn to him and then turn away, as if he had come to them with some old and terrible engine of destruction cradled in his arms, something a thousand times worse than the plastic explosive made in the basement labs of renegade chemistry students or the black market arms obtained from some greedy army post supply sergeant. It seemed that he had come to them with a device gone rusty with blood and packed for centuries in the Cosmoline of screams but now ready again, carried to their meeting like some infernal gift, a birthday cake with nitroglycerine candles. . . .

People know they can trust the man who dared to write this —*they know*. Trust him not to lie because it is easier sometimes than telling the truth, not to take the facile, melodramatic way out when the opportunity exists to say something honest about the real world, not to reassure with pious sentiment even in the face of the pure evil that threatens every heart. Trust him not to bullshit. Certainly not for money, which he does not need.

At that meeting in Maine, I asked what he would do if tomorrow morning every critic turned on him and the public stopped buying his books. Would he go on writing?

You can guess the answer.

What all this adds up to is more and less than comforting; it is a reminder to readers and writers alike that what is worth doing ought to be done, and can be done, for its own sake. These are traditional Yankee values, and King honors them every day in his life and in his work. Can't we? Only then will our lives and our literature be worth a damn.

DIGGING IT

Introduction by Whoopi Goldberg

*B*efore you open the book IT, there are a few traits you must possess.

1. You must have patience to follow the story. Like, through chapters that alternate from past to present.

2. You must have a keen memory for what happened to whom and when and why and how it all connects to what you're reading at the moment.

3. You must have a strong stomach. Some descriptions are so vivid they can replace will power for dieters.

4. You must have a sense of humor—ideally, a *strange* sense of humor.

All this, I stress, *before* you start reading Stephen King's longest and (take it from a longtime fan) most complicated book.

IT begins in 1957, eight months before the horrors begin and 28 years before the final showdown. We are introduced to one of the main characters, Stuttering Bill, early on. Bill's younger brother, George, is the first to succumb to It's wrath. After a flood in town, George is playing outside with a toy boat, watching it float down the street and eventually fall through a grating. He kneels down to look for it and hears a voice, the voice of a clown speaking to him. George reaches down to touch the clown and . . . is never seen again alive.

Next we find ourselves involved in a present-day murder investigation. The victim was gay. During the course of the investigation, we meet both the murderer and the victim's boyfriend. Both mention seeing a clown. One police officer, only one, contemplates the significance of the clown.

Now it's back to the past, where we begin meeting the other main characters, a group of kids growing up in a town named Derry. As the kids become aware of It and the harm It can cause, they begin to share their individual experiences. They develop camaraderie in the common fear and desire to eliminate It. The boys discover, too, that they share an admiration for Beverly. Experiencing the "firsts" together—first kiss, first *etc.*, they begin to take care of each other. Time passes. The bond among them strengthens.

Eventually, they grow up and go their separate ways, establishing themselves in successful careers all over the world and losing touch until they decide to reunite back in Derry. They have decided to figure out how to kill It and prevent It once and for all from doing any further harm.

As adults, the characters do not remember specific events that occurred when they were growing up. It is not until the Derry reunion that things begin to be revealed to them—and to us.

In a scene to be read in a well-lit room only, It confronts the group in a Chinese restaurant, approaching each character in turn, attempting to break down their confidence individually and collectively. King's characters are so real, you feel you are reading about yourself. And he has a tremendous ability to create fears that readers can identify with, the strange fears of childhood such as: Will the flesh fall off my face?

When Beverly returns to her childhood home, she is greeted by an old woman, who informs her that her father no longer lives there. The old woman invites Beverly in for tea. But during the course of the conversation, Beverly realizes that there is something distinctly amiss with this woman. Beverly becomes progressively more uncomfortable, and then odd things start to happen. The tea begins to taste strange. The woman slowly starts to disintegrate before Beverly's eyes. Horror fantasy? Yes, but if you have ever had a feeling that someone or something just didn't seem quite right, you will be able to relate to this incident.

I wait for each new King novel as an alcoholic waits for that next drink. I am addicted. If you are not, I suggest you introduce yourself to King's work through one of his earlier novels — CARRIE or THE SHINING. If, however, you are already a King addict, IT will overwhelm you.

KING OF THE COMICS?

Introduction by Marv Wolfman

S tephen King owes me big. He owes me a large percentage of his income, and one way or another I intend to get it. Why? How? Well, to explain, let's watch the calendar sheets clutter up the floor, let's observe the seasons slip by in reverse, and move back in time through cheap special effects.

So there I was – 1966, and I was a kid of maybe twenty and I was publishing four different fanzines, and pretty much losing money or just breaking even on all of them. Back then fanzines were reproduced on cheap ditto machines and you printed – if the ditto master held out – maybe one hundred fifty copies, maximum. I published *The Foob* – a funny-animal satiric strip about a bunch of little blue guys living in a fairytale village that is remarkably like the current day Smurfs; *Super Adventures*, which was a super hero fanzine filled with stories and articles on comics; *What Th–?*, an opinion and critique fanzine; and finally *Stories of Suspense*, a horror fanzine, featuring both comics and prose horror stories.

One day a friend named Jeff Gelb sent me a story he thought I should print, a little piece called "I Was A Teenage Grave Robber." The title immediately turned me off, but I enjoyed the story somewhat. A little predictable in places, but better than most of the stuff I had been sent. At any rate, I decided to print the story. I did, however, insist the title be changed, and so I took a line from the story "In a Half World of Terror," edited the piece somewhat, and had it typed up.

In my editorial for that issue I remarked that the story had the feeling of the kind of movies one saw on *Chiller Theater* or its like. There was little special in it, and I had no reason to remember the story again once I printed it and sent out my complimentary copies to its author, a kid named Steve King.

Many years passed and I became something of a name in comics for my work at DC Comics and Marvel, but especially for one comic I wrote for eight years called *Tomb of Dracula*. TOD (its initials, and the German word for death) was the first horror series published in comics. Previously, there was only horror anthology titles with non-connected stories.

I was immersed in writing Dracula stories as well as other tales when I received a letter from Jeff Gelb reminding me of that old fanzine I had done so many years before and that the writer of "In a Half World of Terror" was now not just teenage Steve King, but Stephen King, arguably the most successful writer in the twentieth century.

My reaction to that was roughly the same look you saw in the Mel Brooks movie, *The Producers*, when the curtain opens on "Springtime for Hitler." I scrambled back to my files and dug out the copies I had of *Stories of Suspense* #2 (now undoubtedly worth zillions), and even though the name listed was definitely Steve King, I had no reason to believe it was THAT Stephen King—after all his is not an uncommon name.

Needless to say, I eventually discovered that I had indeed published Stephen King's first short story, and after Jeff Gelb printed that fact in a weekly comics newspaper, everyone else seemed to know that as well, and congratulated me on my foresight and my ability to pick talent, and I'd smile as if I did indeed have some precognitive power.

Had I known what I was doing back then I would have printed more copies and saved them for sale today, or I would have signed up that kid to an exclusive contract, and I'd be rich instead of just available for writing articles on other writers' careers. There was little in special skill or knowledge that I've somehow been given that said this was some story of classic importance. Frankly, it was just an okay first effort and I had room in my fanzine. But, because somebody had to be first, and because I went on to be a semi-successful writer myself, there is this "*Isn't it a small world*" magic behind this.

So, the fact that I published Stephen King's first story isn't at all special. What was to come next, however, well, I doubt if even Justice Learned Hand himself would argue that I am completely responsible for Mr. King's subsequent career and, in fact, deserving of a percentage of his income for my work on his behalf.

Stephen King was a semi-starving teacher who in 1972 learned that I had been appointed editor of Warren Magazines, a black and white publisher of horror comic magazines. As Mr. King wrote to me years later, he needed money and felt that he could play up the fact that I had published a story of his several years before, and perhaps sell some comic scripts to me now. And so he sent off several story ideas.

Well, by the time Stephen King learned I was working for Warren Magazines, I had already quit and was working at Marvel Comics. My successor at Warren, a man who obviously didn't have my incredible foresight and uncanny judgment, never bothered to forward the stories to me, or to read them himself, or to reject the stories or to even write back to Mr. King that he had received the submitted material.

No receiving any reply from me, not knowing I had never seen his stories, King turned what were supposed to be comic book stories into very early prose sales. And that is why Stephen King owes me money—had I been at Warren Magazines I most likely would have fallen for Mr. King's blatant nostalgic pitch, I would have bought his stories, and today Stephen King would be a comic book writer and not the most prolific and probably wealthiest writer in the history of mankind. Surely, for my second bit of foresight—leaving a company before I could buy his material—Mr. King owes me . . . and owes me big. I'd say that was fair, wouldn't you? And if one of you convinces Mr. King of that fact, I'll give you, oh, say two percent of whatever I get.

In actuality, although all the statements above are true, Mr. King's interest in comics goes back long before his submission to *Stories of Suspense*. King was a fan of the EC horror comics of the fifties, and much of his work shows that influence. Indeed, *Creepshow* is an homage to those early EC stories, complete with the comic book look and poster by EC Artist Jack Kamen.

King, too, has written comics—for a special Stephen King magazine published by Marvel Magazines, and his comics work was crisp and clean and showed a strong understanding of the medium. I point that out because not all prose writers have been able to write comics. Mario Puzo, while waiting for money from THE GODFATHER, tried writing for Marvel Comics only to give up in hopeless confusion. Some incredibly talented science fiction writers have tried writing comics, only to fail to understand the needs of the comics medium. That one is a talented, or even a brilliant writer in one field does not mean that *ipso facto* the talent will translate into another medium. But King understood comics, and he understood how to write for them.

Then again, were it not for your humbleness here, *he* might very well be writing *Teen Titans* today and I might have written MISERY (if I had half his prose talent, of course, but let's not talk about that, shall we?).

At any rate, that's my connection with Stephen King, and how I obviously was brilliant enough to publish his first story and thereby assure myself a place in literary history. The connection is there, though even as I smile when people mention it in awe to me, I still keep thinking—'Why didn't I print *more copies*? I could clean up in the marketplace today!"

IN PROVIDENCE

Introduction by Frank Belknap Long

"The imagination is an eye—a marvelous third eye that floats free."
—King, DANSE MACABRE

*C*ircumstances seem to have a way, at times, of drawing together to create an unanticipated, close to miraculous occurrence. At the Fifth World Fantasy Convention in Providence, Rhode Island, over the weekend of October 12-14th, 1979, my role as Guest of Honor was shared by Stephen King. My presence on that occasion was largely by rote. In Texas the previous year I had been accorded the World Fantasy Convention's Life Achievement Award, their highest honor, established with the first convention, also held in Providence, in 1975.

We had just finished dining, and sat on the speakers platform overlooking the rest of the banquet assemblage, together with seven or eight others, soon-to-be-called upon. Although my reading of my co-Guest of Honor's work in general had been extensive, I had just perused, for the first time, THE SHINING and his quite extraordinary short story, "Children of the Corn."

For those moments as the repast drew to a close it was the chilling vistas opened up to me by the short story that I most wanted to discuss with him. I've always felt there is something about the cornfields of the Middle West that sets that region apart from all others in the United States. Miles upon miles of

15

blowing corn, providing evil sanctuary for every small, scurrying creature of the night, with the desolation alone, the immensity of it, casting a pall on human travelers, temporarily lost. . . .

King was turning the pages of a manuscript and his wife seemed unoccupied for the moment. I turned to her and said: "I thought 'Children of the Corn' a simply terrific story. It's curious, although it would have been no problem for me to hop a train and explore that region for myself, I've never done so. Not at any time in the past half century. After reading that story I began to understand *why*. Stephen has captured the spirit of the entire region as marvelously as he has done with the more ominously chilling, desolate regions of Maine. It's almost as if he felt just as much at home there."

"Yes," she said. "You're not the first to have stressed that. The story has just been made into a movie. We're both hoping it has turned out well."

She nodded toward her now unoccupied husband, aware that I wanted to talk to him directly about the story at more length. Before I could do so my turn to address the gathering arrived.

As I walked toward the center of the platform to address the assembled fantasy conventioneers, I experienced a kind of "let down" from the way I'd been feeling a moment before. Compared to the imaginative lift discussing "Children of the Corn" had given me, the notes I'd made for my talk seemed dull and uninspired. "This isn't going to be too good an address," I told myself. "If only I had something of dramatic importance to the whole body of *King's* work to anchor it on. If only—."

It was then that the near miracle happened. THE SHINING supplied what I needed most at precisely that moment, and the feeling of horror, mystery, fear and strangeness I'd experienced on reading it for the first time came flooding back into my mind. I've since been told that at least five or six recordings of my remarks were made, but I do not possess one, and reconstruct them from memory, certain that the substance remains unchanged.

I remember speaking slowly and weighing each word with care.

Since my arrival this morning, I said, I've found myself dwelling on a thought that must have occurred to many of you. I'm sure you couldn't have read THE SHINING without feeling that all hotels are, in at least a few respects, quite unlike the businesses you've customarily thought them to be. Such feelings as a rule present no problem, because you can dismiss them in short order as imaginatively fictional illusions. Before you do that, however, consider for a moment this banquet hall of the Biltmore Plaza Hotel in which we have all been dining.

On this platform with me sits the author of what is undoubtedly the most legend-haunted, terror-shadowed, time-paradoxical hotel in recent supernatural horror fiction, the Overlook. And surrounding him and all of us are other legends just as strange, dark or memory-haunted—literary phantoms that can only be thought of as imperishable.

It was here, in Providence, that Edgar Allan Poe courted Sarah Helen Whitman in his last tragic love affair, and was picked up in a badly shaken, almost helpless state and escorted back to his lodgings. And at this very moment from the Ancient Hill overlooking the town comes another presence, a ghostly form to most of you, but to me as alive as the last time he greeted me when I came visiting from New York. I have only to close my eyes for a moment to hear my good friend H. P. Lovecraft say: "Welcome to Providence Plantations at a very good time. I've been up since seven o'clock, because I knew when I received your phone call you'd be arriving early. I hope you can persuade your parents to stay a little longer this time. I'm going back to sleep now, but if you'll knock at my door at noon we'll take another look at the Shunned House, and settle that argument we had about it—"

As I stand here now the way I feel about the haunted hotel in THE SHINING is far from unrelated to just memories of the past. Seated in this hall—I do not say this to be flattering but simply state it as a fact—are at least twenty of the most talented writers and artists in the entire fantasy and supernatural horror story fields. And if hidden demons and dreads and secret fears and all manner of mysteries, hauntings in shadowlands remote in time, can sometimes escape from the mind and mingle, as has been claimed—well!

I beg you not to become too alarmed. A moment ago the base of this platform seemed to vibrate and shift a little, and my hand on this microphone became unsteady enough to be noticed, I'm sure. . . . But I'm refusing to let that disturb me unduly, and *I think it most unlikely we have anything to fear.*

I returned to my seat and another speaker took the microphone. King himself did not address that gathering, as he had an urgent appointment elsewhere, and I returned to my home in New York City later that evening.

It was during those moments in Providence that my views concerning Stephen King's writings solidified, and remain unchanged today. At that time he was just a little more than halfway to his present fame.

I am convinced that from a *purely literary* point of view, his best work bears the unmistakable stamp of authentic genius. To others some of his other qualities may seem of more importance—his immense popular appeal, his several bestseller triumphs or most important cinematic triumphs, but it is the very serious literary quality of his best work that, for my chips, will carry his fame, undiminished, well into the twenty-first century.

STEPHEN KING AND THE AMERICAN DREAM: ALIENATION, COMPETITION, AND COMMUNITY IN *RAGE* AND *THE LONG WALK*

by Burton Hatlen

I.

*I*n the preface to THE BACHMAN BOOKS, Stephen King tells us he began to write what can properly be regarded as his first novel in 1966, during his last year of high school. The original working title for this novel was GETTING IT ON, but when it was finally published in 1977 under the Richard Bachman pseudonym it was titled RAGE. King seems to have worked on RAGE intermittently during his undergraduate years. He told Douglas Winter in STEPHEN KING: THE ART OF DARKNESS that he "reworked GETTING IT ON during his Junior year"—i.e., 1968-69. And in the preface to THE BACHMAN BOOKS he says that he returned to the manuscript in 1970 and finished it in 1971. Exactly how much of RAGE was written in 1966, how much in 1968-69, and how much in 1970-71 is difficult to reconstruct at this time. But in any case the *conception* of the book seems to date from around the time King entered the University of Maine, and for this reason I feel justified in calling it his first novel.

During King's freshman year at the university (1966-67) he completed his second novel, THE LONG WALK, published under the Bachman pseudonym in 1979. Here a brief autobiographical note may be in order: King was a student in my Modern American Literature course in the Fall of 1967. One day after class he told me that he had written a novel, and asked if I would read it. That novel was THE LONG WALK, essentially complete as it was published, although King later changed a few details and added some new epigraphs to give the book a 1970s' aura. During King's undergraduate years at the University of Maine, he began other fictional projects. For example, he worked for over a year on a long novel called SWORD IN THE DARKNESS, which I also read in manuscript. But King regards this novel as a failure, and he has no plans to publish it. Around the time he graduated from the university, King completed another rejected novel, called BLAZE, which he has described as a "reworking of Steinbeck's OF MICE AND MEN." But RAGE and THE LONG WALK are the only novels that King wrote before CARRIE which he regards as worth saving.

What critic Michael Collings calls "the Stephen King phenomenon" begins with CARRIE, the novel in which King first created that blend of gritty social realism and supernatural horror which is his unique contribution to American fiction. In RAGE and THE LONG WALK, King is beginning to move toward the territory that he would make his own, but only somewhat tentatively. Neither novel proposes the kind of supernatural premise which we find in CARRIE, 'SALEM'S LOT, THE SHINING, or FIRESTARTER. Rather, in RAGE King attempts to work, a bit clumsily, within the conventions of the "mainstream" or "realistic" novel, while in THE LONG WALK he moves—more confidently, I think—halfway into the territory of science fiction.

Both RAGE and THE LONG WALK are also more self-consciously "literary" than the later books; and as King notes in his preface to THE BACHMAN NOVELS, both books are laden with "windy psychological preachments (both textual and subtextual)." Nevertheless, these two early novels already possess that sense of narrative pace which we find in all of King's work, and which seems to be an innate gift. Further, these early novels can tell us, I believe, a great deal about the preoccupations of the *young* Stephen King, a writer who was as yet neither rich (indeed, he was very poor) nor (except within the University of

Maine community, where he *was* well known) famous. These preoccupations are largely social and even political, although the language of these novels sometimes veers into a somewhat superficial Freudianism. Many of these social and political concerns reappear in the later novels, but in RAGE and THE LONG WALK such concerns are in the foreground, whereas in some of the more supernatural novels they move into the background. In this respect a study of the social and political implications of these early novels can help bring into focus certain qualities of the later novels that are sometimes overlooked.

King wrote these books in the late 1960s, the years of the Counter-Culture, the New Left, and the great wave of youth protest against the Vietnam War—the years of "the Movement," which crested in the nationwide war protests of Spring, 1970, and which ran out into the sands in the McGovern debacle of 1972. King spent those years in and near Orono, Maine—not exactly the Berkeley of the East, but the home during this period both of a lively SDS chapter and a burgeoning drug culture. In 1969 and 1970 the campus was the scene of several war protest demonstrations and two student strikes, one in protest of the firing of two radical sociology professors and another during the Cambodian spring of 1970, when the student movement briefly transformed the University of Maine, along with most other American universities, into a non-stop teach-in on American imperialism.

King's relationship to these movements was decidedly ambivalent. King had grown up in a Maine mill town, raised by a mother who was intermittently dependent on AFDC and who for a long period supported her two sons by working in the kitchen of the Pownal State Hospital. With such a background, he was understandably skeptical of the "more radical than thou" stance which became, in the last years of the 1960s, fashionable among upper middle class young people. When student protestors screamed abuse at the "pigs," when the hard hats organized counter-demonstrations to shout down the student radicals, at least some of King's sympathies were with the police and the hard hats. Yet as a student government leader and a very visible figure on campus (columnist for the student newspaper, actor in Maine Masque plays, *etc.*), King knew well the leaders of the student anti-war movement, including the two SDS leaders who in the Fall of 1969 publicly announced their decision to join the Communist Party. King himself, after some hesitation, voiced his opposition to the war, and I have a vivid memory of him sitting on the edge of the stage in Hauck Auditorium, watching (along with hundreds of other students) as the Arts and Science faculty debated whether to support the student strike, and applauding wildly when the faculty "radical" carried the day. During these years, he also experimented with most of the drugs circulating on the campus, and his hair and beard were long and lank. Indeed, he briefly considered giving up his hopes of a teaching career when Hampden Academy refused to permit him to begin his student-teaching assignment until he had cut his hair and beard. While King stubbornly preserved his loyalty to the world of millworkers and hard hats, then, he also immersed himself in the student culture of the 1960s, and the radical currents running through that culture certainly touched his thinking.

An incident from 1968 typifies King's ambivalence toward the "conservative" and "radical" currents in the America of that epoch. In this election year, King at least briefly decided to support Nixon, and he went to a meeting of Students for Nixon, where he was, he afterwards told me with considerable delight, the only long-hair in the room. King's impulse to support Nixon suggests the pull within him toward traditional American values, even toward "Americanism." At the same time, his hair and beard represented to him, as to other young people of that moment, a symbolic protest against the hypocrisy of the American establishment.

A similar ambivalence is, I believe, at work in the two novels which King has saved from this phase of his life. These novels develop a searingly critical view of American life. Specifically, the books see American society as forcing young people to forego their natural impulse toward community and to commit themselves instead to a dog-eat-dog battle for "success," or even merely for survival. Yet the rage against the powers that be, even against the adult world itself ("don't trust anyone over thirty," the proponents of the Youth Culture proclaimed), which runs through these books in the end comes to nothing. In these novels the structure of American society is presented as, however violent and hypocritical, nevertheless inevitable, and all of King's young rebels are defeated or destroyed. Further, the rebels themselves are often ambiguous figures, for they buy into the very dream of success which American society uses to manipulate the young, and they are often infected by the spirit of competition and the pervasive violence characteristic of American society at large.

These novels are not, then, revolutionary texts. Rather they are small tragedies, in which flawed but sympathetic human beings come into conflict with a society which insists upon dividing human beings into "winners" and "losers," and which thereby frustrates the hunger of all people, especially the young, for community.

II.

RAGE centers on Charlie Decker, a high school student who feels a not unjustified rage against his brutal father, but who acts out his anger against all adults. The immediate objects are the principal and two teachers at the Placerville, Maine, high school which Charlie attends. After venting enough verbal abuse (most of it sexual) on the principal to get himself expelled from school, Charlie goes to his locker, loads a handgun stolen from his father, walks into his algebra class, and shoots the teacher dead. A little later, he shoots another teacher through the classroom door. Then Charlie spends most of the day conducting "class" for his fellow students. By the end of the day, all but one have come over to Charlie's view of the world. The classroom becomes a liberated zone, where the young can tell one another the truth about their lives.

Indeed, most of the novel is given over to extended flashbacks. In several of these Charlie narrates to his classmates episodes from his own life. Some of these stories elaborate Charlie's relationship with his parents. Charlie's father, we learn, was committed to a macho ethnic which led him to treat women with contempt, and to abuse his son as what young people of the 1980s like to call a "wimp," while Charlie's mother passively accepted this abuse, and tried to force her son to live up to certain arbitrary norms of respectability. In other flashbacks, Charlie narrates some of his earlier rebellions against adult authority and tells of a visit to the University of Maine campus, where he briefly immersed himself in the drug- and rock-saturated youth culture of the period.

As Charlie tells the story of his life, several of his classmates gradually join in, to reveal what they feel about one another, sex and the adult world. Only one student refuses to participate: Ted Jones, handsome, confident, a football player, the boyfriend of the most beautiful girl in school. Charlie, who in the adolescent political maneuverings of Placerville High has heretofore been a distinct outsider, gradually unites the class against Ted Jones, and leads them in a kind of ritual sacrifice. The members of the class attack Jones not only physically but (although how this happens isn't fully clear) also psychologically, and he is reduced to a state of blubbering catatonia—which is, the novel implies, permanent. Having destroyed Jones, Charlie decides that he has achieved what he set out to do, and he allows his classmates to leave.

Charlie then confronts the state police captain who has commanded the forces besieging the school, and who has come to embody official Authority, tricking the captain into shooting him. Charlie does not die—in part because the novel is written in the first person, so Charlie must live on to tell his story. At the end we leave Charlie in the mental hospital where he will, presumably, spend the rest of his life. But the final chapters also suggest that Charlie has permanently changed the lives of some of his classmates. His only real friend goes on to become an English major at Boston University—in the terms of this novel, a clear act of rebellion. And another classmate becomes a political radical, and attempts to "brain Robt. Dole with a Gus Hall campaign sign." The ripples of Charlie's moment of rebellion thus continue to spread.

As my plot summary suggests, RAGE consistently portrays the adult world as brutal and hypocritical. The principal embodiment of this world, a walking symbol of Patriarchy, is Charlie's father. In the first flashback of the novel, Charlie recounts a conversation which he overheard at age nine, when his father, intending to "make a man" of his son, took Charlie along on an all-male deer hunting trip. (For King as for Faulkner and Michael Cimino, the deer hunt is the supreme ritual of American machismo). In the conversation, sexuality and violence blend together:

> ". . .You know what I'd do if I caught somebody with my wife?"
> "What, Carl?" That was Randy Earl.
> "You see this?"
> A new shadow on the canvas. My father's hunting knife, the one he carried out in the woods, the one I later saw him gut a deer with, slamming it into the deer's guts to the hilt and then ripping upward, the muscles in his forearm bulging, spilling out grue and steaming intestines onto a carpet of needles and moss. The firelight and the angle of the canvas turned the hunting knife into a spear.
> "You see this son of a bitch? I catch some guy with my wife, I'd whip him over on his back and cut off his accessories."
> "He'd pee sitting down to the end of his days, right, Carl?" That was Hubie Levesque, the guide. I pulled my knees up to my chest and hugged them. I've never had to go to the bathroom so bad in my life, before or since.
> "You're goddam right," Carl Decker, my sterling Dad, said.
> "Wha' about the woman in the case, Carl?" Al Lathrop asked. . . .
> The hunting knife that had turned into a spear moved slowly back and forth. My father said, "The Cherokees used to slit their noses. The idea was to put a cunt right up on their faces so everyone in the tribe could see what part of them got them in trouble."

Horrified by this model of masculinity, Charlie "wants his mother."

On a psychological level, the novel asks us to believe that the sight of the knife in his father's hand creates in Charlie what Freud would call a castration complex. But we never get far enough inside Charlie to become seriously interested in his psychological processes, and so the recurrent emergence of such Freudian hypotheses becomes, as King himself has noted, an annoying distraction in the novel.

Yet in the quoted passage King creates a resonant image of

American machismo. And Charlie's revulsion from this masculine ritual, climaxing when his father finally kills a deer, *is* persuasive. Watching his father rip open the deer's belly, Charlie

> . . .turned around and heaved up my breakfast.
> When I turned back to him, he was looking at me. He never said anything, but I could read the contempt and disappointment in his eyes. I had seen it there often enough. . . .

To Carl Decker, Charlie's behavior at this moment suggests a lack of "manhood," and in some measure King seems to share this judgment: on his visit to the University of Maine campus, Charlie tells us later, he attempted intercourse with a "hippie" girl, only to discover that he was impotent. But what comes through most strongly in the hunting episode is King's judgment, not of Charlie himself, but of Charlie's father, whose equation of masculinity with violence is defined for us as perverse and destructive.

Nor does Carl Decker direct his violence only toward deer. In another flashback we learn that at age four Charlie decided to break all the storm windows which his father had lined up around the house, preparatory to hanging them. Catching Charlie in the act, Carl Decker picks up the boy and throws him to the ground as hard as he can. A moment later he is apologizing, but the incident seems to give Charlie a model for expressing rage in acts of violence. And in the final confrontation between the two, Carl Decker attempts to strike his son with rake—only this time Charlie fights back. In his commitment to a macho ethic, it should further be noted, Charlie's father is typical of several men in the novel—especially Captain Philbrick of the Maine State Police, who becomes Charlie's principal antagonist in his climactic act of rebellion. And it is Philbrick who finally shoots Charlie—thus doing what Charlie's father apparently wanted to do all along.

If Carl Decker and Captain Philbrick represent the brutality of American society, other adult characters, especially the teachers and the officials of Placerville High, exemplify the hypocrisy of that society. Here the principal issue seems to be sex:

these exemplars of propriety are determined to keep sex a dark, dirty secret, and Charlie is no less determined to unmask these hypocrites. Summoned to the principal's office to receive the school administration's judgment of him, Charlie demands instead that the principal, Mr. Denver, look into his *own* soul:

> Mr. Denver had gone on, something about proper counseling and psychiatric help, but I interrupted him. "Mr. Man, you can go straight to hell."
>
> He stopped and put down the paper he had been looking at so he wouldn't have to look at me. Something from my file, no doubt. The almighty file. The Great American File.
>
> *"What?"* he said.
>
> "In hell. Judge not, lest ye be judged. Any insanity in your family, Mr. Denver?"
>
> "I'll *discuss* this with you, Charlie," he said tightly. "I won't engage in—"
>
> ". . . immoral sex practices," I finished for him. "Just you and me, okay? First one to jack off wins the Putnam Good Fellowship Award. Fill yore hand, pardner. Get Mr. Grace in here, that's even better. We'll have a circle jerk."
>
> "Wh—"
>
> "Don't you get the message? You have to pull it out sometime, right? You owe it to yourself, right? Everybody has to get it on, everybody has to have someone to jack off on. You've already set yourself up as Judge of What's Right for Me. Devils. Demon possession. . . . Why don't you admit it? You get a kick out of peddling my flesh. . . .

Mr. Denver, the archetypal bureaucrat, custodian of The Great American File, actually "gets it on" by "jacking off on" the students over whom he rules—this is how Charlie sees it, at least.

Charlie further suggests that Mr. Grace, the school psychiatrist, is no less perverse in his behavior, and no less blind to his own motives. After the shooting, Mr. Grace attempts to talk to Charlie over the school intercom. "Let us help you," Mr. Grace begs, but Charlie replies sardonically, "By letting you help me, I would be helping you"—that is, he would be confirming Mr. Grace in his "official" role. And in the course of their conversation, Charlie systematically shifts the focus away from Charlie's presumably disturbed behavior and onto Mr. Grace's own sexuality:

> "How long have you been a practicing psychiatrist?"
> "Five years."
> "Have you ever eaten your wife out?"
> "Wh . . ." Terrified, angry pause. "I . . . don't know the meaning of the phrase."
> "I'll rephrase it, then. Have you ever engaged in oral-genital practices with your wife?"
> "I won't answer that. You have no right."
> "I have all the rights. You have none. . . ."
> "No!"
> "Has your wife ever had an affair with another man?"
> "No."
> "Another woman?"
> "*No*. . . ."
> "Has your wife ever given you a blow-job, Don?"
> "I don't know what you—"
> "You know goddamn well what I mean!"
> "No, Charlie, I—"

Charlie's responses to Mr. Denver and Mr. Grace suggest that he sees the "helping behavior" of these adults as merely another power trip. These adults do not beat him or threaten to shoot him, but they too want to control him, and impose on him their assumptions about proper human behavior. Charlie refuses to recognize their authority, for they are, he believes, lying to themselves and to everyone else about their own motives and about what sort of people they are, and therefore they are as unworthy of trust as the more overtly violent Carl Decker and Captain Philbrick.

King's consistently negative portrait of the adult world swings our sympathies toward Charlie, who becomes the embodiment of a justifiably rebellious younger generation. Among college students of the late 1960s, a self image of the young as being heroic by virtue of youth alone was widespread. RAGE, as I read it, vividly dramatizes the feelings of that epoch. These feelings all circle around Charlie, who becomes heroic simply because, in the face of the violence and hypocrisy of the adult world, he insists on *speaking the truth*.

The other young people in the novel, except for Ted Jones, share this hunger for the truth. For the adults, as the passage quoted above suggests, "getting it on" (the original working title of the novel, and a phrase that recurs like a refrain in the published version) means exercising power over someone. For the "kids," "getting it on" means, initially at least, simply telling the truth. Charlie's classmates have so deeply repressed their sexual fears and their anger at the humiliations which they have endured that the very opportunity to say what they feel induces in them a kind of ecstasy. Here, for example, is a boy nicknamed Pig Pen, expressing his feelings toward his mother:

> "She grinds and grinds and grinds, and she always beats you. Be-Bop pencils that break every time you try to sharpen them. That's how she beats you. . . . and she's so *stupid* that you know everybody laughs at her behind her back. So what does that make me? Littler and stupider. . . . I don't think I'd mind if she snuffed it. . . . I wish I had your stick, Charlie. If I had your stick, I think I'd kill her myself."

So, too, the girls in the classroom finally reveal how deeply alienating they have found their sexual experiences up to this point in their lives. Carol Granger tells her classmates that the sound of a voice yelling "Hi, cunt" to her from a car made her feel that her whole life was "wrecked. Spoiled. Like an apple you thought was good and then bit into a worm hole. 'Hi, cunt.' As if that was all there was, no person, just a huh-h-h. . . . And that's like being bright, too. They want to stuff things into your head until it's all filled up. It's a different hole, that's all." And a little later Sandra, Ted's girlfriend, tells her classmates that sex with Ted made her "feel like a doll. Not really real." Sandra then tells of a casual sexual encounter with a stranger who picked her up at a dance, and she says that this experience was "very real. I can remember everything—the music, the way he smiled, the sound his zipper made when he opened it." And then Sandra adds, "But this has been better, Charlie."

A chance to "tell it like it is," as we used to say in the 1960s—this is what Charlie offers his classmates. And telling it like it is allows them to escape, at least briefly, from the alienation that has heretofore been the condition of their lives. Since it is

Charlie's actions that make it possible for others to speak the truth in this way, he emerges as a kind of hero.

Further, the story of Charlie's visit to the University of Maine establishes him as a representative of an entire "youth culture" which is, like Charlie in the classroom, dedicated to affirming the truth in the face of adult hypocrisy. In this chapter Charlie finds himself, for the first and only time, in a world of kindred spirits: indeed, he describes his visit to Orono as "the last really happy time I can remember." In Orono he has a first, ecstatic experience with grass, and discovers a music (bluegrass) which speaks for him. Charlie then moves on to a totally '60s party ("Dana produced a huge scrolled waterpipe from a low bookcase that was fairly groaning with Hesse, Tolkien. . . .") where he has his first, albeit unsuccessful sexual experience. In this counter-culture world, we are to believe, people are honest about their sexuality, and if Charlie had been able to get past his hangups maybe he wouldn't have had to shoot anyone. The Woodstock generation liked to see itself as having achieved a freedom, spontaneity, and honesty unprecedented in the history of the world, and his description of the Orono party scene suggests that King accepted these claims, at least in part.

Yet while Charlie is in certain respects a hero, his impotence at the Orono party also suggests that he has been crippled by the cultural conditioning imposed on him by his parents. In his own view (and it would appear, in King's as well, to some degree) Charlie has been dreadfully put upon by the world, to the point where he is a sacrificial victim, a scapegoat. Charlie's father loathes his son. At times the senior Decker seems to see Charlie as evil, and some of the latter's behavior may be motivated by a perverse desire to prove his father right: "OK, you tell me I'm bad, so I'll be *really* bad." At other times Carl Decker treats his son with contempt, as a sissy. Charlie has entered adolescence with a severely damaged ego. The non-parental adults that he has met in school haven't helped matters any, for Charlie sees these adults as "getting it on" at his expense, as "jacking off" on him. In short, Charlie sees himself as a victim of the adult world, which has systematically eroded his sense of self.

As Charlie sees it, he has been victimized not only by adults but by other young people who have bought into the adult value system. At least, such seems to be the primary point of a long flashback in which Charlie tells the story of the corduroy suit. At age twelve, Charlie was invited to a birthday party for Carol Granger, and his mother forced him to wear the suit. Charlie "had a little crush on Carol," and so he was particularly anxious to look confident and competent. But as he had surmised, no one else at the party is wearing a suit, and instantly Charlie begins to "feel stupid." Some of the children make comments about the suit, and finally Charlie ends in a fight with Dicky Cable:

> He was astride my back in no time. I tried to turn, but I couldn't.
>
> I couldn't. He was going to beat me because I couldn't. It was all senseless and horrible. I wondered where Carol was. Watching, probably. They were all watching. I felt my corduroy coat ripping out under the arms, the buttons with the heralds embossed on them ripping off one by one on the tough loam. But I couldn't turn over.
>
> He was laughing. He grabbed my head and slammed it into the ground like a whiffle ball. "Hey, pretty boy!" *Slam*. Interior stars and the taste of grass in my mouth. . . . "Hey, pretty boy, don't you look *nice*?" He picked my head up by the hair and slammed it down again. I started to cry.

Finally, Charlie's friend Joe McKennedy pulls Dicky Cable away from Charlie.

Joe, to whom we are introduced on the first page of the novel, seems an anomalous presence in RAGE. Charlie says that Joe "was a friend, the only good one I ever had," because Joe was never "revolted by my weird mannerisms." Joe was, it seems, one of the most popular kids in school, and "because everyone liked Joe, they had to at least tolerate me." But Joe, for reasons never explained, is not present on the day that Charlie takes over the school. In effect, the "straight" friend of the "weird kid" that we see in several King novels—Dennis in CHRISTINE is a clear example—is here split into a "good" version and a "bad" version, Joe and Ted Jones respectively. And in the scene within the school, the "good" friend is exiled, leaving the weird kid free to act out his latent hostility against the "straight" kid.

But Joe's rescue of Charlie merely compounds his humiliation, and he runs from the party to hide in an empty house and cry. This incident becomes emblematic of Charlie's entire life. He was, as the chorus sings in Handel's MESSIAH, "despised and rejected of men, a man of sorrows and acquainted with grief"—i.e., a kind of Christ figure. Along with being an heroic truth-sayer, then, Charlie is also a victim of a world which in various ways "gets it on" by dumping on him. Between these two roles Charlie oscillates for much of the book. But note that both as hero and as victim Charlie remains innocent.

However, the sympathy for Charlie which King evokes is by no means unqualified. Charlie may long for a world of truth and love, and he may even create such a community for a moment, but that community is destroyed as much by its own internal dynamics as by the adult world outside the school. For Charlie is not only both hero and victim. He is also, King regularly reminds us, crazy.

In the years around 1970 when King was finishing this novel, Manson's murder cult was much in the news, and Charlie Decker shares more than a common first name with Charlie Manson. Decker's killings, like Manson's, are random and cruel, and the fact that both Charlies kill in the name of a vision of love cannot excuse the brutality of the act itself. Throughout the scene in the classroom, the body of Mrs. Underwood, high school algebra teacher, is lying under Charlie's feet, and at one point he realizes that he has added insult to injury by casually leaving a footprint on her body. Of all the possible objects of Charlie's rage, Mrs. Underwood seems the *least* culpable, as Charlie himself acknowledges. Thinking of his father, he says, "I wish it was him I'd killed, if I had to kill anyone. This thing on the floor between my feet is a classic case of misplaced aggression."

King's ambivalence toward Charlie emerges most clearly in his detailed description of his protagonist's transformation from victim into victimizer, scapegoat into scapegoater. For there are *two* primary victims in this novel, Charlie and Ted

Jones. The relationship between these two parallels certain male/male relationships in other King novels, including CHRISTINE: the straight kid and the weird kid, the insider and the outsider, Dick and Tommy Smothers, Shem and Shaun. But if Dennis in CHRISTINE is the object of Arnie's ambivalent love, RAGE is (like CARRIE later) a version of THE REVENGE OF THE NERDS, for Charlie loathes Ted and deliberately sets out to destroy him.

Charlie's hatred of Ted seems initially justified. Ted has bought into the adult world that Charlie detests, and he is totally confident of his strength and his sexual prowess. At one point, Charlie asks himself what has evoked all this hatred within him. He replies, "Maybe it was only Ted himself, handsome and brave, full of the same natural *machismo* that keeps the wars well-attended. Simple jealousy, then. The need to see everyone at the same level, gargling in the same rat-race choir, to paraphrase Dylan. *Take off your mask, Ted, and sit down with the rest of us regular guys.*"

In Ted's bland self-assurance, Charlie at one point sees a younger version of his father:

> Ted was grinning at me, but I don't think he knew it. I looked at his face, at the flat, conventionally good looking planes of his cheeks, at the forehead, barricading all those memories of summer country-club days, dances, cars, Sandy's breasts, calmness, ideals of rightness; and suddenly I knew what the last order of business was; perhaps it had been the only order of business all along; and more importantly, I knew that his eye was the eye of a hawk and his hand was stone. He could have been my own father, but that didn't matter. He and Ted were both remote and Olympian: gods. But my arms were too tired to pull down temples. I was never cut out to be Samson.
>
> His eyes were so clear and so straight, so frighteningly purposeful — they were politician's eyes.

Absolutely confident, complacent, infinitely condescending — such is Ted Jones. And those of us who spent our high school years as outsiders may empathize with Charlie's hatred of Ted.

Within the classroom, Charlie and his classmates are eventually united in their shared sense of alienation from the adult world, and by a recognition that all of them have felt degraded, humiliated, flawed in one way or another. At this point Ted Jones, who will admit neither his own weaknesses nor the corruption of that "real" world beyond the classroom, becomes the enemy: and in the climactic scene of the novel, everyone gathers around Ted, to subject him to a ritual humiliation. The beating reduces Ted to a state of drooling idiocy, and one of the epilogue chapters suggests that two months later he is still in a "flat-line catatonic state with some signs of deterioration." Thus it is Ted —not Charlie himself or even Mrs. Underwood—who becomes the ultimate victim in this book, the victim, not of the violence and hypocrisy of the adult world, but rather of the rage of the "kids" themselves.

The scene in which Charlie and the other students turn on Ted Jones is, as Michael Collings has noted in STEPHEN KING AS RICHARD BACHMAN, chillingly reminiscent of "The Lottery" (Shirley Jackson was one of King's favorite writers during his undergraduate years) as well as of the opening scene of CARRIE. "The Lottery," CARRIE, and RAGE all turn obsessively on the theme of scapegoating, the propensity of human communities to derive their strength from subjecting certain individuals to a ritual victimization. And King's description of the sacrifice of Ted Jones makes clear the dynamics of victimization:

> They were smiling at Ted, who hardly looked human at all anymore. In that brief flick of time, they looked like gods, young, wise, and golden. Ted did not look like a god. Ink ran down his cheeks in blue-black teardrops. The bridge of his nose was bleeding, and one eye glared disjointedly toward no place. Paper protruded through his teeth. He breathed in great white snuffles of air.
>
> I had time to think: *We have got it on. Now we have got it all the way on.*
>
> They fell on him.

The young people in this room can become "gods" only by reducing one of their number to something less than human. Indeed, the final phrase in the quoted passage suggests that they have turned into vampires, and both the image and the cadences of the language here anticipate 'SALEM'S LOT. And it seems to me important to recognize that the victimizers in this scene are, not the oppressive and repressed representatives of the adult world whom we have met in the course of the book, but rather the members of the youth culture itself.

There are at least two ways in which we might read this scene. On the one hand, we might see Charlie and his confederates as simply doing to Ted Jones what people like Carl Decker and Mr. Denver have done to them. Taught by his father that rage and violence are normal, Charlie has, in attempting to rebel *against* his father, ended by acting just as his father would like to act: "The sins of the fathers. . . ." Such a reading emphasizes the social dimensions of the novel. The young, from this point of view, are no less caught up in the violence and hypocrisy of American culture than are their elders.

On the other hand, we might conclude that the violence of people like Charlie Decker and like his father before him is the consequence, not of certain social values, but of a "natural" instinct. This "naturalistic" reading tends to exonerate everybody—and at this point the novel's critique of specifically *American* social patterns begins to dissolve: the problem becomes not Carl Decker's macho ethic, but rather "Human Nature."

I believe that King himself wavers between these two ways of looking at the ills that humans do, and the ills done unto them. Later books like THE DEAD ZONE and FIRESTARTER engage in an explicit critique of certain aspects of American society. On the other hand, King has repeatedly expressed his admiration of the naturalistic novelists—Douglas Winter quotes his praise of Hardy, London, and Dreiser, and he has spoken to me of his enthusiasm for Frank Norris. RAGE balances between a social and a biological explanation of violence.

But whether we see Charlie's assault on Ted Jones as a consequence of "social" or of "natural" causes, what seems to me most interesting here is simply King's refusal to allow us to see Charlie *either* as a hero *or* as a victim *or* as a crazy kid. Rather he demands that we see him as all three at once. In 1966, there were plenty of young people who had become convinced that they enjoyed, by virtue of their youth itself, a kind of purity that would allow them to create, instantly, a Brave New World. The young Stephen King, I have proposed, felt some sympathy with the world-view of the Youth Culture. But even in 1966 he was also able to test that world-view, and to look at its potential consequences. In this way, RAGE enacts the tragedy of the Youth Culture itself, which passed in a few years from a dream of a universal family of love (I am thinking especially of Woodstock) to the nightmare visions of Manson's "family." That a college freshman in Maine was able in 1966 to intuit this whole tragic arc seems to me very remarkable indeed.

III.

Aesthetically, THE LONG WALK, King's second novel, represents a major step forward from RAGE. RAGE restrains itself, somewhat reluctantly, within the limits of "mainstream" or "realistic" fiction. But THE LONG WALK initiates a break from these conventions by proposing an alternative history and thus an alternative present. Through a series of allusions, King predicates, perhaps in imitation of Philip K. Dick's classic THE MAN IN THE HIGH CASTLE, a partial German victory in World War II. Germany, it seems, conquered Eurasia and attacked the East coast of the United States during the last days of World War II. Germany also conquered Latin American. In response, the United States itself has developed a militaristic, quasi-Fascist system of government. In a remarkable forecast of later practices in Latin America, dissent is controlled by the "Squads," which "disappear" people. (The father of the novel's central character has been "disappeared.")

King's Fascist America is ruled by "the Major," who always wears dark glasses when out of doors, and whose picture is omnipresent. To keep the people docile, the government provides bread and various kinds of circuses, including the "long walk." This annual competition is open to boys in their late teens. The rules are simple. One hundred boys start walking from the Northern border of Maine. They walk until they can walk no more. If they fall below the minimal speed three times within the space of one hour, they are shot by one of the soldiers who patrol the line of march. This process continues until one walker remains alive, and this boy receives "The Prize"—which is, simply, "everything you want for the rest of your life."

THE LONG WALK centers on Ray Garraty of Pownal, Maine. Ray is competing in the walk as "Maine's own." Since he is the point of view character, it seems more or less inevitable that he will win the walk: in this respect the suspense that King tries to maintain seems a little contrived. Yet the focus of the novel is not so much on who will win as on what happens among these boys as they walk south. Drawn together by their youth and by the prospect of impending death, bonds of mutual loyalty spring up among the boys. Yet at the same time, the boys are locked in a war of each against all, a war to the death; for the walk is indeed a Darwinian struggle for survival, and only one walker will live. The tension between the will to community among the walkers and the external forces which demand that they rejoice when one of their number falls gives THE LONG WALK a raw force that is, even on a third or fourth re-reading, deeply unsettling.

We stare in fascinated horror as the first boy is shot. At each subsequent shooting, our horror diminishes only a little; and like the boys themselves, each time we are glad it isn't us. There is in our response a stifled scream of denial. "No, this *can't* be. No one, certainly no *American*, would let this go on." Yet at the same time the whole scenario seems in some awful way plausible. In part, the book seems plausible because King's narrative powers richly evoke a world he knows well—the world of teenagers in small Maine towns, and the Maine landscape through which the walkers move. But another part of the plausibility of the book comes from our sense that indeed this is the way things are in the world, except here they have been pushed just a *little* further, to become an awful caricature of the way we live.

In some ways, THE LONG WALK reproduces the Innocent Youth versus Adult Exploitation theme of RAGE. Now we have not merely one victim but one hundred, and we have an entire nation "getting it on" by watching these boys die one by one. But the "alternative history" format of THE LONG WALK moves us immediately into a new dimension. Since the world King here offers us has obviously been *invented*, we find ourselves asking—in a way we do not while reading a novel like RAGE, which purports to be telling us about the "real world"—what all this might *mean*.

THE LONG WALK slips, indeed, perilously close to allegory. But if we ask what the walk "stands for," we find ourselves most immediately entangled in a web of possibilities. In some ways, THE LONG WALK, like RAGE, invites a "naturalistic" or even an "existentialist" reading. We can read the walk as an image simply of human life itself. The parallel here is simple: Life is, obviously, a journey. We set out on it without really knowing why—we go because we *must*. As we go, our companions fall away one by one, but we walk on until we ourselves die. Garraty tries to articulate this "existentialist" point of view early in the novel: "'We don't bring anything into the world and we sure as shit don't take anything out'," he proclaims, and the period in between is neither pleasant nor unpleasant—it's simply a matter of putting one foot in front of the other:

> "Potato soup or sirloin tips, a mansion or a hovel, once you're dead that's it, they put you on a cooling board like Zuck or Ewing and that's it. You're better to take it a day at a time, is all I'm saying. If people just took it a day at a time, they'd be a lot happier."
> "Oh, such a golden flood of bullshit," McVries said.
> "Is that so?" Garraty cried. "How much planning are you doing?"
> "Well, right now I've sort of adjusted my horizons, that's true—"
> "You bet it is," Garraty said grimly. "The only difference is we're involved in dying right now."

But this "existential" reading of the novel runs up against a major problem. The walkers are all young, and they are presumably—with one exception—going to die, not eventually but *now*. And conversely, the spectators who line the route of the walk never seem to reflect on their own mortality. Rather they have come to watch *someone else* die. So in the end, this "existential" reading does not seem to me very satisfactory.

That all the walkers are male opens up another interpretive

possibility: at times the oppressing force in the novel becomes the entire female sex, for most of the boys seem to feel that they have embarked on the walk for the sake of a woman somewhere, or because a woman pushed them to do it, or perhaps to escape from a woman. *En route*, the boys encounter several women who seem excited at the thought of arousing the sexual desire of someone who is about to die. And there are several incidental images of what seem to be death mother figures, such as the following:

> One old lady stood frozenly beneath a black umbrella, neither waving nor speaking nor smiling. She watched them go by with gimlet eyes. There was not a sign of life or movement about her except for the wind-twitched hem of her black dress. On the middle finger of her right hand she wore a large ring with a purple stone. There was a tarnished cameo at her throat.

If we focus on the images of women in the novel, it begins to seem that perhaps the walk represents an elaborate mating dance which males perform for females—analogous, perhaps, to the flight of the drones after the queen bee, which climaxes when the last surviving drone mates with the queen and then, like all the other drones, falls back to earth dead.

But while some archetypal overtones hover over the extraordinary metaphor which King creates in THE LONG WALK, nevertheless these meanings do not exhaust the implications of the metaphor, for there are also metaphoric linkages between the walk and life in capitalist America. For example, the long walk has all the attributes of the mass spectator sports which dominate contemporary American culture. The competition is the object of intensive TV coverage, so that for the term of the Walk, as during the World Series or on Super Sunday, the attention of the entire nation is focused on the walkers; the walkers are greeted as they go by huge, cheering crowds; there is frenzied betting on the competition, and Las Vegas quotes odds on the various walkers; as Garraty, "Maine's own," passes through a series of Maine towns, he is even greeted by organized cheerleading squads; the Major, who personally greets the walkers several times *en route*, looks and acts not only like a Somoza or a

Pinochet, but also like a football coach, perhaps Vince Lombardi ("Winning isn't the most important thing, it's everything"); and both participants and spectators are obsessed with records—even though they are embittered and angry, the last survivors of this walk are proud to learn that they have broken all distance records from previous walks, and I have a strong suspicion that King wants his readers also to cheer at this moment. (There are also some specific football allusions: At one point, one of the characters tells Garraty, "You're going to win this one for the Gipper." And scattered references to Roman gladiators remind us that throughout history the line between sport and combat has been fuzzy. Insofar as the novel offers up the walk as an exaggerated picture of the role of spectator sports in American society, it pushes us toward some painful reflections, especially on the systematic moral and physical torture which football players undergo, in the hopes of becoming stars.)

The long walk also serves as a metaphor for the role of the military in American life, and even more specifically, as a symbol of the Vietnam war. The participants are draft-age young people, selected in part by a lottery, as were the draftees of the Vietnam era. Like these draftees, the walkers set off to the accompaniment of the cheers of the crowds and blasts of patriotic rhetoric; but both groups go off to death, and both begin to feel like victims of a society drunk on its own illusions.

More broadly, the walk serves as a metaphor of what we used to call the "rat race": the race for the brass ring, the struggle to end up on top of the American pyramid. None of the walkers can quite remember the dream of fame and fortune which first lured them into signing up for the walk, but many of them continue to talk, sometimes hopefully but more often bitterly, of "the Prize." Their society has told them that the world is divided into Winners and Losers, and that the tough and the strong are totally committed to the struggle to win; and at some point all the walkers have bought into this image of human life. None of the walkers know clearly why they are walking: they have joined the walk because, simply, "everyone" sees this competition as splendid and exciting.

So too, to live in America at all is to be caught up in the pursuit of "success." Films and television shows glamorize the lives of the rich and powerful, and Regis Philbin tells us about their lifestyles. Thus even those Americans who don't commit themselves to the pursuit of success are obsessed by those who do—only the lives of the latter seem truly real. Yet King's metaphor suggests that life in the fast lane is a brutal struggle for survival, that "success" for some means "failure" for everyone else, that the winners themselves are twisted into inhuman shapes by the battle to end up on top. At this final level, King's metaphor encompasses both the walk-as-spectator-sport and the walk-as-war levels of meaning, to become, simply, an image —a fiercely critical one—of life in capitalist America.

THE LONG WALK, I have proposed, dramatizes a struggle between competition and co-operation, a struggle that lies at the heart of the American experience. The obsession of American society with the competitive struggle and with victory is suggested principally by the rules of the long walk itself, which literalize Vince Lombardi's famous precept: here winning is indeed *everything*, for the losers are not just metaphorically "dead meat." Yet as we see happening again and again among American athletes, soldiers, and even corporate executives, a considerable degree of camaraderie and mutual loyalty develops among the competitors.

The tension between the principle of competition and the principle of co-operation emerges early in the novel:

> "Ray." McVries was still smiling. "What's your hurry?"
> Yeah, that was right. Hint 6: Slow and easy does it. "Thanks."
> McVries went on smiling. "Don't thank me too much. I'm out to win, too."
> Garraty stared at him, disconcerted.
> "I mean, let's not put this on a Three Musketeers basis. I like you and it's obvious you're a big hit with the pretty girls. But if you fall over, I won't pick you up."
> "Yeah." He smiled back, but his smile felt lame.
> "On the other hand," Baker drawled softly, "we're all in this together and we might as well keep each other amused."

And somewhat later, watching a walker named Harkness drift

into the daze that precedes a final collapse, Garraty finds himself thinking as follows:

> The sooner Harkness stopped walking, the sooner he could stop walking. That was the simple truth. That was logic. But something went deeper, a truer, more frightening logic. Harkness was a part of the group that Garraty was a part of, a segment of his subclan. Part of a magic circle that Garraty belonged to. And if one part of that circle could be broken, any part of it could be broken.

The reality of the competitive struggle in which they are engaged means that each walker must see all the others as in some way his enemies. Even Garraty, our sympathetic central character, decides finally that he wants to win, even if his winning means that his new friends must die. And late in the walk, Garraty and the other surviving walkers all join in a compact: "No help for anybody. Do it on your own or don't do it."

Yet their common situation draws the walkers together. Garraty resists the "No help for anybody" pledge because another walker, McVries, has already rescued him on two occasions, and he feels he "owes McVries a couple." Further, when he finally does join in the compact, he thinks, "Now I'm an animal . . . You did it. You sold out." The friendship between Garraty and McVries becomes, indeed, the center of the novel. McVries, whom Garraty sees as "quite grown-up, really," repeatedly offers wholly gratuitous help to Garraty and to others, and at the end Garraty will turn back and try to carry McVries forward with him.

The growing solidarity among the walkers leads them to see the crowd that lines the route rather than the other walkers as their principal enemy:

> Garraty had a vivid and scary image of the great god Crowd clawing its way out of the Augusta basin on scarlet spider-legs and devouring them all alive.
>
> The town itself had been swallowed, strangled, and buried. In a very real sense there was no Augusta, and there were no more fat ladies, or pretty girls, or pompous men. . . . Only Crowd, a creature with no body, no head, no mind. Crowd was nothing but a Voice and an Eye, and it was not surprising that Crowd was both God and

> Mammon. Garraty felt it. He knew the others were feeling it. . . .
> Crowd was to be pleased. Crowd was to be worshiped and feared.
> Ultimately, Crowd was to be made sacrifice unto.

The walkers become scapegoats for this ferocious crowd, and at some points King's language even suggests a parallel between the walk and the ascent of Golgotha, while the walkers are compared to Jesus. The walkers also come to see the Major as their enemy, a mere "murderer." Passing out of Old Town, the walkers are greeted by the Major (a Pattonesque figure, he likes to ride past the walkers in his jeep, standing at attention as he goes), and they respond with "a forty-six-man raspberry" — although, of course, the futility of this gesture merely re-emphasizes the powerlessness of the boys.

At least some of the boys do, then, learn to love one another, and to see that their enemy is not the other boys, but the system that has forced them to struggle with one another, not for the Prize but simply for survival. Yet how much good the burgeoning sense of community does them remains an open question.

Each individual walker mediates this conflict between competition and community in his own distinctive way, and the range of these responses becomes King's primary method of characterizing the individual walkers. At one extreme we find Gary Barkovitch, the (almost) pure egoist. Barkovitch rejoices in the deaths of his fellow walkers. When Ewing, a black walker, dies, Barkovitch merely sneers, "What the hell can you expect from a dumb nigger?" And later he shouts to Garraty, "I'll dance on your grave." At one point, Barkovitch causes, more or less directly, the death of a fellow walker, and he seems to feel no regret. Garraty finds himself wondering whether Barkovitch's aggressive hostility toward his fellow walkers might be the only sensible approach to this situation: "He plays to win," Garraty suggests, with a shade of envy, but only a little later Garraty decides that "Barkovitch was crazy." This judgment is shared by McVries, who describes Barkovitch as "running on high-octane hate." Perhaps, McVries implies, it isn't so much the desire to win as the desire to see others destroyed that impels Barkovitch forward. But before the end we learn that even Barkovitch feels a hunger for community ("I just wanted to tell you . . . a guy's got to have some friends . . . Who wants to die hated?") and that his bitterness arises, not from a sense of his own superiority, but rather from a deep anger over real or imagined rejections. (In THE STAND, we will see a similar psychological pattern in Harold Lauder.) Even Barkovitch, then, feels the conflict I am describing, although his desire for community can emerge only in a twisted, bizarre form.

At the opposite extreme we find McVries, who even before the walk begins has seen through the Major and the whole competitive ethic he incarnates. Because McVries seems totally indifferent to the competitive ethic, his participation in the walk seems a little mystifying. He offers only one explanation: he has been rejected by a girlfriend, and therefore he "wants to die." But whatever his motive, among the walkers McVries exemplifies a disinterested spirit of brotherhood, and as such he becomes a kind of spiritual leader. In particular, he serves as an almost magical guide for Garraty, rescuing his naive friend from various dangers, and gently leading him toward a recognition of the truth about the walk and about the world the Major has created.

Between the extremes represented by Barkovitch and McVries, the other major characters distribute themselves, depending on the distinctive ways in which they bring together the impulses of competition and co-operation. For example, King devotes a fair degree of attention to Scramm, who knows exactly why he is here: he has a wife and small child, and he has joined the walk purely for the money. Scramm is a superbly trained athlete and is absolutely confident that he will win. In this respect he seems like Barkovitch. But Scramm feels no hatred for his fellow walkers. Indeed, he voices contempt for Barkovitch, whom he sees as "just walkin' to see other people die." Midway in the walk, Scramm develops a cold which deepens into pneumonia. (This ironic touch reminds us of King's admiration for the American naturalists, especially Crane and Norris.) Scramm is as detached about his own impending death as he was earlier about his prospect of victory, and at the end he and Mike, an American Indian, simply sit down together and talk until they are shot. Thus Scramm is capable of a pure act of brotherhood worthy of McVries. Combining Barkovitch's competitive drive with McVries' selflessness, Scramm also has one attribute that is distinctively his own, and which enables him to combine these two contrary sets of attributes: he has the almost mystical sense of detachment which we see in many athletes.

Another example is a walker named Stebbins. At the beginning of the walk, Stebbins is established as a loner, a loser, a weirdo a bit like Charlie in RAGE, perhaps. Unlike Barkovitch, Stebbins feels no hatred for his fellow walkers, only indifference. Like McVries, Stebbins seems to "see through" the walk: early on, the Major appears to tell the walkers, "I'm proud of you, boys." To this statement, Garraty hears a voice behind him respond, "Diddly shit," and he is sure that the speaker is Stebbins. Stebbins' mixture of indifference to the other boys and cynicism concerning the walk as an institution is finally explained in the penultimate chapter, where he reveals that he is the Major's illegitimate son and that he has been driven to join the march by a fantasy of being accepted at last by his father.

As a final example of how the principles of co-operation and competition here come together in individual characters, I will point to Garraty himself, who is torn by this conflict throughout the walk, who at the end violates the "everyone for himself pledge" by turning back to help McVries—but who then, when he finds that McVries is dead, says to Stebbins, by now the only other survivor, "I'm going to walk you into the ground," and then does just that. Garraty too locates himself somewhere between the extremes represented by Barkovitch and McVries. And it is, King implies, mostly in this middle range, where the spirit of competition and the spirit of community fight it out, that almost all Americans live.

The victory of the "nice guy" Ray Garraty may suggest a possibility of reconciling the principles of competition and community. In this book, *pace* Vince Lombardi, nice guys don't finish last. Indeed, they seem to finish first (or, more precisely, to die last) precisely *because* they are nice. Yet any sense of triumph which we may feel at the end (and we *do* feel such a sense, for consciously or unconsciously we have been rooting for our point of view character, Maine's own Ray Garraty) is savagely undercut by a sense of how much we have lost *en route*.

Almost all the walkers come to feel that they have been had, that the ethic of competition and the American dream of success are nothing less than a con job. McVries, the true hero of the book (whose death seems not so much a defeat as a sacrificial act—he keeps going long enough to ensure that Garraty will survive, and then he offers himself as a sacrifice to ensure that Garraty will live), sees through "the system" as early as anyone, telling Garraty, "It's a fake. There's no winner, no Prize. They take the last guy out behind a barn somewhere and shoot him too."

Garraty resists his friend's bleak message, but McVries keeps hammering this point home:

> "Why are you here, Garraty?"
> "I don't know." His voice was mechanical, doll-like. . . .
> "You don't know." McVries said, "You're dying and you don't know why."
> "It's not important after you're dead."
> "Yeah, maybe," McVries said, "but there's one thing you ought to know, Ray, so it won't all be so pointless."
> "What's that?"
> "Why, that you've been had. You mean you really didn't know that, Ray? You really didn't?"

And slowly even trusting Garraty begins to wonder:

> He had wondered a great deal about what McVries had said. That they had all been swindled, rooked. But that couldn't be right, he insisted stubbornly to himself. One of them had not been swindled. One of them was going to swindle everyone else . . . wasn't that right?

Yet the bitterest, most categorical repudiation of the walk and everything it represents comes not from McVries but from Stebbins, the Major's son. Garraty, thinking that he sees through Stebbins, tells him, "You like to think the game is rigged. But maybe it's a straight game. That scare you, Stebbins?" To which Stebbins replies, "Any game looks straight if everyone is being cheated at once."

To say that Stebbins' comment represents King's (even the young King's) final judgment of American society would be untrue. Yet this startling statement does invite us to consider the possibility that we are all being cheated all the time—that our entire society has bought into a mass delusion which we are unable to recognize simply because we are *all* deluded. Further, only the possibility of some delusion of this sort seems to offer an answer to a question that hovers over the entire novel. "Why did we do it, Garraty?" So McVries, twenty-five pages from the end.

We have been asking this same question from the moment that the first walker is shot. However, when we pause at the end and think back over the journey, we realize a little uneasily that the book has offered no answer. For there *is* no good answer. The culture within which these boys live has told them to walk, and walk they have. "We must have been insane," McVries says in reply to his own question. And sensible Ray Garraty responds, "I don't think there was any good reason." At this point McVries draws the inescapable conclusion: "All we are is mice in a trap."

Because this disillusioned, even despairing vision of what American culture does to people gradually prevails, no "victory" is here possible. Garraty, Maine's own, does "win." Of the 100 boys who started, he alone remains alive at the end. And despite McVries' prediction, no one takes him behind a barn to shoot him. Yet it is also clear that he is not going to savor the fruits of his triumph. As we leave Garraty, he is running toward a dark figure who seems to be moving before him, beckoning him on. Is this figure death? Will Garraty too now die, of simple exhaustion? (The last two walkers to fall, McVries and Stebbins, fall dead without being shot). Is the dark figure the shade of his friend McVries? Has Garraty perhaps gone mad?

King gives us no definitive answers to these questions. But whatever may happen next to Garraty, it seems clear that the great American dream has turned to ashes not only for the ninety and nine who have lost, but also for the one who has "won."

IV.

There are undoubtedly some serious flaws both in RAGE and in THE LONG WALK. In its formal structure, RAGE is in many ways an awkward piece of work. A first person narrative by a protagonist who is theoretically "crazy" can be effective, as writers as different as Vladimir Nabokov (DESPAIR) and Jim Thompson (POP. 1280) have demonstrated. But these writers achieve their effects through a consistent *textual* irony: we identify with their narrators *before* we know that the narrators are insane, and the power of the text comes from the author's ability to sustain this identification even as we begin to realize the depth of the narrator's madness. King, on the other hand, defines Charlie as insane almost immediately, and as the narrative proceeds we are never quite sure whether we should identify with him or see him as a psychiatric "case." Further, RAGE relies excessively on the flashback, a technique which becomes in the end a bit mechanical, even though several of the individual flashbacks have the grace and economy of well-crafted short stories.

The narrative of THE LONG WALK, unlike that of RAGE, rushes forward vigorously. Yet the *idea* of THE LONG WALK seems in the end more compelling than the novel. Once we figure out what is going on, we know all too well what will happen in the next chapter, and in the next: one by one they will all fall, all but one. There is a horrifying inevitability about this process, but also a certain monotony. (Agatha Christie, after all, limited herself to ten little Indians.) And with a hundred walkers to keep track of, inevitably King is unable to do much more than sketch in their characters in the briefest and most conventional of terms before they are shot. Even the primary characters become, as we have seen, more like allegorical personifications than like flesh and blood people.

Nevertheless, these two novels, both of them conceived and in large measure written by a young man not yet twenty years old, also have remarkable strengths. In particular, they display an extraordinary imaginative courage. The power of all of Stephen King's novels comes primarily from his willingness to imagine the worst, most terrible thing he can conceive of. By doing so, he in effect invites us to release our own darkest fantasies. We read on, helplessly enthralled, as if we were watching the depths of our own minds unfold before us. "No, it can't be," we say, for what we are watching is all that we never dared, *could* not dare to imagine. Yet Stephen King *has* so dared, and so we celebrate him.

The range and power of King's imagination has steadily increased in the course of his career. Each novel, down to and including IT, represents a courageous movement forward into some *new* territory. Yet as early as RAGE and THE LONG WALK he knew *how to do it* Charlie says and does the absolutely forbidden: he insults, assaults, and symbolically murders the Father. Watching, we want both to applaud and to cringe in horror. Of course, Charlie remains in large measure a "case": we look at him through the window of the classroom, rather than fully participating in his rage. In THE LONG WALK, by contrast, we are *there*, with the boys on their journey. Just as they can't quite believe this is happening to them, so we can't believe it either. And yet here we are, walking south from Caribou, through the rain.

And just as these novels show that even at twenty young Stephen King already knew "how to do it," so they also tell us something important about the nature and function of imagination. In releasing in us our deepest fears, all the novels of Stephen King also inevitably release our deepest hopes. Knowing what we fear, we also know what we desire: safety, mother, friends—a place within what Hawthorne called the "magnetic chain of humanity." Some of King's novels, THE DEAD ZONE in particular, are overtly "about" politics; all of them are, I would argue, political in a much deeper sense. For in acknowledging all the forces within and outside us which assault our humanity, King's novels also celebrate our humanity. In all these novels it always turns out that to be human is to find a place within that magnetic chain.

Beginning with RAGE and THE LONG WALK, all of King's novels celebrate the possibility of community by looking at all the forces arrayed against it. It is his consistent concern with the way we live together that makes King—not, as Thomas Edwards suggests in a recent *New York Review of Books*, an "almost 'serious'" writer—but rather one of the most truly serious novelists writing today.

WHEN COMPANY DROPS IN

by Charles Willeford

By the time I received my review copy of MISERY, the novel had already been on the bestseller lists for five weeks, so I decided not to review it. After all, when a first printing of a million copies has been announced, it doesn't make much difference whether the novel is praised, panned, or treated with indifference. The readers of horror fiction are unlikely to peruse newspaper book pages to see what looks promising this week, or any other week.

Horror fiction depends, for its maximum effects, on believers—those who believe in God, in reincarnation, in astrology, the afterlife; people who capitalize heaven and hell as if they were talking about San Francisco and Wichita. For nonbelievers, a novel like King's PET SEMATARY, for example, isn't frightening, it's ludicrous. To enjoy fiction of any kind, some suspension of disbelief is required, but for PET SEMATARY to work as scary fiction, the reader must believe in the supernatural and reincarnation; that an Indian god can bring animals and people back to life (slightly altered; after a person's been dead for a while, King says, and then lives again, his personality is never quite the same). Non-believers simply can't suspend their disbelief this far, and they feel that King is insulting their native intelligence.

MISERY, happily, doesn't play on the fears of the Bakker,

Roberts, Falwell or Billy Graham followers; most of the events in this novel, although there are exaggerations, *could* happen. At least they stay within the limits of probability. Certainly, these gruesome events will make every reader who writes, or tries to write, squirm in his chair.

The plot of MISERY is a combination of John Fowles' THE COLLECTOR and Evelyn Waugh's A HANDFUL OF DUST, without the latter's emphasis on mortal sins. Paul Sheldon, the protagonist-narrator, is a best-selling writer of potboiling nineteenth century historical romances that feature Misery Chastain, the eponymous heroine of King's novel. Paul hates writing these potboilers, and considers himself as a "serious" novelist. After making a pile of money on his Misery novels, he kills her off in the last book, and then spends a year writing a "serious" novel about a car thief. From the description, this new novel sounds like another story about a juvenile delinquent, with sociological overtones, written in a literary style. Celebrating the completion of FAST CARS with too much champagne, Paul skids off the highway during a Colorado snowstorm. When he awakens, both of his legs have been severely crushed, and he is in a farmhouse bedroom of a madwoman named Annie Wilkes. Annie is a dough-faced, shapeless, asexual woman, and a Registered Nurse. She has spent most of her adult life moving from hospital to hospital, from Bakersfield, California to Denver, Colorado, killing off patients surreptitiously in each new post. After a well-publicized trial in Denver, where Annie beats the rap, she retired to this isolated farm in Colorado. She is also, unhappily for Paul Sheldon, his "Number One fan." She learns who he is from his wallet, and she is furious that he killed off her beloved Misery in his last book. (She has read the paperback version, of course, not the hardcover, a sore point for most novelists, when people tell them they are going "to wait for the paperback.") Now that she has Paul in her clutches she makes him burn his only manuscript copy of FAST CARS, having read it and become offended by what she considers the coarse language. She demands that Paul bring Misery back from the dead, and write another Misery Chastain romance just for her, her own private book.

Because of his crushed limbs and the steel splints she has fastened them together with, Paul is in agony. She hooks him on pain pills, threatening to withhold the pills if he doesn't do her bidding, and she shows her mastery over him by making him drink dirty soap water with his pills. King obsessively details Sheldon's dislocation, despair, and finally his willingness to compromise on anything to stay alive.

Paul begins to write another Misery novel, and the story becomes a duel between the writer and his reader. Annie is a good reader, however, and she doesn't let him cheat. The new Misery novel must be logical, well-plotted, accurate historically, and have believable situations, together with valid, suspenseful complications and resolutions.

To make his situation worse, the second-hand typewriter she buys him has the 'n' missing. Paul has to fill in the 'n's' by hand with a pen as he finishes each page. As the book progresses, the 't' and the 'e' (the most common letters in English) fall off the ancient Royal typewriter, and he must fill these in as well. For a while, Annie agrees to fill the letters in for him, but she soon quits because it's too distracting to fill in the letters and read, too.

Typescript is an ugly typeface, and unpleasant to read on 8½ by 11 inch typing paper, but when it is reduced in size to a book-sized sheet, with the 'n's, 'e's and 't's filled in with ink, the long samples of the new Misery novel are almost too tedious to follow. (One wonders, too, whether King filled these in himself, or had some of his kids do it for him.) Fortunately for the reader, these long examples can be skipped over because King provides short summaries of the plot as the new novel progresses. What King has to say about writing, and the differences between reader and writer, are impressive, but the major point he makes is that both of them, reader and writer, want the same thing from fiction. They want to know the answers to the dramatic questions posed, but they also want to delay the ending and prolong the pleasure of suspense as long as possible.

Paul also learns something important about himself. The ease with which he slips into the new Misery novel, considering his unpleasant circumstances, makes him realize that he isn't a "serious" novelist after all; he's a romance novelist—the best at what he does—and he wants to live and publish this new book because it's the best of the Misery series so far. He also suspects—indeed he knows—that when he does complete the story he will be killed by the insane nurse.

In a battle like this one, the reader knows that one or the other must win, and King has given us a formidable villainness in Annie Wilkes. Where Paul is intelligent, she is shrewd and cunning, and she keeps a good jump ahead of him at all times. By rewarding him with decent meals, or by punishing him by giving him poor food, by withholding his pain pills, and by lopping off various parts of his body and sealing the stumps with a blowtorch, she is in complete control of this horrible situation. Although she threatens him with the loss, she wisely spares his balls, however, knowing that he will need both of them if he is to complete the novel. When we consider Paul's poor physical condition; his kidney infection; his dope addiction; his weakened state from lying in bed for months; we doubt that he could survive the amputation of his foot with an ax—and the blow-torch —without dying from shock. But the motivation of completing the novel is enough, King says, to give Paul the will to survive.

There is a metaphor here about the relationship of the writer and the editor as well, the editor wanting changes the writer doesn't want to make, and the writer, who must write every day, no matter how badly he feels, turning out his daily stint of a thousand words or more, once he has been hooked on his book and becomes the prisoner of the characters he has created. As Fred Allen used to say to his sponsors, when they wanted changes in his scripts, "Where were you bastards when the pages were blank?"

King's novel is padded, of course, first with the boring passages of typescript of the new Misery novel, which Paul has to finish, finally, in longhand when the typewriter no longer works; and with Paul's detailing of his deteriorating physical condition. It would be a better book at half its length, but it doesn't have King's trademark pop culture references and interminable lists of brand names. King needs a tough editor, but where will he find an editor bold enough to suggest cutting when the editor knows in advance that the book will be printed in a million-copy edition, and will become a best seller in advance of the publication date? As the book approaches the climax, King proves once again that he is a master of suspense, and MISERY is undoubtedly King's best novel so far. He proves that the horror of reality is much worse than anything that smacks of mysticism and the undead.

What Henry Miller said about his own writing applies equally to Stephen King: "In an age marked by dissolution, liquidation seems to me a virtue, nay a moral imperative. Not only have I never felt the least desire to conserve, bolster up or buttress anything, but I might say that I have always looked upon decay as being just as wonderful and rich an expression of life as growth. . . . Like the spider, I return again and again to the task, conscious that the web I am spinning is made of my own substance, that it will never fail me, never run dry."

Let us hope so, especially now, now that King has finally got the hang of it.

THE CYCLES (TRICYCLES AND HOGS) OF HORROR

by J. N. Williamson

*T*o begin to comprehend Stephen King and his accomplishments completely requires, I believe, the passage of considerable time—decades, at least—or a vantage point rather different from standard literary exegesis. It's all so much; one becomes a boggled five-year-old at his first three-ring circus. King and his probably unsurpassable success surprise more than awe me, possess my ungrudging respect; but what gives me a near-unique view of the circus is the fact that I am a full-time horror professional who made his start in novels after Stephen King and one who happens to be his elder by a dozen winters.

Steve—who calls me by my initials or, in rare letters, "old slyboots"—and I are not friends or enemies, we don't have the same agent, and our close acquaintanceships are largely with different writers. I'm not one of the worshipful fans who wait with (to me) unfathomable patience for him to sign something, nor am I, say, Peter Straub or Charles Grant, Douglas Winter or Dennis Etchison: confidants. Neither, as yet, am I a Richard Matheson, Bob Bloch or Ray Bradbury; someone who has been around longer, and to whom both Steve and I lower our heads deferentially.

And while we are both full-time professional wordworkers who earn most of our livelihoods from creating horror fiction and claim devoted readerships, any comparison of King and me on the only measuring stick that matters to most modern Americans would be absurd. In terms of the sport he cherishes, baseball, Steve is MVP Roger Clemens of the Red Sox, and I'm the last pitcher in the rotation. Using basketball as an analogy (my sport; I'm a Hoosier like Larry Bird), King is a younger Kareem; I play for the Indiana Pacers. Fact is, the one thing I can imagine to shake in Stephen's bespectacled face, and laugh sneeringly, is that *my* state houses both a pro basketball team and Coach Bob Knight of Indiana University. Bangor'll have an NBA franchise when Clemens' and Larry's grandkids have gone out for soccer — if King gets lucky!

I have no more passion for the decades spinning away than another man, but it's possible my particular pro's-eye look at Kingana can be valuable: I think that his novels have sold the way they have partly because of the particular time frames of King and his predecessors, and partly because of the ages of his initial body of readers.

Let's begin by considering the ten, scary "bears" which King, in his foreword to Underwood-Miller's KINGDOM OF FEAR, itemizes as those phobias which frighten the most people: fear of 1) the dark; 2) "squishy things"; 3) deformity; 4) snakes; 5) rats; 6) closed-in places; 7) insects; 8) death; 9) others ("paranoia"); and 10) fear "for someone else." Compare them with the following two lists which one of my readers discovered a few years ago in a psychologists' publication and sent to me without attribution:

Men	Women
1. Castration	1. Disfigurement
2. Blindness	2. Blindness
3. Lack of all physical functions	3. Rape
4. Being alone; friendless	4. Being alone; friendless
5. Disfigurement	5. Lack of physical functions
6. Mental deterioration	6. Mental deterioration
7. Loss of all income	7. Spiders
8. Failure among one's peers	8. Failure among one's peers

Men	Women
9. Venereal disease	9. Loss of all income
10. Total domination by others	10. Unsought pregnancy

Nowhere on the psychological "expert" list for either gender is fear of the dark, although an argument might be made for numbers two and four. The psychologists' citations, for example, of income loss and unsought pregnancy cannot be fitted into King's ursine catalog even with the most charitable allowances. And considering current headlined apprehension about AIDS, both King's total exclusion of social disease and the shrinks' one-list allusion in ninth place may seem to be extraordinary (or outdated) oversights.

Both on balance and track record, nevertheless, I think the King list is more in harmony with the facts and the truth of King, the man and author, and of his primary and initial readership.

Look: Neither a 45-year-old man with his offspring grown or practically on their way out the door nor an elderly person fretting about social security, and what lurks beyond that, is apt to place "the dark" or "squishy things" at the top of a scary list. Castration and disfigurement, unless he or she is infected or infirm, aren't apt to rank higher. That makes all three lists appear dubious to those in their middle years. At 45, one is twenty years too young—or five years too old—to worry much about death, while at 65, observation instructs me, rats, snakes, and fear for somebody else aren't among the great bugaboos. (It is to King's credit that he at least *cited* dying as a human concern!)

But to a generation of readers who have discovered anew the pleasures of comic books, endured or possibly enjoyed innumerable low-budget splatter flicks and the thought-jarring dissonances of rock, King's ten bears look just about right to me. In my opinion recent youth have been uniquely influenced by what they touched, saw, heard, or were told by their peers to *be*. Conformists in many ways, they've tended to tool their trikes, bikes and hogs where they pleased, smooshing things *en route*, behaving the way those of their age who shared the trip conceived or preferred them to be. Some have ducked confrontation and real peril—yet have felt backed into the corner of closed-in circumstances from which they might successfully flee only in company with someone who'd keep quiet, even under torture, about shared secrets. A pimple has terrified them, even while they've loyally closed ranks rather than betray a friend, and worried themselves sick lest they be considered, by peers, hesitant to do *anything at all* for them.

I happen to be the right age to notice that, in such a context, a social outcast is seen as virtually deformed. It's not so much that this generation of readers is more immature than preceding generations than that it is different.

Now, the writers acknowledged as masters in the horror field who immediately preceded King ranged in age roughly from their almost-late forties to mid-fifties when CARRIE (1974) and 'SALEM'S LOT (1975), Stephen's first published novels, came out. (For the record, he was twenty-six and -seven when these books appeared). What had frightened them, because they grew up in another era, was not necessarily or not always the same ground King has deftly mined. Possibly one example of what I mean will be sufficient: King's predecessors did not grow up to "discover" the Bomb; they experienced a world without it, then—however fleetingly—cheered it for ending a devastating war.

Although there was no actual interregnum in modern horror after Robert Bloch's seminal PSYCHO, before King and CARRIE there was a relative moratory dearth of such fiction. Since CARRIESALEMSLOTTHESHINING, the situation has changed. There is more and it's lengthened. Many of yesterday's publishers and writers alike believed it was not possible to write a successful horror novel, partly because they didn't know how to target an audience, or package such books. Consequently, post-PSYCHO pre-CARRIE horror was usually found in short story form.

The product of such self-fulfilling negativism was that writers were obliged to create—and compete—in a restricted, censorious marketplace at a time when failure to keep up with new fictive ideas and trends were potential sources of personal unpopularity, even a certain social ostracism. If you're a fantasy writer, or would like to be, try to imagine how challenging it was—in markets that often paid no more than today's small press magazines—to find yourself in direct competition with Ray Bradbury, Robert Bloch, Robert Heinlein, Richard Matheson, Fritz Leiber, *etc.*, *etc.*! Until the last few years, I believe it's nearly indisputable that the short horror stories of the fifties through mid-seventies explored as much fresh thematic material as the average novel contains today; possibly more. These stories were the most original and inventive written anywhere this century, works which remain durable, powerful, filled with wonder—and wonderfully readable.

Even some of the finest contemporary short-form dark fantasy, viewed in a narrowly critical fashion, is often in reality: 1) *compressed novels*, not true short stories, or 2) ingenious reworkings of familiar fright figures. But post-CARRIE readers want their horror lengthened, quantified.

King's most significant collective achievement, therefore, may tentatively be regarded as bringing back the crass tendency to make an outcast of those peers who aren't keeping current! Whether or not this translates entirely to keeping up with what's been called "the Stephen King reader" remains to be seen.

Yet most full time current horror novelists are swift to admit, sometimes gratefully, that it was the King phenomenon which beat back the publishing doors and paved the way—if not rolled out the red carpet—for a warmer reception. While I don't know if King's readers also buy the books written by the rest of us—or to what extent—not every publisher has access to the newest King manuscript, and most will eventually try with all their promotional might to invent a "new"—or "the next"—Stephen King. Because those who toil in the same villainous vineyards privately hope to claim that role, the arrangement is mutually felicitous.

It remains for sociologists with a working knowledge of psychology, literary historians, or writers who are more brazen than I feel this particular day, to check up on a theory of mine: that Stephen King may, literally, have discovered or invented a new *kind* of readership.

The notion, unquestionably, is not mine alone, but I doubt anyone wonders about it more earnestly or more literally than I have just expressed it. Because it not only says a lot about the mediums which principally motivate people now, about the real popular level of the genre and the degree of esteem in which my friends and I are held, but a great deal of the *truth* concerning our whole society, our tastes and preferences, our directions of the future, and how the younger generations both differ from and are like their predecessors.

It isn't my intention to say that Stephen King's only readers are comic book or movie junkies nor to condemn them if that proves to be the case. Good news, gang: there were comic books and motion pictures when I was a boy, and I gobbled them up.

But I wonder if the novels and story collections King has written have made many readers of people who otherwise might not have read books at all; if they've turned only-occasional readers into those who, at least, consume whatever King scribbles; and if they've caused more than a handful of people to become would-be writers. My guess, in each instance, is *yes*.

I wonder, on the other hand, if these readers are any spiritual kin whatsoever to the kind of people who—before CARRIE—frequented and ransacked the library stacks and old used bookstores for the masters who preceded Stephen King, collected them, learned from them, and passed into realms of reading beyond the genre; became, in short, what used to be called "well-rounded" readers or, less onerously and plainly, book lovers.

I wonder if King's faithful readers are persons, of any age at all, who take a bus or drive a heap downtown and browse, not for making-money autographs or "finds" but for treasures of the spirit.

Or are these good people those who—presumably plugged-in to riotous sounds every mile of the trip—climbed off their trikes a dozen years ago, their bikes last year, and their motorcycles an hour ago?

THE GLASS-EYED DRAGON

by L. Sprague de Camp

As fantasy mavens know, fantasy, neglected for over a hundred years, was revived in the eighteenth century by Galland's translation of THE ARABIAN NIGHTS and by the Gothic novel, invented in Germany and brought to Britain by Horace Walpole. It was further developed by the codification of peasants' tales by Hans Christian Andersen, the Grimm brothers, and others; and finally by the writing of original juvenile fantasies by Lewis Carroll, George Macdonald, and their successors.

In the 1880s William Morris, a romantic medievalist among many other things, sought to revive the medieval romance, dormant since Cervantes' Knight of the Rueful Countenance struck it down. The result was the modern heroic fantasy. This sub-genre was taken up by Lord Dunsany and Eric R. Eddison in the U.K. and eventually by Robert E. Howard in the U.S.A. It blossomed wonderfully in the 1960s, with the appearance in paperback of J.R.R. Tolkien's LORD OF THE RINGS and of Robert Howard's Conan stories. Now the presses pour out a vast spate of sword-and-sorcery novels. They come in all degrees of competence. Many combine the juvenile plot of pure good versus pure evil with a decidedly adult degree of sex, sadism, and slaughter.

Then where stands THE EYES OF THE DRAGON, a fantasy novel of nearly 100,000 words by Stephen King, the current master of horror fiction? The eyes in question are glass ones in the mounted head of a dragon on a wall in Roland the Good's palace, and THE EYES OF THE DRAGON is a most beguiling story, told with King's skillful use of language, which carries the reader along in a raptorial grip.

Roland the Good, King of Delain, is really a mediocre monarch, neither very good nor very bad. Though well-meaning, kindly, and sympathetic to the lower orders, he is not very bright and is easily swayed by his sinister magician, Flagg. Unwed at fifty, Roland at last is persuaded to take a bride. In time Queen Sasha gives him two sons but dies in the birth of the second. Flagg arranges this death, because Sasha has turned out entirely too good and with too much influence on King Roland for Flagg's liking.

The jacket flap says that the story will "captivate readers of all ages." This suggests that it lies somewhere on the continuum between the child's fairytale and the modern adult heroic fantasy. Although enormously readable, the tale does not fit quite comfortably into either category.

For instance, an adult reader may be a little put off by the author's use of "dear reader" mannerisms, such as many novelists of the last century used but which are now confined to tales for the very young. In Chapter 66, for example, the author addresses the reader: "We'll speak more of this room later; let me tell you now only. . . ." Again, in Chapter 70: "By now I am sure you have guessed Peter's plan of escape. . . ."

Also, observe the occasional use of contractions like "You'll" or "doesn't" not only in quotations, where they belong, but also in the body of the text. This usage is more suitable to a work for juvenile than to one for adult readers.

Another juvenile feature is the unquestioning acceptance of a feudal state, topped by a more-or-less absolute monarchy, as the political norm. It was the norm in fairytales of medieval European origin, since outside of Italy that assumption reflected political reality in Europe. In other times and places the norm has been different. Even in medieval Europe, class conflict and peasants' revolts were frequent enough to modify the conventional fairytale picture of a "rightful" king, gallant nobles (save for a few wicked dukes or counts), and loyal commoners.

On the other hand, the novel contains some things that most writers of children's stories would not have used. Although the narrative is no sexier than Tolkien's LORD OF THE RINGS (which is to say practically not at all), consider Chapter II. On King Roland's wedding night, he confronts his seventeen-year old bride. "She had never seen a man with his drawers off before her wedding night. When, on that occasion, she observed his flaccid penis, she asked with great interest: 'What's that, Husband?'" I am not here referring to a current type of adolescent novel dealing with contemporary social problems. At a librarians' conference I heard one speaker complain of some of these books that "Every fourth word is 'fuck'!"

Neither, I think, would authors of kiddie books go into the subject of nose-picking in quite such nauseant detail.

King's tale, however, is adult-oriented enough to have a tragic sense of life. Virtue is not always rewarded; neither is villainy inevitably punished. Sometimes good guys come to a bad end, as they often do in the real world. In Chapter 2, Roland's mother, the Dowager Queen, chokes to death on a piece of lemon when a juggler entertaining her drops one of his crystal balls with a crash. The otherwise blameless juggler is promptly beheaded, which does seem a little severe for mere clumsiness.

To ginger up suspense, King sometimes employs what in the cinematic art is called the alternating syntagma. He switches point of view back and forth from chapter to chapter, as Edgar Rice Burroughs did in his Barsoomian stories. ERB would have Deja Thoris go traveling and get into some frightful predicament; then cut to John Carter, frantically seeking his spouse until he in turn gets into a fix; then back to Deja. King overdoes it a little in Chapters 117-130, where he alternates p.o.v. between chapters as short as three or four lines.

For Lovecraftians, King drops a little in-joke. On page 60, Wizard Flagg reads in his grimoire, "bound in human skin." He has studied the work "for a thousand years and had gotten through only a quarter of it ... written on the high, distant Plains of Leng by a madman named Alhazred. . . ." (I understood that Lovecraft's Alhazred, author of the dreaded NECRONOMI-CON, was a Yamani Arab and that Leng was somewhere in Tibet, 4,000-odd kilometers from Arabia; but never mind. "Abdul Alhazred" is not a real Arabic name anyway, although it could be a corruption of Abdallah Zahr-ad-Din, "Servant-of-God Flower-of-the-Faith.")

In due time, Roland's two sons grow up. The elder, Peter, is the parfit gentle hero: tall, strong, handsome, brave, virtuous, and intelligent. He is so able that, when he has been framed for murdering his father and imprisoned, and the head warden tries to beat him up, he beats up the warden instead.

The younger son, Thomas, becomes king in Peter's place. But Thomas takes after his father. At the time he is still an adolescent, a pudgy, pimply, awkward nose-picker, mostly well-meaning but not very bright. He is weak, given to drink, and easily manipulated by Flagg. The wizard would naturally prefer the pliable Thomas as Roland's successor to the stalwart Peter.

Roland, Thomas, and several minor characters are well-drawn and plausible, with the usual mix of the virtues and faults of real human beings. In fact, the least believable characters are the two main antagonists, Prince Peter and Wizard Flagg; Peter because he is too good to be true, Flagg because he is too totally evil to be credible. He reminds one of Thurber's villainous duke, who excuses himself by saying "We all have flaws; mine is being wicked." In our post-Freudian era, absolute evil is hard for a literate adult to believe in. Whether or not God is dead, Satan is certainly terminal.

People who have lived through the reigns of Hitler and Stalin are cautious about setting bounds to human depravity. But Hitler and Stalin were driven by comprehensible if wildly exaggerated lusts for power and glory and by implacable hatreds. Besides that, each pursued his own perverted vision of a better world. Flagg's desire is for simple chaos and destruction, to no intelligible advantage to himself or to anyone else.

Flagg's quirk is explained by his being, not a human being, but a Thing from another plane. An adult reader might wonder: If the fauna of this other plane includes demons, wouldn't they seek to survive, to dominate each other, and to make little demons as other organisms do? Perhaps Flagg needed a good shrink, of which there were none in his native milieu.

Altogether, we have a delightful and hypnotically readable tale, narrated with the invincible plausibility of King's works, as far as I am acquainted with them. This is not much. I have not read any of his other novels, only shorter pieces in magazines. Some of these I liked, others I did not. I was especially taken with "The Ballad of the Flexible Bullet," which asks: Is the typewriter haunted or is its owner paranoiac?

My reason for not reading the novels is that straight horror does not much entertain me. I lately found out why, when I read King's introduction to Underwood-Miller's earlier symposium, KINGDOM OF FEAR. King explains that he bases his stories on the elementary fears that people carry in the backs of their minds from childhood. He lists his own top ten phobias: fear of the dark, of squishy things, of deformity, of snakes, and so on.

The trouble is that only two of the ten give me even faint, vestigial qualms, while the rest do not bother me at all. I *like* snakes, though I am not so foolish as to pick up a venomous one with naked hand. Having yearned as a boy to become a naturalist, I find all organisms interesting. If I believed in spirits, I should want to know about their physiology, metabolism, and ethology.

This is not to portray myself as fearless as a John Carter. I have a couple of phobias, which I often have occasion to beat down in the course of everyday life. They are acrophobia (fear of heights, which I exploited in an episode in my historical novel, THE BRONZE GOD OF RHODES) and erythrophobia (fear of embarrassment); but they do not appear on King's list.

As for the qualifications mentioned, THE EYES OF THE DRAGON can be justly compared to THE LORD OF THE RINGS, with which it shares virtues and faults. The first volume of LOTR, THE FELLOWSHIP OF THE RING, starts in the same juvenile tone as that of its frankly children's predecessor, THE HOBBIT. This tone persists through the first chapter of fifty pages, telling of Bilbo's eleventy-first birthday party and his startling disappearance. Thereafter the tone little by little becomes more adult, although the story takes another fifty pages to start moving briskly.

When THE LORD OF THE RINGS appeared, the brilliant but opinionated literary critic, Edmund Wilson, gave it a scorching review in *The Nation*, calling it "balderdash" and "juvenile trash" among other noncompliments. He said: "It is essentially a children's book—a children's book which has somehow gotten out of hand."

Wilson was hard to please in fantasy; he was equally severe with H. P. Lovecraft, whose "invisible whistling octopus" he ridiculed. If he had to read fantasy, he wrote, he preferred James Branch Cabell's archly cynical futilitarianism and *Weltschmertz*. (Later in life, Wilson took a more indulgent view of Lovecraft.)

One has a feeling that, if King wished, he could write straight adult heroic fantasy, without the smattering of juvenility, as well as anyone writing in that sub-genre today. But he would need to tell his story straight, without all that vague and never truly resolved portentousness of his "Gunslinger" series.

I am sure, however, that King will go ahead on his own track, regardless of anything I say. In any case, the ending of THE EYES OF THE DRAGON leaves the door wide open for a sequel. I look forward to this potential novel with the sort of eager anticipation I felt for the second volume of THE LORD OF THE RINGS. Since I am, to put it tactfully, well past my first flush of youth, I hope King does not take too long about it.

THE BIG PRODUCER

by Thomas Tessier

As the publishing phenomenon of the last ten years, enjoying an extraordinary success that shows no sign of abating, Stephen King has spawned not only a flock of pale imitators but also a growing corps of amateur critics. Amateur, I think, because nothing I've read yet about King's writing approaches true literary appraisal. On the contrary, most of it is enthusiastically uncritical, often to the point of adoration. That's understandable, since we're dealing with a remarkable string of bestsellers and no one buys CARRIE expecting to get a modern-day TESS OF THE D'URBERVILLES.

But there is more to the coverage than just fan reaction. We have already had DANSE MACABRE, a nonfiction book in which King tells us at least as much about himself as he does the horror genre, and since then he has continued to provide a running commentary on his life and work in the form of newsletters, magazine articles, interviews and book introductions. Even if King doesn't do it himself, someone else will surely get around to collecting and publishing his extemporaneous thoughts from these other sources.

Is there anything left to say that he and his admirers have not yet put on the record? Perhaps. Stephen King is a big producer, and the history of big producers is one of the most curious diversions in all of literature. Prodigious output, widespread success, fame and wealth—it all makes an irresistible combination. The big producer is a cottage industry that puts money in the pockets of many people (including the authors of articles like this). In some cases the facts and numbers are so dramatic that it's impossible to avoid using the language of the GUINNESS BOOK OF WORLD RECORDS in discussing them.

Georges Simenon is a good example. He wrote more than 400 novels under his own name and various pseudonyms. He has probably earned more money than any writer in history, and he is certainly the most widely read and translated novelist ever. A UNESCO survey estimated that 500 million people have read Simenon—and that was as of 1972.

There's a common but unfortunate prejudice against the big producer. It is assumed that quality is lost in achieving such quantity. The best these books can offer is the temporary escape of a good read. Plot tends to be formulaic, characterization ranges from nonexistent to stereotypical, and the result, however entertaining, is forgettable. This criticism is often perfectly valid, regardless of genre. Edgar Rice Burroughs, Zane Grey, Doc Smith and John Creasey may still have their readers, but very few will go so far as to defend their work on literary grounds.

Still, quality doesn't have to suffer. Dickens and Balzac were big producers who created classic, enduring literature. The same can be said of Anthony Trollope, Arnold Bennett and Henry James—James being the rare example of a big producer who never enjoyed more than a modest success in his lifetime. Perhaps the most recent big producer who is also a fine writer is Joyce Carol Oates, who pours forth an astonishing stream of stories, poems, essays and novels.

The big producer, then, can be found at every level from the sublime to the ridiculous, but is there any point in relating the hacks to the artists? There is a dreadful and pernicious notion about these days that we actually have two kinds of literature. One might be termed proper literature, consisting of the great and serious books that are read by a dwindling number of people. The other is "mass" or "popular" literature (Anthony Burgess calls it prolefodder). But this is an artificial distinction, one that would be quite meaningless if it didn't carry the damnable message that pleasure, fun and thrills are to be found only in one kind of book and not another.

Stephen King offers good writing and bad. At the age of forty he has published more than twenty volumes of prose, many of them quite lengthy. More novels are said to be completed and awaiting publication—at the time of this writing we seem to be in the middle of a four-book blitz; the second such in King's short career. It is the pace of a big producer, and the enormous, still-growing audience his work has found underscores the need for careful consideration.

Accounting for great success is always tricky, much more so when it is accompanied by huge output. It may be the creation of an appealing central character like Erle Stanley Gardner's Perry Mason, who has remained popular for more than fifty years now. Or it can be the overwhelming effect of detail; James Michener, for instance, lards his narratives with a wealth of encyclopedia facts and potted history. It may even be something as simple as nostalgia—there's no denying that Barbara Cartland, whose novels make Greek tragedy seem like improvisation, has tapped a vast longing for the virtues and rituals of old-fashioned courtship.

Whatever the device, we are frequently dealing with something that requires more than just literary analysis. The big producer services an intense need that is peculiar to the time in which he or she writes. Reliability is only a small part of it; big producers are in fact more susceptible to ups and downs than their less prolific colleagues. Whether the product is quality literature or hackneyed rubbish is almost beside the point. In BLOODY MURDER Julian Symons said that the best way to understand the success of a big producer is to examine the work in its sociological perspective.

Stephen King started out as a writer of horror fiction but soon became something more, and less. CARRIE, 'SALEM'S LOT and THE SHINING were the best news the genre had had in decades. The writing was fresh, natural and thoroughly contemporary. The books had terrific pace and energy, and they were wonderfully free of the cynicism and calculation that marred, for me at least, novels like ROSEMARY'S BABY and THE EXORCIST. It's worth dwelling on King's first three novels for a moment because they show him at his best.

CARRIE, as many others have remarked, strikes a true and deep chord of adolescent experience, in spite of stylistic crudities and a cobbled-together structure. Anyone who attended high school in America in the last thirty years can understand CARRIE viscerally. The staples of teenage experience—fear, innocence, cruelty, loneliness, peer pressure, sexual awakening—are all honestly dealt with in a novel that also stands squarely in the horror tradition.

'SALEM'S LOT may be highly derivative of Dracula but it may also be the most entertaining vampire novel since DRAC-ULA. It was definitely a leap forward in technique for King. The real strength of its appeal, though, is in its classic confrontation between idealistic youth (Ben and Mark) and the corrupt, dead world of adults (Barlow and his converts). The ending was defiant and challenging but not really hopeful, which made it perfect. We all know that things get worse, not better, as we grow up.

In THE SHINING the terrors of the Overlook Hotel prompt, mirror or confirm exactly the nightmarish disintegration that is taking place in Jack Torrance's mind. THE SHINING is very much a book about how adults, and their families, can go wrong (which is perhaps why the ghostly twin girls, echoes of a previous doomed family, are so frighteningly effective). The real monsters are alcoholism, pipe dreams and personal failure, and their inescapable consequences.

In all three of these novels the external horror is rooted in profoundly personal matters. In each case the point of contact, the conflict, is precisely where the central characters bump into the harsh wall of reality. There are no happy endings here, not even credible reassurance; at best there is survival, a temporary respite. King used the horror genre with instinctive skill to get at real human problems, concerns and weaknesses, which of course is what good literature is all about. True psychological terror is one form of that literary essential, the shock of recognition. King's first three novels revealed a writer who could do more than merely scare or thrill his readers: he could disturb them.

After THE SHINING scaled the bestseller lists two kinds of King books began to appear, those that were genuinely new and those that had been written earlier but deemed unpublishable, at least until success created a demand. The best of the older work is undoubtedly "Apt Pupil." Like CARRIE, it is a short, sharp, powerful novel that achieves what it sets out to do with a minimum of fuss and bother. It does not engage our sympathies in the usual way but it has a nasty fascination that works quite well. The other works in DIFFERENT SEASONS and many of King's short stories are nearly as effective.

There are some fine passages in every King novel. He has an enviable gift for sketching familiar middle class people. He has a cinematic sense of timing, suspense and structure, and he can orchestrate his special effects most impressively. If all this can be summed up as technique, then King has refined his technique with great professionalism.

Still, many of the big bestselling novels that followed THE SHINING left me feeling disappointed in one way or another. There were no more moments of bright terror, and even the lower grade horrors that were served up often had a routine, ready-made air about them. Substantive characterization, which seemed to be where King was heading, did not materialize. Some of the novels—CUJO, THINNER, CHRISTINE—had almost no psychological density whatsoever.

It was as if King deliberately turned away from the intensely personal core that gave his early work such strength, and chose instead a series of topical but abstract issues on which to hang his tales. So we got apocalypse (THE STAND), fascism and assassination (THE DEAD ZONE), a sinister government agency (FIRESTARTER), and the dual American obsessions, cars (CHRISTINE) and diet (THINNER). These things are of more than passing interest in the post-World War II era, but the books have nothing original or thoughtful, much less provocative, to say about them. They're there for convenience only, to trigger a glib sense of familiarity in the reader. They are not "sub-texts" by any stretch of language or imagination.

None of that would matter so much if these novels gave us a few engrossing, moderately complicated human beings among the dozens of minor figures. There *are* many fine touches in King's characterizations—it is one of his real strong points. But there is also an unfortunate reliance on brand name identification: cars, bikes, jewelry, restaurants, chain stores, hardware, food and beverages, even musical groups, to mention but a few in the parade. THINNER can almost pass as a mail order catalogue. King claims to be fascinated by the iconography of our modern consumer culture, but all he does is invoke it and hope for the best, like an ancient Roman enumerating the minor deities. The names are there for the same reason as the "subtexts": to facilitate a spurious feeling of recognition. This is stickerism masquerading as characterization. Any reader who can recognize a character by such trappings is a very lazy reader indeed.

But there's more to it. Compare CUJO with THE SHINING. In each novel we have a struggling family that is suddenly, drastically besieged. In each novel death claims its victims before the ordeal is over. We might expect CUJO to be the more devastating book, if only because in it the central child dies, but that is not the case. THE SHINING is a far better novel in every way. True, the Overlook Hotel may offer more possibilities than a rabid dog, but THE SHINING is emotionally convincing whereas CUJO is not—and most of the difference ultimately comes down to characterization.

Something else happened after THE SHINING. King discovered the happy ending, which, in our ultra-cool times, means discreet reassurance. THE STAND employs the Curtis LeMay solution to the problem of evil—an atom bomb; the irony seems sadly unintentional—after which the good people can begin to build a new and better world. At the end of FIRESTARTER the whole terrible story is going to be made public via *Rolling Stone* magazine. Never mind that *Rolling Stone* had already lost any semblance of being countercultural or oppositionist, and had transformed itself into the unofficial house organ of the emerging yuppie class. It was, let us say, a good icon. Even CUJO finds the silver lining. A mother loses her child but her framing perspective, from first page to last, is that she has made it into *People* magazine. It is impossible *not* to believe that the survivors in THE SHINING are scarred for life; in CUJO it is impossible to believe that they *are*.

My last point about this group of novels is that not one of them can honestly be described as horror fiction. They use certain horror elements, sometimes quite well. Randy Flagg in THE STAND is an inspired creation, but he is all too often offstage. THE DEAD ZONE and FIRESTARTER contain variations of paranormal activity, but by the end of each book they are nearly irrelevant to the main drama. CUJO has a trusted and beloved part of the natural world striking back at man, as in much better works like DuMaurier's "The Birds" and Roueche's FERAL, but by explaining it away as rabies caused by a bat bite King undercut any real horror possibilities and ended up with nothing more than a freaky incident. Machinery taking charge is a science fiction and horror golden oldie, and CHRISTINE could have been a barbed short story or novella — but at 500+ pages it is like a dwarf pumped up with steroids.

In each case the horror element has the reduced status of being part of the scenery, rather than arising as an integral part of the emotional conflict. The best horror literature is ultimately subversive, anarchic, and it seems to me that this is exactly the quality these novels lack. In reaching out for the widest possible audience, King has produced several big books that are neither good horror fiction nor good serious novels in any other sense. They are hybrid entertainments. There's nothing wrong with entertainment, but it is *not* something separate and apart from well-written, well-conceived literature — unless you subscribe to prolefodder. Compared with King's first three novels, these later ones are simply mediocre.

But they are spectacularly successful in the marketplace. Since THE SHINING (1977) very few weeks have gone by without at least one King book on the bestseller lists, and nearly every year has seen a new film based on his work. What lies behind the marketing triumph? What need is King servicing so well that his addicts number in the millions?

He is giving middle class America to middle class America,

and he has learned how to do it painlessly for all concerned. He is the scribe of the baby boomers and, to a certain extent, their kids. King *knows* childhood in the fifties, adolescence in the sixties, maturing and settling down in the seventies. This is what he offers his audience, in the form of hundreds of memories, echoes, pictures and names. Forget the melodrama and the varying frights; what's really happening is that King is holding up a mirror to his generation. They see themselves and for the most part they like what they see. His international success is no mystery, considering how much the world has been Americanized in the last forty years. Nor should it be a surprise that his books appeal to today's teenagers: King's embrace of the prevailing commercial culture is perfectly attuned to the narcissism and materialism of the Reagan eighties.

I do not mean to belittle his achievement. King has managed a rare feat, and in some ways he is unique among the regular residents of the bestseller lists. But in too many of the later novels he has neglected his most precious talent, the ability to challenge himself and his readers. All writers inevitably reflect the times in which they live, but good writers distort the mirror to reveal truth rather than mere fact. When King takes the easier way the results are finally predictable, even in an ambitious and well-intentioned novel such as THE DEAD ZONE.

Big producers disappear just as quickly as other authors. Consider E. Phillips Oppenheim and Edgar Wallace, the two hottest novelists of the twenties. Altogether they wrote more than 300 books, of which less than half a dozen are still occasionally reprinted. King is so intimately locked into the tastes and trappings of his generation that his work may suffer the same fate, most of it eventually fading into dull quaintness, clogging up the second-hand shelves and tag sales of the future.

Perverse as it may seem, Arnold Bennett might be a useful example at this point. If anyone had logorrhea it was Bennett. He made his fame and fortune with sensational, crowd-pleasing serials, and he continued to produce them throughout his life. But from time to time he would haul himself up and create a major work: THE OLD WIVES' TALE, CLAYHANGER, RICEY-

MAN STEPS, among others. Bennett never lost his fans, and whenever the critics got to the point where they were ready to dismiss him as a sell-out, he confounded them. His was one of the most intriguing careers in literature.

The third novel in the four-book blitz has now arrived. It is called MISERY and it sounds promising, a non-supernatural confrontation between two characters in an isolated setting. If nothing else it should be welcome change from the gargantuan excess of IT and the modular fantasy of THE EYES OF THE DRAGON. It is still possible to approach a new King novel with some measures of anticipation. But it seems no accident that the promotional material for MISERY specifically describes King as the author of the horror classics, CARRIE and THE SHINING. Twenty books later, those are the two that still linger vividly in the mind, and the marketing people know it.

Regardless of whether MISERY is something special or just another Stephen King novel, he has plenty of time and talent. Perhaps he should consider what Bennett understood, that being a big producer can in itself be a form of laziness. The hope here is that King will find his way to delivering a few more genuine shockers, books that disturb and unnerve us. He does not need a dazzling prose style. He does not have to stop entertaining; Graham Greene used to distinguish between his "serious" novels and his "entertainments" but eventually saw the foolishness in it. Good books are always entertaining and good style is always natural.

It would be a mistake, even in a dissenting report like this, to criticize King for failing to meet goals and expectations that are not necessarily his own. But he has already demonstrated that he can write excellent fiction that is frightening, tough, personal and uncompromising. It has been too long since he has done so, and he should stop settling for less.

THE KING AND HIS MINIONS: THOUGHTS OF A *TWILIGHT ZONE* REVIEWER

by Thomas M. Disch

I.

"*T*he time has been," Macbeth reminisces in Act V, "my senses would have cool'd to hear a night-shriek, and my fell of hair would at a dismal treatise rouse and stir as life were in it." Read a few too many dismal treatises, however, and you may find, along with Macbeth, that: "I have supp'd full with horrors; direness, familiar to my slaughterous thoughts, cannot once start me."

It may be, however, that this disclaimer, coming just before his "tomorrow and tomorrow and tomorrow" speech, is the theatrical equivalent to the obligatory false alarm in every horror movie when the cat leaps out from behind the curtains and we all shriek, and then have to laugh to reassure ourselves that "It's only the cat!"—though we know quite well that there is enough direness ahead of us to cool our senses to freezing. Not only such basic physical direness as death, disease, the frailty and corruption of the flesh, the hunger of various predators, and the dangers posed by psychopaths at loose after dark, but the further, horrible suspicion that the social system we are necessarily a part of, which is supposed to keep these dangers at bay, may instead have formed some kind of unholy alliance with them—the suspicion, to put it another way, that Macbeth may be the person who's answering the phone when we dial 911.

Those would seem to be enough different varieties of direness to guarantee some degree of timeliness and universality to the genre of the horror story. This plentitude explains why the range of the horror story, in terms of literary sophistication, should be wider than that of any other literary genre, running the gamut from the elemental night-shrieking nastiness of EC Comics to the highbrow *frissons* of James's TURN OF THE SCREW or Kafka's METAMORPHOSIS. Horror, like his brother Death, is an equal opportunity employer.

To the degree that a theme is universal, it is in proportion exploitable, and the proliferation of schlock horror novels in the wake of such box office successes as THE OMEN series, *et al.*, is hardly to be wondered at. So long as there are rustics to buy ballad-sheets there will be balladeers to supply them, though as the mean reading speed of the audience and the technology of printing have both greatly advanced in recent centuries, it's not ballad-sheets that are hawked nowadays but paperback originals.

Without dwelling on the easy irony of the word "original," let's take a quick peek inside a recent 329-page ballad-sheet brought out by Pocket Books, THE DEATHSTONE by Ken Eulo, author of THE BLOODSTONE and THE BROWNSTONE (and, doubtless, if the market holds up, of THE HEADSTONE, THE WHETSTONE, and THE RHINESTONE). There is nothing intrinsically unworkable in the book's premise of a small town keeping up the pagan tradition of human sacrifice; it's done yeoman service for Shirley Jackson's story "The Lottery," and the movie *The Wicker Man*. Horror stories are usually reenactments of favorite myths. What sinks Eulo's book to the rock-bottom of the sophistication spectrum (from savvy to sappy) is the style of his reenactment, a style that is equal parts soap-opera mawkish and button-pushing portentous, graduating to dithering hysteria for the big moments:

> They were circling the fire now, dancing in a madman's frenzy, delirium, their huge animal heads weaving in and out of shadows. The fire blazed up with a roar, sending a column of red flames soaring. They moaned and wailed and shouted. Even though the words

were unintelligible. Ron felt that their hideous shrieks were like a hand held toward him, a handshake with death.

Don't worry, though, kids. Ron doesn't die. He saves Chandal and little Kristy from the Widow Wheatley and the other wicked Satanists and returns to his talent agency in Hollywood.

* * *

If there is one key to prejudging books and consigning them, half-read, to the holocaust, it must be Style, and Style is the single word most likely to provoke hack writers and hack readers to postures of defense. Story-telling and yarn-spinning are simple, wholesome crafts, they would aver, to which questions of Style are irrelevant. Style is to be left to stylists, like Hemingway or Faulkner or Joyce, the writers you have to read in school.

Nonsense. Style is simply a way of handling yourself in prose so as to signal to an attentive reader that he is in the presence of someone possessed of honesty, wit, sophistication, irony, compassion, or whatever other attributes one looks for in a person to whom one is about to give over n-many hours of one's mental life. People who insist otherwise usually have mental halitosis.

Which is why I think it's fair for reviewers to indicate which books they have found unreadable. Otherwise the longest, dullest, worst books would only be reviewed by people able to read them, i.e., unable or unwilling to recognize their gross defects. Only creative writing teachers would review John Gardner. Only Scientologists and veterans of the Golden Age of science fiction would review BATTLEFIELD EARTH. Only authors' friends would review, say, such a book as John Shirley's CELLARS. And publishers would come to think that no one ever actually noticed what they were doing.

I might suggest burning CELLARS, though, as it's a paperback, it will yield at most only enough heat to roast some marshmallows. The tell-tale elements are the willingness to fill a blank space with any cliche that comes to mind ("like a thundering symphony"), an urge to dress up the text with portentous guff ("And the sage remembers . . ."), a merciless determination to recycle said guff, and an emotional sympathy lavished exclusively upon the first person singular. To these attractions the novel proper adds a couple wheelbarrowfuls of standard-issue splatter-movie grue ("A woman spread-eagled on her back. Her blouse had been torn away . . . Her breasts had been symmetrically quartered like fruit sections in salad."), and a misogynic regard for the fair sex to a degree that makes Mickey Spillane look like a radical feminist—all smoothed over with mystic mummeries so false they're probably intended as comic relief, as when our hero explains to the Keystone Cops the killing style associated with the mayhem quoted above: "The lettering on the circle looks like ancient Persian to me, and I suspect the ritual has something to do with the demon Ahriman." Ah so!

So CELLARS goes, the grue alternating with the hokum for 295 pages of prose that is eighty-five percent pulp padding and fifteen percent amplified scream (under another hat Shirley is the head of a punk rock group called Obsession). There is, I admit, an aesthetic to screaming, and Shirley's shriller screams can get to your crystal ware, but screaming is, as a general rule, less effective on the printed page than in rock music, where the silly lyrics are blessedly incomprehensible and the beat goes on. Novels, alas, don't have a rhythm section to keep them moving—so when the pages refuse to turn: burn, baby, burn.

* * *

Let me state clearly here that I am not disparaging "escapist reading" in order to promote "serious literature." I have a keen appetite for entertainment novels of all kinds. For some readers, it may be, the very unnaturalness and ineptitude of the lower grade of occult novels are welcome distancing devices from what might otherwise be too scary, too close for comfort. For them, mustache-twirling villainy and dime-store Halloween masks serve the same sanitizing function that the code of genteel taste serves for readers of more middlebrow spine-masseurs (tinglers they're not), such as Jonathan Carroll's VOICE OF OUR SHADOW, a preppy ghost story as decorously conventional and capably tailored as a Brooks Brothers suit. Carroll just doesn't believe in ghosts, and his disbelief is contagious. But does anyone believe in ghosts, after all?

Spiritualism flourished in the 19th century and lingered into the early decades of the 20th. Since it was the chief tenet of spiritualist faith that there *are* ghosts, many writers of ghost stories in those years expropriated for their own use much of the spiritualists' genteel intellectual baggage. This new breed of ghosts was not specters of the damned, like Hamlet's father, nor bleedin' 'orrors, beloved by readers of the penny dreadfuls. They were, instead, Lost Souls—most in transit to the Other Side, confused about but not necessarily ill-disposed toward creatures of the flesh.

Under this new dispensation, ghosts were domesticated and made to conform to the decorous tastes of a middle-class, middlebrow audience. In the American pulps there was still full-frontal ghastliness, but British ghosts were expected to comport themselves like ordinary people. When an ex-wife wished to haunt her faithless husband (as in Mary Treadgold's "The Telephone"), her reproaches were conveyed over the phone, in what we must imagine to be a subdued tone. The theory is that ghosts are credible in proportion to the gentility of their manners. The brush of a sleeve, a stifled sigh—these are to be the stuff of horror, and in the hands of a good writer they serve very well. The greatest of all ghost stories, James's THE TURN OF THE SCREW, doesn't bother with horrid shrieks and rattled chains.

Yet if they were on their oaths, I'm sure most of the best ghost-story writers would admit that their ghosts are symbols of Something Else. Which is a roundabout way of saying that, finally, Eulo and Shirley and Carroll (and unnumbered others) fail for this reason—a reluctance to make eye contact with their fears. Instead of real horrors to sup upon, with meat and maggots on their bones, they offer plastic skeletons.

II.

Stephen King is another matter. He has enjoyed his success precisely because he's remained true to his own clearest sense of what is fearful, fearfuler, fearfulest. What King fears is his own and other people's capacity for cruelty and brutality; madness, loneliness, disease, pain, and death; men, women, most forms of animal life, and the weather. When King introduces supernatural or paranormal elements into his tales it is as a stand-in for one of the above-mentioned "natural" fears. Thus, Carrie's telekinetic powers in his first novel are emblematic of the force of a long-stifled anger erupting into rage, and the horror of 'SALEM'S LOT is that of witnessing the archetypal Our Town of Rockwell, Wilder, and Bradbury electing Dracula as mayor and appointing his wives to the Board of Education.

King's DIFFERENT SEASONS is a collection of four quite separate tales, only one of which (and that, thankfully, the shortest) failed to shiver my timbers perceptibly—though King has throughout DIFFERENT SEASONS kept to the hither side of the natural/supernatural divide. The other three, in ascending order both of length and personal preference, are: "Rita Hayworth and Shawshank Redemption," a quietly paranoid curtain-raiser that persuaded me *never* to be framed for murder and sentenced to life imprisonment; "The Body," a vivid if sometimes self-consciously "serious" account of the rites of passage practised by the aboriginal teenagers of Maine's lower-middle class (and a telling pendant to the novel 'SALEM'S LOT); finally, the hands-down winner of the four and, I think, King's most accomplished piece of fiction at any length, "Apt Pupil." (In his book's afterward, King complains about the difficulty of publishing novellas of 25,000 to 35,000 words. Yet "The Body" and "Apt Pupil" are respectively, double those lengths, and even the shorter tale would have made a weightier book than Carroll's VOICE OF OUR SHADOW. I don't mean to look a gift horse in the mouth, only to point out that DIFFERENT SEASONS is more nearly a collection of novels than of stories.)

The premise for "Apt Pupil" could scarcely be simpler. A bright, all-American thirteen-year-old discovers that one of his suburban neighbors was the infamous Kurt Dussander, commandant of a Nazi death camp. Instead of reporting Dussander to the police, this paragon of the eighth grade begins to blackmail him—not for money but just "to hear about it":

"*Hear* about it?" Dussander echoed. He looked utterly perplexed.

Todd leaned forward, tanned elbows on bluejeaned knees. "Sure. The firing squads. The gas chambers. The ovens. The guys who had to dig their own graves and then stand on the ends so they'd fall into them. The . . ." His tongue came out and wetted his lips. "The examinations. The experiments. Everything. All the gooshy stuff."

Dussander stared at him with a certain amazed detachment, the way a veterinarian might stare at a cat who was giving birth to a succession of two-headed kittens. "You are a monster," he said softly.

To tell more of how this oddest of all couples leapfrog down the road to damnation would be a disservice to anyone who hasn't yet read the book. I'm told by those who have a hand on the pulse of sf and fantasy fandom that "Apt Pupil" has not been exactly taken to the hearts of King's usually quite faithful subjects. I can only suppose that this is a tribute to how closely it cuts to the bone. Surely, in terms simply of generating suspense and keeping the plot twisting, "Apt Pupil" cannot be faulted. I hope Losey gets to make the movie, or that Hitchcock could return from the grave for just one more production. Not since STRANGERS ON A TRAIN has there been a plot so perfectly suited to his passion for ethical symmetries.

* * *

As I write this, Stephen King's PET SEMATARY has already been on the *New York Times* bestseller list for ten weeks. The considerable interest (and ultimate failure) of PET SEMATARY is directly related to the themes I've been dealing with above. The story concerns a doctor disordered by his grief for a loved child, and who succumbs to the temptation of "resurrecting" the child by interring its corpse in an Indian burial ground that has the spectral property of reanimating the dead. King does his usual skillful job of seducing us into accepting his unlikely story, and at the same time creates an atmosphere drenched in the fear of death. One would have to be a very guileless reader indeed not to foresee that the author has doomed his hero's child to an early death. The real element of suspense is how the child will behave in its resurrected state, and King's answer is to have the little zombie go on a rampage of homicide and dirty talk that was like watching a cassette of THE EXORCIST on fast forward. My objection to this denouement is neither to its strain on credibility nor to its mayhem, but to the way it fails to carry forward, still less to resolve, the novel's so powerfully stated themes—the human need to believe, at any cost, in an afterlife, a need that can drive those who lack the safety valve of a religious faith to such bizarre excesses as spiritualism.

King's opting for a conventional splatter-movie resolution to the question, "What if the dead were to live again?," is all the more regrettable, since in the figure of Church, a zombified cat, he has prefigured a possibility that is both more harrowing and more pertinent to the central themes of loss and grief, though in Church's case it is the loss of those vital energies that together constitute the soul. From having been the *beau ideal* of cattiness, Church degenerates into a sluggish, surly scavenger; not at all a demonic cat, just spoiled meat. If the dead child had returned from the grave similarly disensouled, the horror would have been infinitely greater, because that loss would be a vivid correlative to a parental fear of a fate truly worse than death, the fear that one's child may be severely mentally impaired.

It's doubtful, of course, whether the public wants to be harrowed. The blustering denouement King does provide is reassuring to readers precisely to the degree that it's conventional; it's King's way of telling us not to be upset: it was only a ghost story, after all.

Part of the problem is simply that ghost stories are by their nature short, since the psychology of most literary ghosts is simple in the extreme: they want to getcha. "Dark fantasy" (Charles L. Grant's high-toned euphemism for "horror stories"; thus undertakers become "grief counselors" and garbagemen "sanitary engineers") is a traditional rather than an experimental or innovative art form, as much a ritual as a form of literature, and its "devotees" bring to bear criteria of judgment and that have less to do with criticism than with incantation and magic. The old ways must not be departed from, nor any traditional rite omitted.

There are undeniable advantages to playing the game by the

rules. Geniuses may fly in the face of tradition, but when their epigones attempt to follow them, the result is likely to lack both the strength of conventional post-and-lintel construction or the energy of first defiance. Traditional values in fiction (a strong plot, believable characters, flowing prose) are a safeguard against major debacle in much the way that wearing evening clothes protects one against sartorial solecisms. They offer, as do the sonnet and the sonata form, the aesthetic satisfaction of *tight* closure. But the chief virtue of a traditional narrative, for most readers, is surely that it is *comfortable*, like a couch one has lived with many years and that has learned the shape of one's head. Since horror stories must deal with subjects that are inherently disquieting, this observance of aesthetic decorums ("Once upon a time...") helps defuse—or at least distance—feelings that could be genuinely dangerous, if given a less circumscribed expression.

At his best, Stephen King has shown himself capable of combining the *frissons* of the supernatural thriller with the weightier stuff of tragedy, but in the present instance he has decided to sidestep that harder task and just lay on the special effects till he's spent his budget of potential victims. I hope it doesn't represent a long-term decision.

III.

In the two-and-fraction years that I reviewed for *Twilight Zone* magazine, I was able to divide my column inches about equally between the genres of science fiction and horror with occasional forays outside those adjoining ghettos, but I confess that I found less and less of it that I could read with pleasure, interest, or vigorous dissent. In the case of horror fiction, this is probably not to be wondered at. Being by definition limited to the evocation of a single emotion, and by hoary convention to a few traditional narrative themes, a steady diet of the stuff is calculated to produce an eventual toxic reaction. As well give all one's musical attention to oboe concerti.

Even in science fiction, while its potential may be undiminished, the actual stuff that sees print has been (with some honorable exceptions) more tepid, more formulaic, and more ill-written than at any time since its last cyclic nadir in the late fifties and early sixties. In part it's the publishers who are to be blamed; they manufacture a product suitable for the most reliable part of their market, the proverbial Common Denominator, who are, not to put too fine a point on it, dopes, or if that seems too harsh, let us say they suffer from reading dysfunctions.

There has been increasingly louder lamentation in the publishing industry during the last few years over the fate of what is euphemistically called mid-list fiction, by which is meant novels not likely to become bestsellers. *Most* fiction of any quality nowadays falls into this mid-list category, as witness the now virtually total disparity between the books the *New York Times Book Review* commends to our attention and those that fill its hardcover and paperback bestseller lists. Consider the sf titles on the *Times* list for the week of, say, January 9, 1983. There is THE E.T. STORYBOOK, titles by Clarke and Asimov (I won't rehash my dissatisfaction with FOUNDATION'S EDGE and 2010 except to say I found the plots of both books numbingly predictable and the wattage of the prose varying between 60 and 15), a prehistoric bodice-ripper, and a new potpourri of toothless whimsies by Douglas Adams. A sorry lot, but no sorrier, in literary terms, than the rest of the list, which contained not a single title remotely conceivable as a candidate for the major literary awards.

Why does dreck so often rise to the top of the bestseller list? Is there some merit in these books that their prose disfigures, as acne can disfigure a structurally handsome face? Or is it (I will propose) precisely their faults that endear them to an audience who recognizes in these novels a true mirror image of their own lame brains?

Meanwhile, in the realm of Something Lower, where books are but numbers in a series, the hacks grind out and the presses print the sf and horror equivalent of Silhouette Romances, the sheer mass of which is awesome in much the same way that Niagara Falls is awesome: there is so much of it and it never stops. The metaphor needn't stop there: it is, similarly, not very potable, and most of it courses through the paperback racks without ever being reviewed. Why should it be, after all? Are sneakers or soft drinks or matchbooks reviewed? Commodities are made to be consumed, and surely it is an unkindness for those favored by fortune with steak in plenty to be disdainful of the "taste" of people who must make do with Hamburger Helper.

This is not the proper occasion to speculate how this situation has come about; whether the publishers by their greed, the writers by laziness or native incapacity, or the audience by its hunger for the swill are most culpable. Yet I can't resist stepping down from the platform without relating one final anecdote that bears on these matters. Recently at an sf gathering where fans and writers were mingling, a younger writer from Texas insisted on explaining to me, at great length, the secret of his success. (His first tetralogy has been through several printings; his second, he assured me, was destined for still bigger bucks.) His secret was that he'd found out the name and address of every sales rep who worked for his publisher and had programmed his computer to write each one of them a warm and personal letter thanking them for the efforts he was sure they were making on his behalf. He said it was especially important to get the sales reps to stock your title at airport book stalls; he knew this because he'd been in the distribution end of the business before he'd turned to writing. He assured me that the quality of a book was quite beside the point and that what mattered most of all was the writer's relationship with the reps. When I was in high school we had a name for that relationship.

Well, it's a good anecdote, but I don't think it explains the smell of the world in general. Some lousy writers—and those usually the most successful—are doing their level best. Other lousy writers kvetch about market forces but are happy for the excuse to produce slipshod work. In many cases, the problem is engine failure.

*   *   *

My tenure of office as *Twilight Zone*'s book critic from the issues of May 1982 until February 1985 was not all as discouraging as those last dire reflections may sound. I may be disgruntled by some of the poorer books that came under review, but not driven to despair by them. Indeed, rereading assorted columns, I am reminded not only of the original pleasure of combat, but also of the simpler, gregarious pleasures of working with *TZ*'s then editor T.E.D. Klein, who offered a reviewer all he could ask for: *carte blanche* in the choice of what I reviewed, decent wages, a sufficiency of applause, and hours of good talk about writers and what they write. Since leaving my post at *TZ*, it is those visits with Ted that I've most missed.

Though I had *carte blanche* at *TZ*, it was nevertheless imperative that I should deal with any new Stephen King book that appeared. He was not only the King of the genre but already, even then, of bestsellerdom as a whole. Ordinarily I would have shied away from reviewing a writer in that position. As someone who tills in the same genres—but for vastly lower wages—enthusiasm for his work can easily look like one is sucking up to the man and his success, while to give him any critical lumps at all can easily be interpreted as sour grapes. In the context of *Twilight Zone*, such reservations seemed to loom less large.

Furthermore, the kind of criticism that King's work most lacks is the kind that deals with more than theme and that awards merits or demerits for "originality" or "style"—that is, a kind of criticism that goes beyond reviewing. But that kind of criticism is hard work, *and* I doubt whether King's oeuvre really requires such attention. For that reason, and also because the latest additions to the oeuvre have not seemed especially tempting (I've read THINNER and thought it thin; I've contemplated the horrid bulk of IT, read its reviews, and shuddered), I have not taken advantage of this opportunity to double my two-cents-worth on the subject, except to note, in as neutral a tone as I can command, that the interest of King's work stems at least as much from its success as a commodity as from its aesthetic merits. King is more than a writer, he is a publishing phenomenon, and as such transcends criticism.

His most salient virtue, as a commodity, is the consistency and reliability with which the Product is produced. Fame hasn't made King slack off *or* aspire greatly. The result is a fictional

Levittown, acres of decent housing all at exactly the same mid-
dling level of accomplishment and ambition. It doesn't give a
critic much to consider.

It's the personality and the situation that are interesting.
King has been very successful in creating a public image of
himself as a Big Kid who's just having fun and goofing off and
filling nickel tablets with million-dollar novels, the latest of
which, IT, concerns a novelist in just that happy situation, yes?
Self-referentiality is supposedly a hallmark of postmodern
writing, and there's King being as self-referential as can be. But
why? Because the Stephen King Story cries out to be told? Or
because he has a canny sense of the market and knows that
every fannish (i.e., addicted) Reader entertains daydreams of
becoming a Writer like King, rich and famous and triumphant
over all those insensitive souls who laughed when he sat down
to play?

SNOWBOUND IN THE OVERLOOK HOTEL

by Guy N. Smith

*D*uring the severe winter of 1979 I was snowbound in the Overlook Hotel! The blizzards came, piled the snow up to the windows, blocked all the routes in and out, and created hedge lions and other creatures of terror which might or might not have moved during those long hours of darkness; it was impossible to tell because the snow was frozen hard, and not even the starving rabbits which crept in to gnaw at the boles of young trees and shrubs left any footprints.

For me it all began back in October. I had lunched with my publisher in London and successfully negotiated a new contract. As I was about to leave the editorial director handed me a chunky paperback off his desk and said, "Have a read at this sometime, you might enjoy it."

I had a browse through the book during the long train journey home to my remote farmhouse high up in the Shropshire, amidst the Welsh border hills. The title was THE SHINING by Stephen King. I'd heard of King, of course, but I had yet to read any of his works. CARRIE hadn't appeared on the bookstalls and I had dismissed 'SALEM'S LOT as yet another overdone vampire theme. Well, I'd read this one sometime, I promised myself, and put it on my bookshelves in a place where it wouldn't get totally overlooked.

Then, two months later came the blizzards, eight foot drifts that cut us off from civilization, stopped the mail from arriving but fortunately left us with the telephone. At the time I was working on LOCUSTS but even the atmosphere I was trying to create of a drought and incessant burning heat failed to keep me warm. The cold was such that the single radiator in my study was not sufficient and I was forced to take the typewriter into the kitchen and work on the table close to the stove.

Without any distractions during the daytime, because there was no chance of going any further than the logpile in the backyard, I kept on schedule and for once had my evenings free. So I decided to have a read at that book THE SHINING.

If ever the atmosphere in a book got through to the reader it did then. That very first evening I was totally convinced that I was marooned in the Overlook; a freezing wind howled inside and lots of things creaked and moved that I could not really pinpoint. My skin prickled the way the author had intended it to, and once I leaped up from my chair because I was sure I heard Danny calling; it was, in fact, my own youngest son calling from his bedroom, seeking an excuse to come downstairs and join us for a while.

I began getting in extra buckets of logs during the daytime because I didn't like going outside any more after dark! Those hedge lions, crouched in the shadows beyond the yard light, surely moved and I began thinking that they might try and cut off my retreat to the back door. And when I went upstairs for a bath I found myself leaning round the door to pull the lightpull just in case there happened to be a bloated old woman floating dead in the bath!

I am a slow reader and in a masochistic sort of way I savored every page, and by the time I was getting towards the end of the book the snowplough had reached us, cut a single channel down one of the narrow lanes with an eight foot wall of snow on either side. Well, we were in need of replenishing our supplies so the next day I decided that, with luck, I could make it to the nearest small town and back in the car. I had to because a further belt of snow was reported to be moving across the Atlantic and we would surely be cut off again; Stephen King was ensuring that I got the full treatment and a proper initiation into his unique world of horror.

I made it to town in the early afternoon and I did not hurry because when you have been cut off for any length of time you appreciate the bustle of people around you. I finished my shopping, lingered over a coffee, and on the way back to the car I called in at a bookshop and bought a couple of paperbacks — CARRIE and 'SALEM'S LOT! If King could do this to me then I was greedy for more.

But my experiences at the Overlook weren't quite over yet. Darkness had fallen by the time I turned off the main road back into the two miles of snowploughed lanes, and that was when the nightmare began all over again. The Cortina wasn't a car any longer, it had suddenly become a snowmobile and I was Hallorann going in search of Danny Torrance. The hedge creatures lined the tops of the ploughed snow ravine in force, not just lions but every imaginable spook shape, big ones, small ones, and they really *moved*. Some slipped and fell, bounced on the rutted track, broke and powdered in the twin beams of the headlights, slithered on the car roof and rolled off, united in their efforts to try and get to me. A huge one blocked my path, I trod on the gas and hit it at full speed, crunched it flat and somehow lurched over it. A nightmare ride, there might just be one big enough round the next bend that would stop me and the track was now so narrow that the car doors were touching on either side so that I wouldn't have been able to get out anyway. I'd be stuck there all night and. . . .

I made it, reversed into the yard down the track I'd dug out the day before, backed right up to the door and unloaded as fast as I could. All I wanted was to get indoors and bar the door against these lurking terrors which King had sent to get me.

During the next fortnight I read CARRIE and 'SALEM'S LOT. I preferred the latter to the former because it opened up a fresh angle on the vampire theme, but Stephen King had given me a lot to think about.

What makes Stephen King tick, why is he so different from all the other horror writers? To begin with I believe that it is the *realism* of his themes and, on reflection, I don't think it really needed a snowed-up farmhouse to bring it all home to me. The claustrophobic terror is all there, the Torrances couldn't just up and walk away from it even if they'd wanted to (which they certainly did!); they were stuck with it, as are all the characters in his other books.

But that in itself would not be enough if the reader could not identify with the characters, really *feel* for them. Cardboard silhouette figures flitting through the pages would not work because you wouldn't give a damn what happened to them. They are *ordinary* people, not distant professors of something-or-other, or politicians or public figures. They are you and I, our friends and relatives, and if they walked in through the door tomorrow we would recognise them and say, "Hi, how goes it?"

So we have characters we can identify with caught up in a plot which isn't just a re-hash of some Lovecraftian idea; it is new and it appeals, scares us, and we love to be scared because we're nice and safe and it could not possibly happen to us. Or, there is a nagging thought which we try to push to the back of our minds, that it just *might*. So we read on and hope that everything will come out all right in the end.

But Stephen King has even more than all this and I'm not just talking about talent; that goes without saying. He has a style all of his own which makes for easy and entertaining reading. I once read somewhere that it was a "colloquial" style and I'm not sure whether that was meant to be a criticism or not. If it is colloquial then that is what his huge readership demands and to take it away would be to reduce him to the ranks of lesser writers in the genre. We are dealing with a phenomenon who will be linked with Poe and Lovecraft many decades hence, except that he is a giant in his own time whereas the other two became legends long after theirs. We are witnessing a legend which will escalate; this is only the beginning, and King is still a young man who will surely turn out many more books.

For me there will never be another SHINING though. I don't want one, a sequel would surely detract from the original book, and that winter fortnight will live with me for the rest of my life.

But what of his other books? I received a present from an American friend of DIFFERENT SEASONS and again I was pleasantly surprised. Different seasons and different themes, none of them truly horror to the purist, yet they were compelling reading, left an impression and an awful lot to think about afterwards. King's books need to be read slowly, I am convinced of that (if that is possible!), for there are many gems which will be overlooked by the "scanner." It is nothing short of sacrilege to read one at a single sitting.

CUJO ranks in my top three although I felt that the sub-plot spoiled it; I wanted to get on with the main story and I wasn't much interested in what was happening away from that broken down car in the burning heat. THE STAND, too, would have had a higher placing in my list of favourites if it had been around 500 pages. But that is a personal choice, others prefer the monster read to the shorter one.

Then one day I had a letter from a bookselling friend in the States asking if I could get him copies of paperbacks by an author called *Richard Bachman*, published in the U.K. by New English Library. He needed as many as I could find because, he claimed, Bachman was Stephen King! My first thought was "rubbish," Stephen King had no need of a pseudonym, but I'd do my best to get the books anyway. I phoned several bookshops without success, and even phoned the publishers, but there were no Bachman books available. A week later the rumour was confirmed as fact and it took me three months to find a copy each of THINNER and THE RUNNING MAN. I would have recognised them as King's work had I chanced to read either before this amazing revelation and King's own confession.

I enjoyed them primarily because they were shorter books, but they would not have found their way into the bestseller lists on the strength of a hitherto unknown writer called Bachman. King is the undisputed king of horror and nothing less than his name will appeal to a worldwide readership. That fact is now proven through Bachman.

Of course there will be books and more books about Stephen King himself, for those who have hungered for his next novel want to know everything there is to know about the author. Other writers will try to emulate him, but that is an impossibility. He has become more than just the world's best-selling author, he has achieved a status beyond that of a writer of horror fiction. He has set a standard which has made life difficult for all other authors.

But for myself he is something more than special. He showed me *real* terror in that fortnight trapped in the Overlook and whatever else he writes nothing can take those frightening, magical two weeks away from me. He has shown me new dimensions which even the old masters of terror failed to do.

BY CROUCH END, IN THE ISLES

by Peter Tremayne

What sort of influence are Stephen King and his work having on my side of the Atlantic, in these islands which constitute the United Kingdom and the Republic of Ireland? Now I am a great believer in being specific and not using convenient labels. So, at the outset, I must be explicit about what is generally regarded in the United States as "British literature." You see, the blanket term actually encompasses several cultural traditions and several languages as well.

The United Kingdom is a multi-national state, with English the dominant language and dominant culture within the islands. But also there are the Welsh, Scottish Gaelic and Cornish languages and their cultures, which are Celtic. The Isle of Man, halfway between Ireland and Britain, a self-governing island, legally a Crown Dependency outside the United Kingdom, is also Celtic; the Manx language is similar to Scottish Gaelic and Irish. And, of course, Ireland, both the Republic and the six north-east counties of Ulster (contentiously part of the United Kingdom), also has a Celtic language and tradition.

Scarcely a day goes by without the name Stephen King registering in my consciousness. Am I such a devout fan, you may ask? No; the fact is that I live in North London. My house—Alan Ryan described it as "a lovely Victorian house near Highgate Cemetery" in HALLOWE'EN HORRORS—is just minutes from the scenic Victorian graveyard where Bram Stoker used to spend his Sunday afternoons, where author Karl Marx lies buried though DAS KAPITAL lives on. As any *aficionado* of horror will tell you, Stoker used the cemetery as the location for the tomb of the undead Lucy Westerna, describing an actual tomb which, for a modest fee, enthused guides will conduct you to, drooling at the mouth while they describe Stoker's moment of inspiration at the tomb one wild, dusk-shrouded evening *when* . . . ah, but that's another story.

Beyond the cemetery sprawls Hampstead Heath, another Stoker location, where you can pretend that you are not in a great concrete urban conubation. Both the cemetery and the Heath are due west from my house, across a high-spanned Victorian bridge, officially known as the Archway, spanning the main Great North Road out of London. Unofficially, it is known as "Suicide Bridge" with the unenviable reputation as the spot where despairing individuals decide to (literally) drop out of life, about 250 feet to the concrete highway below.

Across the brow of the hill to the north, again just a few minutes away, is a district of London called Crouch End. Once a shy, retiring hamlet amidst the farmlands which surrounded London of yesteryear, it was suddenly overwhelmed by the flood of late Victorian concrete and bricks. Now it is not simply a suburb, it is part of metropolitan London itself. You can just see the remains of a village. The streets of Crouch End spiral away from a central clock-tower where the main street, Broadway, channels the winding, narrow road down Crouch Hill and then forks it into roadways leading to Muswell Hill and to Tottenham. Until a decade ago it was still fairly sleepy, an area more or less bypassed by the hustle and bustle of London life.

Towards the end of the 1970s or early 1980s Stephen King visited Crouch End. I believe the main purpose of the visit was to spend a few days with Peter Straub, author of GHOST STORY, FLOATING DRAGON, *etc*. Now what Peter Straub was doing living in Crouch End, I have no idea. I'll tell you the fascinating truth about this neck of the woods—it has more publishers, agents, journalists, illustrators and writers populating it per square meter than any other comparable area in the country.

You can't go for a walk without falling over someone in the business. Take my street as an example. It contains some forty plus houses. Now I have not done a survey to give exact figures but offhand, from encounters in the corner shop, I can name one publisher, two editors, two agents, an illustrator and five writers inhabiting those houses. Pretty incestuous, isn't it?

One of Crouch End's most distinguished luminaries until recently was horror-writer *extraordinaire* Brian Lumley, who used to live just around the corner. Have you read his short story "Late Shopping"? I remember Brian writing that after a visit to our local supermarket. If you want to know the sort of people we are in this neck of the woods, read it. I guess it was soon after this that Brian decided to pull out of atmospheric Crouch End and is now holed-up in a nice little house beside the sea in Devon. Maybe "Late Shopping" had something to do with his moving. . . .

After Stephen King's visit to this little corner of the world, he too wrote a short story about it, putting Crouch End on the international map. I hope you've all read "Crouch End," first published in NEW TALES OF THE CTHULHU MYTHOS, edited by Ramsey Campbell for Arkham House in 1982. I suppose that Crouch End and its environs is a place conducive to horror writing.

So you see, whenever I walk abroad on the streets of my neighborhood, I am always reminded of Stephen King, a writer who first intruded into my life back in October, 1979. I was *en route* for the Fifth World Fantasy Convention in Providence, Rhode Island. I flew into New York first, to see my publishers, do some radio and television chatshows and launch the U.S. editions of my Dracula trilogy. It had been a wearisome flight with a remarkable degree of turbulence as we crossed the Newfoundland coastline and headed down towards JFK. Certain brown paper bags were much in evidence in the closing stages of the flight. I must have looked pretty disreputable as I staggered towards the Customs Control.

A tight-faced young man homed in on me.

"These your bags?" he barked. I was about to be flippant and deny all knowledge of the bags I clasped in my sweaty paws.

Then his dark, gimlet eyes met mine and I simply mumbled: "Yessir!"

Surprisingly, he demanded my passport, even though I had been through the passport control. He raised an eyebrow when he saw my profession.

"What do you write?" Words? No, no. Be civil. I told him. A curious expression crossed his face. Horror fantasy?

"Yes. I'm on my way to the World Fantasycon in Providence." His harsh face crumbled.

"Ah . . . I wanted to go but I'm on duty. I'm a fan."

Words were obviously inadequate to comfort him.

He regained control sharply: "Do you know Stephen King," he barked.

Regretfully, I denied any acquaintance. I knew *of* him, I confessed. Indeed, back in 1975 an eager publisher has pressed 'SALEM'S LOT into my hands and told me to read it. I did. I was impressed. Subsequently I picked up his first novel CARRIE and then THE SHINING. The Customs man showed intense disappointment that I did not move in the right circles.

"You'll meet him at Providence, I expect?"

I expected.

"Tell me, don't you think he's the greatest thing to hit horror fantasy since John Webster?"

Jesus, Mary and Joseph! *John Webster*?! I was doubtless in the presence of a true FAN! Webster (*c.* 1580-1625) is regarded as the first true writer of horror fiction with such numbers as THE WHITE DEVIL (1612) and THE DEVIL'S LAW CASE (1623).

To cut a long story short, there was I being grilled by a JFK Customs official on the finer points of Stephen King's fiction. If I did not make the right answers I had little doubt that I would be refused entry into the country. An hour later I was able to disengage myself and emerged cursing the name of King and all his works. I can claim to have suffered on behalf of the man. . . .

On that trip and others I have noticed a habit in the United States of lumping everything that comes out of these islands as "British," by which is meant "English." The literary traditions in the languages other than English are very strong and, indeed, Irish is the third literary language of Europe, pre-dated only by Greek and Latin. Generally speaking, literary traditions in the Celtic languages of these islands tend to be ignored by the English literary tradition, a subject of much sadness.

Particularly in the horror genre the English and Celtic traditions are extremely clear. It is a curious fact that, on taking any cross sample of the leading horror-fantasy writers under the general label of "British," we find that the preponderance of them are Celtic or of Celtic origin. I have examined this curiosity in an essay in Roman Iswaschkin's HANDBOOK OF POPULAR BRITISH CULTURE (Greenwood Press, 1987), asking whether it is a mere nationalist indulgence to attribute some cultural influence to the fact that macabre fiction seems to be the forte of the Celtic nations within "British" culture.

I believe that it is no accident. That element of cosmic horror and fantasy appeared as an intrinsic ingredient in the earliest Celtic myths and folklore and crystallized in Celtic literature. In particular, we find this to be true among the Irish literary traditions where fantasy always has been and is still a strong element. The themes of the supernatural, the break in the natural laws of our universe, have been stock in trade of Irish writers from earliest times, writing in both the Irish and English languages. I would argue that this element is more predominant than it is in the work of their more "down to earth" English counterparts. It is this exploitation by Celtic writers, or writers of Celtic background, of the cultural traditions handed down to them which provides an ability to present breaks in natural law as vivid and realistic.

Charles Maturin, Fitzjames O'Brien, Sheridan LeFanu, Bram Stoker, R. L. Stevenson (DR. JEKYLL AND MR. HYDE), John Buchan (THE WATCHER ON THE THRESHOLD), Sutherland Menzies (author of the first werewolf story in English), Oscar Wilde (THE PICTURE OF DORIAN GRAY), M. P. Shiel, Arthur Machen, Algernon Blackwood, A. Conan Doyle, Dorothy Macardle (of THE UNINVITED fame), William Morris, Lord Dunsany, George Macdonald, C. S. Lewis, John Cowper Powys . . . well, the list of Celts in the fantasy field is endless. And when you examine some of those accepted as English then you have more fun — the Brontës, for example (dad was Irish from Co. Down and mum was from Cornwall). Even William Blake's father was from Rathmines, in Ireland.

The point is that whichever language the Celts choose to write in—their mother tongue or the *lingua franca* of English—they produce a powerful school of fantasists. There is a long tradition of horror writing in all the "British" languages going back to our friend John Webster in the early 17th century. Works from Celtic writers working in English and English writers have brought the genre to an exceptionally high standard.

The sad thing is that in recent years there has been a decline of those standards generally and I believe that this decline is not only reflected in literature in these islands but in the United States as well. So before we take off about Stephen King's influence on "British" horror fantasy, let us be sure that we know what we are talking about.

The enduring masters of the genre have achieved acclaim because they dealt with "horror" not as an end in itself but as a means of social moralizing. This should not be taken at its crudest level but in acceptance of the fact that all art is comment. These masters have dealt with the horror element in a subtle way, producing works which skillfully prick at the subconscious until the reader is fearful without being aware of why he is afraid, drawn on with terrified tread until it is too late to turn back to safety.

Today, especially in the "British" tradition, we find too many writers substituting sheer nausea for subtle fear of the unknown. In stating this, perhaps I risk being torn limb from limb by some of my fellow scribes in the same gruesome way as they would dissect their own characters. I do not seek to attack them individually nor impugn their motives. But within these islands I find a disturbing rejection of our own not inconsiderable traditions in the genre. More and more we are tending to become pale imitations of modern American writers in style and theme. There is a frustrating tendency for our writers to become "mid-Atlantic," but they are not even emulating the best of American horror writers, only echoing the worst aspects. Technicolor gore rather than the stealthily creeping terror of something unseen and shapeless is the ingredient being used to make people react.

In his famous essay "Supernatural Horror in Literature," H. P. Lovecraft, speaking of his contemporaries, believed that horror stories had profited by the long evolution of the type and possessed naturalness, convincingness, artistic smoothness and skillful intensity quite beyond comparison with anything in the genre of previous years. Technique, craftsmanship, experience and psychological knowledge had, so Lovecraft believed, advanced tremendously with the passing years so that much older work seemed naive and artificial.

Lovecraft died in 1937. Unfortunately, if he had lived into the 1980s he would have seen a total reverse of his estimation in the process of much horror writing, especially during the last twenty years. In general things have got worse, not better.

The trouble is that most writers are trying to compete with films or, indeed, actually write their works with the hope of a film in mind, rather than be content to produce a literary work. As filmmaking has become more sophisticated in terms of technical approach, filmmakers have become more explicit. A close-up of a severed hand actually looks like a severed hand. Teenage filmgoers have come to expect blood, gore and vomit, violence and sheer nastiness. The crass gruesomeness of many horror movies, the utterly sick stupidity of video-nasties, has had a remarkably negative effect on many writers moving into the horror genre. They believe that is what horror literature is all about, but that is not what it is all about.

Think of one of the most horrifying passages in DRACULA (1897). It is not a passage about cascades of blood, torn flesh or sexual nastiness. It is the simple scene where Jonathan Harker peers out of his bedroom window in Castle Dracula to see the Count crawling down the wall . . . *head first*!

Or take, as example, one of the most horrifying tales of all time, "The Voice in the Night" by William Hope Hodgson, a fearful tale in which not one drop of blood is spilt. A ship is becalmed in a mist. The sound of a dinghy being rowed comes from nearby. A voice hails the ship, pleading for provisions. Subsequently, the voice tells a story of how its owner and his fiance have been shipwrecked on an island covered with fungus. Supplies gone, they have been forced to eat the all pervasive fungus. The effects are terrible, and they are resolved to their doom. The dinghy begins to row away. The story ends:

> I glanced about me. I became aware that the dawn was upon us.
> The sun flung a stray beam across the hidden sea; pierced the mist dully, and lit up the receding boat with a gloomy fire. Indistinctly, I saw something nodding between the oars. I thought of a sponge—a great, grey nodding sponge—The oars continued to ply. They were grey—as was the boat—and my eyes searched a moment vainly for the conjunction of hand and oar. My gaze flashed back to the—head. It nodded forward as the oars went backward for the stroke. Then the oars were dipped, the boat shot out of the patch of light, and the—the thing went nodding into the mist.

Ah, when the "Blood, Gore and Vomit" brigade have been forgotten or are some curiosity in the eyes of a literary mortician of 20th century popular literature, the work of those who see the genre as something more than merely a means to momentarily shock readers or make them sick will still be remembered. Their stories will remain quite rightly as masterpieces, not only of this genre in particular but of literature in general.

Now where does Stephen King enter this sad state of affairs which I see within "British" horror literature?

When King made his entrance into the genre it was already, generally, in decline. There were several worthy individuals writing in the field but once again let me stress I am speaking in general terms. King appeared as a bright star in a tarnished firmament. He succeeded in reintroducing the element of *literature* into the genre. And if writers, in whatever genre they practice, are not concerned with literature, then what the hell are they doing putting pen to paper?

King shot to fame as a phenomenon. No other writer in the genre has ever produced such a series of bestsellers in both hardcover and paperback nor scored the amazing amount of box office successes with films based on his work. Yet he is not writing with the purpose of a film in mind, not trying to compete with technicolor gore and filmic tricks. He is first, foremost and above all things a writer.

"Good writing in itself is a pleasure," he once wrote, "and it can seduce you into the story. I'm not very concerned with style, but I am concerned with the balance. Language should have a balance the reader can feel and get into—rhythm to the language as it moves along. Because if the reader is seduced in the story then it carries him away."

King, therefore, is a man who takes his craft seriously. He is not writing merely for money, in spite of the immortal intelligence pronounced by the learned Doctor Sam Johnson! He is writing with passion, with consummate literary skill, and he uses the allegory of horror-fantasy to comment on the outrageous state of modern society. He brings his skills together so that they become a literary *tour de force*.

Whitley Streiber placed his finger on the heart of the matter when he wrote:

> . . . his work is also important both as literature and as culture matter. He writes from the heart of the American experience. There is something in his voice that fits our American ear very well. We feel comfortable with a guy like him telling us a good story, and we know he comes to us with truth. We like justice, and to see it done fulfills one of our deepest longings. King talks American. . . .

Herein is the message that I want to put across. In being true to his own cultural ethos, Stephen King is true to all cultures and can therefore appeal to and be accepted by them. King does not betray his own cultural background, his own social experience and therefore his own intellect.

This is the essential lesson that writers in the genre must learn—whether in these islands writing in English, Irish or Welsh, or in America. They should remain rooted in their experience and culture, if they want to succeed internationally. King is clearly an American who loves his own cultural ethos—that is precisely what makes him acceptable and accepted in other countries in the world.

There are many "British" writers who have opted to become "mid-Atlantic," neither one thing nor another. I, too, have heard agents softly whispering that if you want to cash in on the lucrative American market, then write about American settings, adopt American ideas—buy a Webster's Dictionary instead of an Oxford Dictionary, alter your prose style and dialogue to sound like a third rate American television series.

King once said that "horror fiction, fantasy fiction, imaginative fiction, is like a dream." He is absolutely right. But if you want to persuade others to believe in your dream, it must, essentially, be *your* dream and not a series of half-digested concepts picked up from television screens or travel books.

The influence Stephen King *should* have on his "British" counterparts, rather than how his success *has* influenced some of them, is to be true to themselves and their own cultural experience; to stop trying to emulate American developments in the genre. We have become awed by the American book and movie market and we want a piece of the action. However, the matter is not resolved by becoming pale imitations of our trans-Atlantic cousins. We have to re-connect with our own literary and cultural traditions—which, in the horror genre, are not inconsiderable. We have to show the world what we can offer. We can take Stephen King's example by firmly grounding ourselves in our culture (or cultures) and making the horror genre *literary* once again.

But now it's time to go for my evening constitutional through Crouch End, a district that really isn't at all like Stephen King's story would have it. We are actually a pretty ordinary crowd of people in these parts. Horror writers, in particular, are warm, generous, able to take criticism without resorting to. . . .

Well, did I mention this man we found up on Hampstead Heath nailed to a tree?

If I don't come back from my constitutional, I'd like to ask Stephen King to write my obituary for the *London Times* (not more than 600 words, please). After all, I feel I am owed for that hour at JFK. . . .

"REACH OUT AND TOUCH SOME THING": BLURBS AND STEPHEN KING

by Stanley Wiater

*I*n an interview conducted by T. N. Murari and published in *Cosmopolitan* (December 1985), the following exchange takes place—

COSMO: In what ways has the fame affected your personal life and your relationship with people?

KING: I'm more wary of new acquaintances than I would be if I was not "famous." When people call me up, the first thing that flashes through my mind now isn't "How nice it is to hear from this person," but "What does he want?"

COSMO: Do you still keep in touch with your old friends?

KING: No.

In spite of this seemingly cold-hearted attitude, Stephen King is widely regarded as one of the most generous and giving of people—especially when it comes to aiding and acknowledging fellow writers. Further, he has used his immense public status as a self-proclaimed "brand-name author" to bring further recognition to other writers, both beginning and established, primarily through the use of book blurbs.

Quite simply, "blurbs" are the complimentary quotes placed on the covers of paperbacks (and, less frequently, on hardcovers) to influence the potential purchaser of the book. Most often it's an effort by the publisher to obtain some early acclaim for a lesser known writer, using either selected portions of published book reviews or direct recommendations by more established authors—usually from writers working successfully in the same genre.

> "If there's going to be an occult bestseller this year, this is surely it! For 10 years I've been waiting for someone who really knows medicine to write an all-out, go-for-broke horror story and the waiting is finally over . . . I didn't put it down until I turned the last page . . . literally wrung out and trembling."—for THE UNBORN by David Shobin.

In his article "A Few Kind Words About Book Blurbs," *Washington Post*, January 17, 1982, Curt Suplee uses King repeatedly as an example of how a known author can help the promotion of a currently unknown author. Referring to the quote given for David Shobin's first novel, THE UNBORN, Bantam Books publicity director Stuart Applebaum tells Suplee that King is "a golden name" to appear on a book. He goes on to say that King is "One of the great blurb-meisters. He's like a guy who says he's going to quit smoking but always wants one last puff."

Although it may seem to some critics that King's name appears as a blurb on every other horror novel that comes out, research indicates that in fact King has blurbed approximately 50 books to date. (In a recent letter, King himself guesses the figure is closer to 75.) His forewords and introductions to other writers' anthologies or collections presently number only about a dozen. He has done blurbs for crime writer Jim Thompson, espionage author David Morrell, and "Batman" artist Frank Miller, but the vast majority of his blurbs have remained in the horror genre. On a statistical basis alone, if one considers that King has had a full-fledged literary career for about fourteen years, the number of books he has bestowed his "U.S.D.A. government brand seal of approval" averages out to only four or five a year—hardly an overwhelming number by anyone's standards. And as we shall see, King has chosen his recommendations very cautiously. Time and again his blurbs go to the same handful of working horror writers.

According to Stephanie Leonard, publisher of *Castle Rock*:

the Stephen King Newsletter and personal secretary to King, he has been cutting back on the number of blurbs he will give. King now believes it will "hurt his credibility" to issue too many, though for someone with his phenomenal reputation, that seems a bit unlikely at this point. Like most sought-after "blurb" authors, King receives bound galleys to read from either his publisher or agent, although occasionally an unpublished manuscript will reach him "over the transom." These average "between four and eight requests a month." Leonard reports that if King sincerely likes the book, he will then call the publisher to give his quote or send out a brief letter with his favorable comments included within. The most flattering remarks are then issued on the book's front or back cover (a single line is usually displayed due to sheer lack of space), often with a tag line identifying King by his most recent novel at the time. However, as King's fame has increased geometrically with every book published, even this use of "by the author of. . ." has since been almost universally discarded.

"One of the best horror novels I've read in the last two years."—for MOONDEATH by Rick Hautala.

Although he has stated repeatedly that he never gives out a blurb merely because he knows an author personally, the fact remains there are not many truly praiseworthy horror writers working today that King is unaware of. (However, it's been reported that Hautala and King went to college together; the only instance we're aware of where King knew another horror writer before either of them were recognized in the genre.) Obviously he is selective, in both the authors he chooses to blurb, and in the precise and calculated way he words those recommendations. He knows all too well—like any other successful author—that a good blurb for a bad book will cast doubts on his own reputation and judgment as well as those of the first-time novelist. So far, it would be safe to say that King has yet to embarrass himself by giving a literary "kiss" to someone else's newly published creation.

King has been charitable in trying to give earnest young

writers a fair break—although, as in any field, outstanding new talents in the literature of fear are few and far between. For example, in his introduction to the 1983 anthology TALES BY MOONLIGHT edited by Jessica Amanda Salmonson, he is clearly at odds in trying to say good things about some of the stories: "How are the stories? Well, I thought several of them were most exquisitely awful—I'll not embarrass either you, me or the writers of the tales by singling them out. If you have read widely in the field of fantasy and horror, you will spot the clunkers almost immediately. . . ." However, King then immediately finds a way to soften that seemingly devastating criticism by stating: "But the bad stories lend their own undeniable authenticity to the volume—like the abysmal performance of the rock-blues group Canned Heat at Woodstock, they form a rough-textured background which may be unlovely but which is nonetheless real and completely felt. And the bad stories are more than outweighed by the good ones . . . and the best of them are better than anything I or any of my so-called 'heavyweight contemporaries' have done in a long time. Oh, maybe not in terms of style, and certainly not in terms of polish, but the energy displayed in this book approaches megaton levels."

King's heartfelt introduction is part recommendation of the book itself, part lament on the lack of places for new writers, especially those who prefer the short story form, to make their voices heard. Indeed, of the smattering of introductions and forewords he has written, it can stand alone as a very personal contemplation on the near-death of the short story scene. Throughout, King is astute enough to not blindly endorse this particular volume as a whole, yet he enthusiastically embraces the idea that a book of short stories can exist when ". . . the sound you hear, that long and melancholy roar, is the sea of literature ebbing from the coastline of popular consciousness." In his autobiographical stance and highly nostalgic tone, he sounds more than anyone else like Ray Bradbury in combining both topical despair with eternal hope.

But if King is cautious with his recommendations toward new authors, he is perhaps more restrained when issuing judgment on his peers. Even with someone as widely known and admired as Harlan Ellison, King has (seemingly) limited his praise:

> "If there is such a thing as a fantasist for the 1980s (always assuming there *are* 1980s) then Harlan Ellison is almost surely that writer."—for SHATTERDAY by Harlan Ellison.

On closer examination, this may be his way of keeping from the general public that he knows Ellison personally, and a blurb—if too praiseworthy—may be cynically misconstrued as merely one friend heaping praise on another. Certainly, in his foreword to the 1982 Ellison collection STALKING THE NIGHT-MARE, King willingly and gleefully goes on at length to demonstrate just what an immense fan he is of the multiple-award-winning author. In a very informal (and also extremely funny) confessional monologue, King states: "For whatever it's worth, Harlan Ellison is a great man: a fast friend, a supportive critic, a ferocious enemy of the false and foolish, maniacally funny, perhaps insecure (I'm not sure what to make of a man who doesn't smoke or drink and who still has such crazed acid indigestion), but above all else, brave and true." Interestingly, as we search for those authors whom King will make reference to elsewhere, he makes mention herein of a short list of writers who have had a "profound influence" on him: "Lovecraft. Raymond Chandler (and, at second hand, Ross Macdonald and Robert Parker). Dorothy Sayers, who wrote the clearest, most lucid prose of our century. Peter Straub. And Ellison."

More importantly, Ellison is one of the small group of writers singled out by King in his book length study DANSE MACABRE (1981) as among the best of our contemporary horror writers. This level of praise surely negates any public sense of hesitation on King's part to write a truly flattering blurb for Ellison; if anything, he is justifiably wary in not letting us know just how "biased" he is on Ellison's behalf.

> "I have seen the future of horror, and its name is Clive Barker. Clive Barker is not merely good; he is great.... He's an original. Never—never in my life have I been so completely shaken by a collec-

tion of stories. I have never experienced such a combination of revulsion, delight and amazement."—for THE INHUMAN CONDITION by Clive Barker.

"Les Daniels tells a hell of a story . . . his books are rewarding, creepy, and fun!"—for THE BLACK CASTLE by Les Daniels.

"Readers will be more than impressed—they will be mesmerized."—for THE WOMAN NEXT DOOR by T. M. Wright.

"DEAD WHITE is tight and exciting and readable. A good tale."—for DEAD WHITE by Alan Ryan.

"THE PARASITE is one of the scariest, most important novels of horror and the occult that I've read in a long time. It ends with a grisly little innuendo that reverberates in my memory. But more importantly, Ramsey Campbell has written a novel using the Lovecraftian themes of survival, the occult, and the things which may live at the rim of the universe (or beyond it) in a way that seems to ring true for our time. It is an accomplishment he can be proud of."—for THE PARASITE by Ramsey Campbell.

Besides David Shobin, some of the other beginning (or unknown outside the horror genre) writers King has blurbed are Clive Barker, Les Daniels, Bari Woods, T. M. Wright, Alan Ryan, Dennis Etchison, Ramsey Campbell, and Michael McDowell. Each has gone on to have viable careers as outstanding horror writers. King was one of the first to recognize the considerable talents of McDowell, and in his short-lived book review column for the men's magazine *Adelena* (November 1980), King discusses McDowell's first novel, THE AMULET, as one "of the best paperback original horror fictions to be found over the last four to five years." An early champion of McDowell (who has since published over 30 books), King wrote a lengthy inside cover blurb for his 1980 novel GILDED NEEDLES, declaring it: "Riveting, terrifying, and just absolutely great. . ." He concludes his blurb/review with ". . .To say that [it] is a great read and that it offers the deep pleasure of going along for the ride with a novelist who is coming to the height of his powers, is to say two-thirds of it. The rest is the simple fact that Michael McDowell must now be regarded as the finest writer of paperback originals in America."

"May be the scariest haunted house novel ever written."—for HELL HOUSE by Richard Matheson.

"Perhaps the finest psychological horror writer working today . . . and never in finer form."—for PSYCHO II by Robert Bloch.

King has repeatedly shown his respect and affection for certain writers whom he greatly admires by blurbing re-issues of their early novels, or paperback editions of newer works. This group includes Robert Bloch, John Farris, Richard Matheson, and Jack Finney. (Finney's THE NIGHT PEOPLE was one of the first blurbs King ever gave out. The paperback edition was published in 1978, and the blurb—"For those who love novels, and they are not apt to find a better one this year"—is tagged with "—Stephen King, author of CARRIE.") More importantly, King devotes several thousand words of discussion—and admiration—for each of these particular authors in DANSE MACABRE, as well as Ray Bradbury, Shirley Jackson, Anne River Siddons, Ira Levin, Ramsey Campbell, James Herbert, Peter Straub, and the aforementioned Ellison. It's evident from his statements that he is very conscious of the influence that Bloch and Matheson have had, not only on himself as a youngster, but on a whole generation of horror writers.

His feelings for Bloch and Matheson go beyond blurbs and mention in DANSE MACABRE: King composed an insightful profile of Bloch for the 1983 World Fantasy Convention program book, and has reportedly already written an introduction for a planned COLLECTED STORIES OF RICHARD MATHESON. It's hardly a great shock to learn that he has also contributed a foreword to the first collection of stories of Matheson's son— Richard Christian Matheson. Once again, he is select in his praise, stating in SCARS: "The stories vary somewhat in execution and effect—a rather too-elegant way of saying that some are better than others. This is to be expected; Richard Christian Matheson is still a young man and still maturing as a writer.

But these stories do more than mark him as a writer to watch: they mark him as a writer to enjoy now."

It's certainly possible that King would have written a foreword to the initial collection of a new young horror writer, someone who is no relation whatsoever to Richard Matheson. However, there is an underlying sense of personal pleasure which King subtly conveys—especially if the reader realizes he has always stated publicly how important an early discovery of Matheson senior's work was to his own literary development. In fact, this short foreword is filled with reference to other formative writers whom King enjoys, including—of course—Robert Bloch and Ray Bradbury. (King has apparently never blurbed a book by Bradbury. Then again, if King is a "literary phenomenon," Bradbury is surely a "literary legend." So in terms of their respective careers, Bradbury actually has no more need of a King blurb than King would require one from Bradbury. Furthermore, both are extremely well-established as "brand-name" writers.)

King always saves his most "definitive" blurbs for those authors whose work he truly admires—and has enjoyed—over the years. Although only briefly mentioned in DANSE MACABRE, John Farris is another author for whom King has long openly expressed his admiration. Beyond allowing the same early blurb ("America's premier novelist of terror. . .") to be used repeatedly by Farris's publishers, King gave one of his earliest critical assessments of a fellow writer by writing a highly autobiographical introduction to a 1981 paperback reprint of Farris's novel, WHEN MICHAEL CALLS (1967). He begins by stating, "It's more difficult for me to write about the work of John Farris than it would be for me to write the work of a number of other writers because, in the years of my late adolescence and early adulthood, I did more than just admire his work—I adopted his career as both a goal to be reached and an example to be emulated." In discussing his early work and the "period of stylistic imitation" he went through as a young writer, King further reveals that "some of the stories I wrote as a teenager would begin sounding like Ray Bradbury and end sounding like H. P.

Lovecraft, with a nice slice of Cornell Woolrich right in the middle . . ."

To date, he has done personal introductions for only two other writers in the field: Joseph Payne Brennan's THE SHAPES OF MIDNIGHT (1980), and Charles L. Grant's TALES OF THE NIGHTSIDE (1981).

> "An electrifying finish: During the last forty pages my hands were as good as nailed to the book."—for IF YOU COULD SEE ME NOW by Peter Straub.

> "The terror just mounts and mounts."—for GHOST STORY by Peter Straub.

> "I thought it was creepy from page one! I loved it."—for SHADOW-LAND by Peter Straub.

Throughout his career, however, King has saved his most lavish praise for someone who has since become one of his best friends, Peter Straub. It's fascinating to consider how Straub and King met one another due to the exchanging of published compliments. (Which was also the case, for that matter, with John Farris.) According to Straub, King had been asked to write a blurb for JULIA, Straub's first horror novel. (Yet it does not appear on either the American hardcover or paperback editions.) It was while visiting England in 1977 that they first got together in Straub's house in the Crouch End district of London—and also agreed to someday collaborate on a project. (Which of course was 1984's THE TALISMAN. The ever prolific King also wrote another story inspired by that meeting, appropriately entitled "Crouch End.")

In his introduction to FEAR ITSELF: THE HORROR FICTION OF STEPHEN KING (Underwood-Miller 1982), Straub stated candidly: "He appeared in my life as a name on a blurb. . . . Along with supportive remarks from Dorothy Eden and Robert Bloch, my editor received a paragraph from Stephen King, 'author of CARRIE and 'SALEM'S LOT.' I had never heard of those two books, nor had I heard of Stephen King, but neither had anyone else. Yet the comment by this obscure author was easily the most insightful of the ten or twelve responses to JULIA. The others praised, and I was grateful for the praise, but Stephen King showed in a few sentences that he understood what I was trying to do—he had a sort of immediate perception of my goals." Straub goes on to describe how their friendship deepened with a second blurb, "nearly two pages of generosity and insight," most of which appeared on the hardcover edition of IF YOU COULD SEE ME NOW.

Since that time, King has also blurbed GHOST STORY and SHADOWLAND. Oddly enough, they are *not* the most colorfully phrased blurbs, with the exception of the wonderfully graphic imagery for the paperback edition of IF YOU COULD SEE ME NOW.

Beyond the lengthy discussion of GHOST STORY in DANSE MACABRE, King has also written "Peter Straub: An Informal Appreciation," published as part of the program book for the 8th World Fantasy Convention (1982). The most telling line in the entire essay being when he calls Straub: ". . . Simply, the best writer of supernatural tales that I know."

> "A riveting and bloodcurdling novel of small-town horror by one of the premier horror writers of his, or any generation."—for THE NESTLING by Charles L. Grant.

While the above blurb is a very high recommendation of this particular novel by the prolific Grant, it also serves as a good example of how publishers will use King's name again and again— and the same blurb again and again—as long as they think no one will notice slight reworkings of the actual quote. In this case, Grant's publisher later modified the blurb so that it could be used on another novel to say ". . . one of the premier horror writers of his, or any generation." This is certainly permissable, if not perhaps wholly ethical. However, the limits of ethics were truly stretched when another of Grant's publishers further modified the original blurb to read ". . . the premier horror writer of his, or any generation." Incredibly, for anyone not aware of the original incarnation of the blurb, it now appears as if King is stating that Grant is the best horror writer there ever was . . . !

Another variation of a blurb's unnatural origins concerns Dennis Etchison, who has had two paperback editions of his books blurbed by King. The way the blurbs originally appeared is unusual—neither was actually intended as a direct recommendation for either book. Rather, Etchison was commissioned by King himself to correct the numerous small bibliographical and biographical errors of DANSE MACABRE when the book was being readied for a mass market paperback edition. In his "Footnote to the Paperback Edition," King explains this situation, then goes on to say ". . . He is also one hell of a fiction writer, and if you have not read his volume of short stories, THE DARK COUNTRY, you have missed one of the great volumes in our peculiar field. . . . The stories are not just good; they are without exception exciting, and in some cases genuinely great, the way that Oliver Onions' 'The Beckoning Fair One' is great. . . . And I advise you to run, not walk, to your nearest *emporium de bookstore* and pick up a copy of it as soon as it's available. And no, I was not paid for the plug; it comes from the heart." One line eventually made its way to the front cover of DARKSIDE; two other sentences appeared on the back cover of THE DARK COUNTRY.

King is fond of making lists, as evidenced earlier by the seemingly informal mention of "profound influences" in his introduction to STALKING THE NIGHTMARE. These include favorite films, fears, and—naturally—books. Although not precisely clones of blurbs, these lists are undeniably close relations in that they are definite endorsements or recommendations for a particular book or author. The best known is entitled "Stephen King's 10 Favorite Horror Books or Short Stories" and was published in THE BOOKS OF LISTS #3 (1983), compiled by Amy Wallace, David Wallechinsky, and Irving Wallace. The list was as follows:

GHOST STORY by Peter Straub
DRACULA by Bram Stoker
THE HAUNTING OF HILL HOUSE by Shirley Jackson
DR. JEKYLL AND MR. HYDE by Robert Louis Stevenson
BURNT OFFERINGS by Robert Marasco

CASTING THE RUNES by M. R. James
TWO BOTTLES OF RELISH by Lord Dunsany
THE GREAT GOD PAN by Arthur Machen
THE UPPER BERTH by F. Marion Crawford
THE COLOUR OUT OF SPACE by H. P. Lovecraft

Previously, in his introduction to Brennan's THE SHAPES OF MIDNIGHT, King contributed another list when he declares: "There are collections of stories that are meant to be read not just once but many times; collections which are not to be loaned out (and when someone asks to borrow the book, summon up all your courage and integrity, and scream into the face of the would-be borrower: 'BUY YOUR OWN, TURKEY!') lest they be lost forever—such loss to be bitterly regretted in later years. Charles Beaumont's THE MAGIC MAN is such a collection; Ray Bradbury's THE OCTOBER COUNTRY; Richard Matheson's SHOCK; Fritz Leiber's NIGHT'S BLACK AGENTS. Here is another, long overdue but finally here." And in his Afterword to DIFFERENT SEASONS (1982) he briefly makes mention of the number of "people who *had* been typed as horror writers, and who had given me such great pleasure over the years—Lovecraft, Clark Ashton Smith, Frank Belknap Long, Fritz Leiber, Robert Bloch, Richard Matheson, and Shirley Jackson. . . ."

Repeatedly, whenever an appropriate forum is found, King honors the recognized masters, most often singling out the works of Bradbury, Bloch, Matheson, and Straub. Beyond any of his peers, he has convincingly declared how he believes these authors are the true giants in this "peculiar" field. Meanwhile, his listing of ten favorite novels or stories would surely suffice as the springboard to a college freshman course in the history of horror literature. (King was once an English teacher, and has taught at both high school and college levels.)

Finally, in presenting an overview of his own critical perspective in DANSE MACABRE, there is an appendix of 100 books he felt were vital to an understanding of the horror scene. (Although the list was restricted to works published primarily within the last 30 years.) While not in any sense a series of "blurbs," it remains his most comprehensive list of recommended writers to date. Not surprisingly, the list includes Bradbury, Bloch, Brennan, Campbell, Daniels, Ellison, Farris, Finney, Grant, Marasco, Matheson, McDowell, Straub, and Wright. One can therefore safely conclude that these are the authors (along with Britisher Clive Barker, who appeared on the scene after the book was published) whom he strongly feels are every bit as worthy of interest as his own work may be.

So besides recognizing new talents and acknowledging old influences (it would not be too much to consider the dedication page of DANSE MACABRE a blurb of sorts: "It's easy enough—perhaps too easy—to memorialize the dead. This book is for six great writers of the macabre who are still alive. Robert Bloch. Jorge Luis Borges. Ray Bradbury. Frank Belknap Long. Donald Wandrei. Manly Wade Wellman."), King has also given blurbs to most of the established writers who are rightfully considered his equals as "masters of fear." It is a short list.

One can also conclude that King is sincerely compelled to champion the cause of well-crafted, entertaining *fiction*—horror or otherwise. The *Washington Post* article quoted him as saying, "You start to feel like a pimp, but if a book is good, somebody ought to say so." Whether acknowledging such "grand masters" as Bloch or Matheson, or lending his magic name to the first time novelist, he has prudently used his immense clout to reach out to those whose first books he senses "the publishing house is about to send . . . out like the Titanic." He is extremely sensitive as to how the general public fervently equates his name with "Grade A Horror," while often ignorant that anyone else is capable of writing as skillfully and powerfully.

Quite simply, King knows we will pay attention to whatever —and whoever—he is pointing out.

This is obviously a (occasionally career-making) responsibility he doesn't shoulder lightly. By pointing out the very best—established or new—talents the field has to offer, he is perhaps assuring us that his response in *Cosmopolitan* was really meant for those who don't understand how a writer's true friends can only be other writers. That, like the old Beatles song, we all "get by with a little help from our friends." He can't forget that, for many readers just being introduced to the genre, the only horror writers they may take a chance on are those he directly or indirectly suggests.

Out of a compassionate sense of duty to his colleagues—and perhaps a little understandable guilt at his own stupendous success—Stephen King is only blowing a fair wind toward his fellow voyagers on that perilous and unknown sea called publishing.

THE MOVIES AND MR. KING: PART II

by Bill Warren

Most writers, even prolific, best-selling writers, usually have only a fraction of their works filmed. There are exceptions, of course: virtually all Zane Grey novels have been filmed *several* times each; a surprisingly large number of Cornell Woolrich novels have been turned into movies. Of living authors, only Stephen King has had so many of his stories filmed; as I write, no fewer than fourteen movies have been based on his fiction. All King's other novels and most of his short stories have been optioned for film.

Some of the films—*Carrie*, *The Shining*, *The Dead Zone*, *Stand by Me*,—are outstanding; most are fair to middlin'; two are stinkers. This isn't a bad track record; I suppose Margaret Mitchell fares better, with 100% of her writing (one novel) filmed very well indeed, but few writers have had four good movies taken from their works.

For a while, King movies were appearing even more frequently than Jerry Lewis telethons. Initially they were popular. But in the short time since I discussed King's movies in FEAR ITSELF, his name has gone from an attractive element for audiences to one that apparently repels them. Perhaps it's because the unifying element of all of the movies based on King since *The Shining* is that, unlike the novels, they are not frightening.

They do not deliver the goods. These trains run with empty boxcars.

Part of the problem lies in the source: King's fiction. He prides himself on being a storyteller, and in one sense, that's exactly what he is—but the word "story" here actually means "situation." King sets up an unusual set of circumstances—a car haunted by an evil old man possesses a lonely teenager; a man discovers a way to bring the dead back to life; a writer is imprisoned by a psychotic fan—and rings interesting changes on the situation until the end. He does not write compelling, intricate plots; the actions of the characters do not lead linearally to consequences that pay off a hundred or two hundred pages later; things develop, but they do not *grow* like the tightly-woven stories of, for instance, John LeCarre. His is the classic horror form, hearkening back to Stoker and Lovecraft, and at his best, King is at the peak of this field. The fear he generates in his most effective work grows out of the situation, not out of a string of escalating events.

But horror movies, to simply be scary, often require plots and clues. King's novels CARRIE and THE DEAD ZONE have his strongest plots, and made two of the best films. Despite whatever weaknesses it has as a film *per se*, the novel FIRE-STARTER is in a genre—misdeeds by a government agency— that needs a strong plot, and it doesn't have one. The novel is one of King's weaker efforts, the film is even worse than that; once Charlie arrives at The Shop, the story is basically over— but neither the film nor the novel are.

Another reason King's name has become a warning rather than an attraction for filmgoers is that King made a six-picture deal with De Laurentiis Productions, a company eager to get as many of the films out as soon as possible. Only one remains to be filmed. Dino De Laurentiis is a shrewd, powerful producer; his films are handsomely filmed in the studio he built in North Carolina. Though some consider him to be the worst thing that has happened to big-budget genre films (*King Kong Lives!* is a convincing argument for this viewpoint), his films generally make money—if not in the United States, then in the international marketplace he thoroughly understands.

De Laurentiis has had little experience with horror movies, which may explain the peculiarly flat tone of four of the films, and his odd choice of directors. Of the five King films made by De Laurentiis so far, two were directed by newcomers (including King himself), one by a director known for action films (if known at all), and two by horror experts—who stepped in at the last moment to take over from directors who knew little about horror.

King's writing style is highly cinematic; there are few writers he's discernibly influenced by, but he's heavily influenced by pop culture in general and movies (and music) in particular. Because ordinary movies have had such an impact on his style, perhaps it isn't surprising that his own screenplays tend toward the ordinary and uninventive. (Based on seeing the films, King's screenplays are not as good as those by other writers adapting his work; judging from the few I have read, the best King screenplays seem to be, in fact, those that were not filmed.) In Jessie Horsting's STEPHEN KING AT THE MOVIES, King himself cites a scene in *The Shining* (when Shelley Duvall discovers the "all work" manuscript) as proving Stanley Kubrick knows nothing about horror movies—because he refuses to do the expected hand-on-the-shoulder shot. Because of these difficulties and limitations, the films made since I ended my first article on King and the movies with a discussion of Kubrick's *The Shining*, have been variable in quality.

David Cronenberg's version of *The Dead Zone*, written by Jeffrey Boam (with additional but uncredited ideas by Cronenberg), is the most intelligent adaptation of a King work; the script is a model of compression, both of the novel, and in and of itself. Unlike the novel, which has side issues and background material, everything in the script is aimed at one end: telling the story of Johnny Smith and his ESP abilities.

The film is handsomely produced, shot entirely in autumnal and wintry landscapes, corresponding to the dying fall of Johnny's life; Cronenberg told Jessie Horsting that he used the paintings of Norman Rockwell as his way into this very American story. The casting is very good, with Christopher Walken giving his best screen performance so far as Johnny Smith.

Martin Sheen is peculiar casting for the earthy Greg Stillson—Sheen looks aristocratic—but the artificiality which Sheen cannot seem to divest himself of works to advantage here; Stillson is, after all, a phony. In short, *The Dead Zone* is a very good film on all levels, but it is the script that is most impressive. Cronenberg told me that he worked directly with Boam on the final draft, writing himself only the scene in which Stillson confronts the newspaper editor, but he also devised the changes from the novel that most impressed me.

Compression was, of course, necessary, but there are other changes as well. Every significant change is an improvement, many working in cinematic rather than literary terms. Not only does Johnny Smith appear in his own pre- and post-cognitive visions, but his painful helplessness when he "sees" Deputy Dodd kill a victim gives him impetus to take action against Greg Stillson when he "sees" Stillson launch a future nuclear war. A visual idea works—placing Johnny in the vision literalizes his power—and it builds his later motivation to kill Stillson.

In the novel, "the dead zone" refers to elements that Johnny's powers do not register, such as street numbers—a portion of his brain has been burned out. In the film, the term refers to a shadowy area of the future which he learns can be altered. He touches Chris Stuart and sees the boy drowning (and sees himself underwater, too); his panic leads Chris to refuse to play hockey that day, and when Johnny again touches his arm, he discovers that he can see into "the dead zone"—Chris will not drown after all. The future, he knows, can be changed.

Other changes, not as cinematic, but also improvements, abound. In the novel, Johnny had a few precognitive visions as a child, following a bad fall on a frozen pond; his later automobile accident and resulting coma brings his power into full play, but the brain lesion that gives him his power slowly kills him. In the film, since the scenes of Johnny as a child were eliminated, Cronenberg removed any suggestion that his power began before the accident—but we see him suffering a kind of seizure earlier the same day. By the end of the film, we learn that his medical problem is not what gave him his abilities, but that the abilities themselves, which he cannot control or switch off, are killing him.

More clearly than in the novel, in the film the murder investigation has several strong plot functions; in addition to the impetus it gives him to stop Stillson later, it also makes Johnny realize that his powers really can help people in ways he was not sure of. By having Johnny's refusal to help Bannerman *precede* Sarah's visit to the farm, the latter scene is given an additional meaning: it brings Johnny back into the world again. And then by having Johnny wounded while helping Bannerman again drives him into a kind of seclusion, one in which he helps children as a tutor. (There are several literary allusions in the film, to Edgar Allan Poe and Washington Irving, but significantly one of Johnny's pupils reads from *Sleeping Beauty*—which is what Johnny has become.)

Other changes are more daring and not everyone has liked them. In the novel, Stillson's assistant is a biker, who recruits other bikers as Stillson's guardians; in the film, the assistant is still a thug, but a thug in a three-piece suit, which Cronenberg felt was more believable. At the climax, the child Stillson shields himself with is Sarah's own son—earlier we had seen Sarah and her husband stumping for Stillson—which is neatly circular, giving us a child we already have some emotional investment in, rather than just a nearby kid. This grew out of a chance remark by Christopher Walken during rehearsals. Cronenberg said Stephen King didn't like that change, feeling it too neat. But it's no neater or more coincidental than having Johnny suddenly become a collector of politician's handshakes, as in the novel— which otherwise takes pains to point out that Johnny dislikes his power.

Apart from the obvious financial incentives, the reasons for adapting a novel or other fiction to a dramatic context are many; two of the most important are an effort to duplicate or mimic the effect of the work in film form, and for the filmmaker to use the story and themes to his or her own ends. *The Dead Zone* is both, but primarily the former, and can be compared to *Firestarter*, entirely an effort to put the book on the screen.

Firestarter does this—even King agrees—but fails at the same time. Part of the problems lie in the novel, not one of King's best, a story of governmental intrigue wedded to an escape thriller (like, say, *The 39 Steps*), fused with a variation on *Carrie*. Cross-genre blendings are often entertaining, but King's forte is novels of situations, not strong plotting. Something like *Firestarter* requires a strong plot.

Government agents pursue Andy and his firestarting daughter Charlie; once they are captured, *nothing* happens until the climax essentially—King has painted himself into a corner, so even his usual situational novel can't develop. Andy's powers are almost useless in this situation. Charlie refuses to use *her* powers on people, despite all kinds of reasons to, so all we can do, in novel and film, is sit and watch her incinerate things in laboratory settings.

Furthermore, the principal villain, John Rainbird, seems to have strayed in from a James Bond movie; he's preposterous. A political assassin, Rainbird is a huge, scarred American Indian with a long fall of hair—not exactly Mr. Average, but assassins have to be inconspicuous. He's about as inconspicuous as a giraffe in a swimming pool. His motives in wanting to kill Charlie are forced and unacceptable. Casting a flamboyant actor like George C. Scott in the role only exacerbates things; based on what you see on the screen, he has no real understanding of the role, yet plays it all stops out, as if energy alone will overcome the weirdness of the character.

What a movie version of FIRESTARTER needed to do was rethink things cinematically, to find new ways of presenting some of King's ideas. Instead, writer Stanley Mann regards the novel as a sacred text and follows it slavishly, and the film is hollow, unbelievable. It is as close an adaptation as any feature based on King, but miles from the book; it's a paint-by-numbers kit of the Mona Lisa—you end up with an exact reproduction that lacks the vitality of the original. King's novel is weakly plotted, treading over ground he's covered before, in a genre he doesn't seem to understand—but it is *readable*. King's novels stick to your hands like they've been coated with Elmer's Glue; even a misfire, you should pardon the expression, like FIRE-

STARTER is compelling from beginning to end. A screen adapter simply cannot duplicate the elements that make the novel entertaining, so he has to find correlatives—and Mann does not.

Mark Lester is primarily a director of action and stunts, and handles that kind of thing here perfectly well. But that's not what *Firestarter* should have been about; we should care about Andy and Charlie, and Irv and Norma; we should fear Rainbird and Hollister. We don't. Drew Barrymore, a good child actress, is forced to play someone a lot stupider than she is, and is uncomfortable, unconvincing. (Compare her dialogue scenes to her silent scenes; in the latter she's very good.) Lester brings little to the film, what ideas he does come up with are weak; at least, I presume it was the director who, to show us when Charlie is using her powers (as if cinderblock walls bursting into flame isn't a clue), blows a wind into her face, or has David Keith as Andy clutch his head when he's putting the whammy on someone. But the biggest blunder is the climax, straight from the book; in the novel, we stay with Charlie, inside her, understanding why she wipes out The Shop in a swath of flame; in the film, we must *watch* her do this. Charlie changes from a sympathetic little girl to a monster whom even we may want to see destroyed.

Firestarter is not a terrible movie, merely a failed one. The score by Tangerine Dream is very good; the photography by Giuseppe Russolini exceptionally rich; the art direction by Giorgio Postiglione intelligent, detailed; the fire effects by Mike Wood and Jeff Jarvis everything the film needs. But the script embalms rather than adapts the novel, unthinkingly cramming what's good and bad into the film without consideration. Action and violence are what De Laurentiis wanted, and what he was given. *Firestarter*, the *ninth* adaptation of a King work in eight years (and the fifth in two), by comparison with the immediately previous King adaptation, however, which it followed to the screen two months later, may have looked like a winner to most.

Children of the Corn held the title Worst Stephen King Movie until King's own *Maximum Overdrive*. King's short story of the same title, included in *Night Shift*, reads like a first draft. At the beginning, the protagonists hear a radio preacher refer to corn, but since the corny religion is made up entirely of children, who runs the radio station? For whom is the broadcast intended? After all, the religion is confined to the town of Gatlin. How'd the kids kill all their parents without anyone from the county, state or federal governments making inquiries? Certainly someone in town had relatives elsewhere—why didn't they show up? Furthermore, it simply is not believable that American children would adopt such a restrictive religion, or that older children adopt younger ones.

The story isn't fueled by logic; it's a mood piece, powerfully effective on anyone who has driven through those endless miles of corn that seem to cover all the flat states with square corners out in the middle of the country. Logically, the story is hopeless; emotionally, it is terrifying—and horror fiction is directed at emotions, not logic. In 30-pages you don't have time to worry about niceties; while watching a film, these questions occur to you—but they didn't to the makers of *Children of the Corn*.

The most intelligent decision made by screenwriter George Goldsmith was to change King's quarreling couple, travelling together in hopes of patching up their marriage, to an unmarried couple who find commitment in what happens to them. In the short story, it is not important that we have likeable protagonists, but it's critical to the film. Linda Hamilton, as Vicky, is appealing and attractive (but somewhat unformed as an actress, at this point); Peter Norton is less well cast, as his taut, smug face is more that of an aristocratic villain than of a hero. The first scenes as they drive past all that corn provide a sense of unease, as if *anything* might be out there in all that foliage.

But Goldsmith has already made several bad decisions, and he keeps on making them. The story is narrated by Joby, one of the Children of the Corn, so we know he will survive the events to come. We see Malachai and other Gatlin children, under the direction of Isaac, slaughter all the adults in town, three years before the events of the main part of the story. This brutal, bloodthirsty scene works against the film; we know Burt and Vicky are driving into danger long before they do. Instead of a gradually building mystery, Goldsmith and first-time director Fritz Kiersch have tried to turn the screws of suspense too tightly, too soon—and simultaneously undercut themselves by having Joby narrate.

The dialogue given these kids is ridiculously Biblical; it would have been more disturbing if they had talked like ordinary but obsessed children. Instead, we get tripe like "I have seen this car upon the road." "Seize her!" "Hah! Sacrilege! Down on your knees, heretic!" "Outlander! We have your woman! She still lives!"

Sarah, Joby's sister (and the only other kid in town not in thrall to Isaac), seems to have ESP—at least she draws pictures of events to come. This adds nothing to the film. The protagonists don't use her ability for anything. But then again, the film doesn't follow any other kind of logic, either. Running from murderous children, Burt immediately accepts Joby as a friend: Why? He leaves Sarah and Vicky behind in the house, although he knows a murderer is at large: Why? How can Burt so easily talk the kids into giving up their religion? Why does Isaac return from the dead after being murdered by Malachai? What is He Who Walks Behind the Rows, anyway? A demon? God? No suggestions are offered, although the entity is rather easily defeated by fire.

Kiersch tries to make the film frightening, but has bad ideas along this line, too. The children advance brandishing blades, which we are shown again and again; there are a few sudden-shock scenes, some of which work, but the last, after everything is over with, is silly. Audiences howl with laughter and the film dribbles to a halt.

Children of the Corn is Stephen King as B-movie, but that's not necessarily a defect—*Cujo* basically is a B-movie, and though hardly outstanding, is acceptable as an adaptation and as a film. Furthermore, unlike virtually all of the other films discussed here, it has some frightening moments. Stephen King, although this startles many, declares that it is his favorite among the films adapted from his work. "It's just this big dumb slugger of a movie," he told Jessie Horsting, "that stands there and keeps on punching. It has no finesse, it has no pretentions."

Lewis Teague inherited a troubled film from director Peter Medak, who left after one day's shooting. Barbara Turner's script was rewritten by Teague's choice, Don Carlos Dunaway, so Turner took the pseudonym of Lauren Currier. The film was shot swiftly and relatively cheaply; this is not surprising, because it really isn't an expensive concept. A woman and her young son are trapped in her car by a rabid St. Bernard for half of the novel and 40 minutes of the film; Teague's problem, like King's, was to make this interesting. The screenwriters' problem was to effectively compress the novel, which some have felt is padded, into a script of the right length.

With *The Dead Zone*, the novel was not only shortened for the screen, but events were given different emphasis; the adaptation of *Cujo* is more like that of *Firestarter*: it keeps everything essential, but it's shorter. However, *Cujo* has a more challenging premise than *Firestarter* and a more interesting structure; the task King presented himself (and, inadvertently, the filmmakers) was to keep the reader's/viewer's attention despite the confined locale. (Alfred Hitchcock liked to do the same thing; notice the confined settings of *Lifeboat* and *Rear Window*; King returned to this idea even more stringently in his later novel MISERY.)

One of King's problems as a writer is that his subplots often do not integrate effectively with the main story or theme; these asides are fascinating and amusing, but stubbornly refuse to reflect or comment on the spine of the work. In CUJO, while the wife's adultery does play a pivotal part in the action, the husband's advertising career and the mishap involving dye in cereal are side issues. The surprising thing in the film is how easily this material slips in and slips by; it's there, it serves the plot function of distressing the father and sending him away from the house, but unlike the novel, we don't become impatient to simply get on with it.

The most important element changed from book to movie is that in the novel, after their ordeal in the car, young Tad dies; in the film, he lives—and this was the correct decision. Perhaps because Stephen King is, by all reports, an especially kind and loving father, his stories often deal with the deaths of parents or young children; it may be the most horrifying concept for this father who grew up without a father. But he violated a cardinal rule of drama in his novel CUJO: deaths must be appropriate, not arbitrary. He defends killing Tad by claiming that children die in real life, but that's a feeble defense—this isn't real life, after all, it's demon-haunted Castle Rock. There's no irony, no sense of appropriate futility or reality; the reader feels cheated, frustrated, not as if some cosmic order has been satisfied, as should be the case with death in fiction.

It's a downer of a novel anyway; poor Cujo, a big loveable animal who wants only to be a Good Dog, is turned into a monster by the rabies he caught while being playful, and you always feel sympathy for the tormented dog. Because King can take us (very believably) into Cujo's thoughts, and the film cannot, we have less sympathy for the dog in the movie; this might seem to allow for a more tragic ending for the people involved, but it forces the opposite. By feeling pity for Cujo throughout the book, we are allowed some relaxation from the tension King so powerfully builds; in the film, there is no relief. To have had the boy die would have overburdened an almost unpleasantly tense situation.

One of the best elements of the film is Dee Wallace; she often has found herself confronting strange menaces or visitors, as in *The Howling* and *E.T.*, and her involved performances have always helped heighten a sense of reality. She is at her best in *Cujo*, always believable, yet with the watch-*me* power that good actors often have. Danny Pintauro is also very good, a child actor who isn't the least bit actory; he's a presence of his own, so at the end, when he is unconscious, it's a bit surprising to see how small he is. Daniel Hugh-Kelly is adequate as the husband, and Christopher Stone (Wallace's real husband) is both creepy and attractive, as he needs to be, in the role of tennis bum-seducer Steve. However, he's not as nasty here as he was in the novel, so his trashing of the family's home seems unmotivated. The other roles are smaller, but Ed Lauter, Mills Watson and Kaiulani Lee are all fine.

As a director, Teague is too fond of moving camera shots; they often tend to imply a watcher when none is there. Early in the film, when Tad dashes for his bed while keeping an eye on the closet door (very witty use of an *actually*-enlarged bedroom set); there's a shot from *inside* the closet, suggesting someone is keeping an eye on *Tad*. This may be intended to relate to the several Cujo point-of-view shots as he lurks around the farm-yard, watching from inside the barn or under the car, but it doesn't, really, since apart from Tad's imagination, there is, in the film, no connection between Cujo and the closet, not even a symbolic one.

Cujo is not a great movie, but it shows that Lewis Teague is, despite his overreliance on that flying camera, a very inventive man. In fact, he may create *too* much tension. When Dee Wallace and the boy are under siege by Cujo, the movie changes from an enjoyable, funhouse ride into a film suffused with a sick, strained tension. You not only want things to end, you want them to end *right now*, never mind about anyone getting away. It isn't scary fun any more, it's genuinely nerve-wracking –but that's better than no scares at all.

No scares is the case in *John Carpenter's Christine*. John Carpenter is a generally overrated director; he has no screen personality or viewpoint, except what he unevenly has bor-rowed from Howard Hawks. Actors seem to be on their own in his films, with no director's vision uniting disparate styles. He rejects the idea of logic, as anyone who has seen his best-known film, *Halloween*, can attest.

Bill Phillips' screenplay, of course, had to discard much of King's novel. Some things needed to go. Arnie's criminal activi-ties are only briefly alluded to, which is okay. The long past of Roland D. LeBay added little to the novel that we needed to know for the film; its lack is not felt. The emphasis on football and other high school activities had to be dropped–but did we have to lose *all* of King's rich insights into high school life? CHRISTINE is another of King's novels that's longer than it needs to be, but it also has, especially in the Dennis-narrated sections, some of his very best prose and most accurate in-sights. There's no equivalent in the film, a plodding retelling of the basic elements of the novel—but with crucial explanations and linking events removed.

The script is less than a *precis* of the novel; at times, you have to have read the novel to know what is going on, to understand motivations. In the novel, Buddy Repperton has several encounters with Arnie, which he *loses*; in the movie, he has only one, which he (basically) *wins*. So why does he come back later and trash Christine? Because he is the Bad Guy. How does he know the car is so important to Arnie? Because the script requires him to know. Christine is a car from the 1950s; naturally, her radio plays only '50s rock—but why does *Dennis's* car radio play only '50s music? Why does the police detective (Harry Dean Stanton) suspect Christine is alive? Why, when he sees Christine roll in on her own, smoking and smoldering, does Darnell climb behind her wheel?

In the novel, why the 1958 Plymouth Fury with a mind of her own is murderously evil is never made clear; it's both alive *and* haunted. The solution offered in the film is no improvement. Here, the car is evil as she comes off the production line, killing people for no reason (a guy opens her hood and is bitten by it; another drops cigar ashes on her upholstery, and later is found dead). In the novel, it's clear that, however she became aware, Christine *is* aware and wants a loving owner. In the movie, she's *buh-buh-bad to the bone*, as the song tells us as soon as we see her. This removes mystery and begs any and all questions.

The most important omissions have to do with Arnie. In the novel, he enters into a kind of dream state, not really aware what is happening to him and Christine. After LeBay's death, Christine and LeBay's ghost begin turning Arnie into a replica of the furious old man, complete with his vocabulary and bad back. In the movie, Arnie simply changes into a cool dude. Clearly, Christine is doing it—but *why*? In the novel, Arnie himself has questions about what is happening to him: Christine seems to cure herself, *but he's not sure*; when he finds that someone has been killed, it's disturbing to him. In the film, Arnie *sees* Christine regenerate herself after the assholes trash her; why is he genuinely surprised when she runs off on her own to kill the bad guys?

Movies have survived worse scripts than this. Better scripts have raised more unanswered questions. But *John Carpenter's Christine* is a pretty slow vehicle; you have *time* to wonder about all blunders. It's just a big clock, wound up in the first scene — see? an evil car — that ticks its way to the predictable ending.

Clearly, it is very difficult to adapt Stephen King. Can *King* do it well? As with so many things, the answer is — it depends. His earliest produced script was *Creepshow*; despite some serious blunders, it's still an amusing, entertaining film. But except for parts of "The Crate," it isn't very scary — despite King's announced intention to make it one of the scariest films of all time. He and director George Romero also wanted it to be as much like the EC comics of the 1950s as possible.

The frame story, with a father throwing out his son's "Creepshow" comic book, is a gleeful attack on all repressive parents who don't understand that kids love blood-and-thunder stuff. (The boy is King's son Joe.) The camera finds the comic in the garbage, and an animated figure, like an old horror comic host, guides us through the pages of "Creepshow" as they flutter in the evening wind. An effort is made to have the film physically resemble a comic book; Jack Kamen, who worked on the EC comics, drew each opening panel for the stories in the film's comic book (which also has ads, letter pages, *etc.*), which then become the first scene of each story. As director, Romero tried to make the film visually like a comic book; not only does he use big splashes of color with jagged edges behind characters in important scenes, but the choice of angles, what is called "breakdown" in comics themselves, is in a comic-book style, especially in the frame story (but this is not followed consistently).

Making the film look so much like a comic book is more distracting than anything else, and very little is gained by it; you can admire the effort, but you also have to wonder why it was done — since it doesn't pay off. Several years before, Amicus Films of England did two anthology movies based on actual stories from EC comics; the first of the two, *Tales from the Crypt*, did a marvelous job of translating the comic stories to the screen, because the filmmakers understood something important—the EC comics horror stories were intensely, even rigidly moralistic. In interviews, Stephen King clearly understands this himself, but it doesn't happen in any of the stories except "Something to Tide You Over." In the others, something terrible happens to bad people, without satisfying any sense of justice or rightful retribution.

In the first story, "Father's Day," there is a very EC-ish walking corpse, but *why* he is walking and *who* he kills are *all wrong*, if this is to be an EC story. He comes out of the grave and kills not only Bedelia, who killed him, but lots of innocent bystanders (they're crude and greedy, but those aren't reasons for retribution). The last shot/panel has the right EC look, but the head on the platter should have been Bedelia's, not Sylvia's, who never did anything to the old man.

However, as with all five of the *Creepshow* episodes, the acting is delightful, with good character actors entering into things with a wink and a grin, exactly the right approach.

In "The Lonesome Death of Jordy Verrill," King himself plays the lead with great energy and glee, a true silent movie-comedy performance. It's as broad as Kansas but entirely appropriate to the material. Some have complained about King's amateurishness, but he really *isn't* an actor, and to demand professionalism of him is pointless. Unfortunately, in neither this nor any of the other stories does Romero find a directorial style that matches the exactly-right playing of his cast; it's as if he can tell other people how to do it, but can't do it himself. Here, he lingers on objects as they get grassier, infected (or something) by the "meteor shit" from the object Jordy finds in his backyard. Again and again we see the room covered in foggily-green grass, including Jordy himself at last. It's merely scenic. This is the kind of EC story found in their science fiction comics rather than the horror titles; as such, it's a perfectly good example. In the sf comics, the EC staff moralized only rarely; usually, something weird happened to someone ordinary and that's what happens here, as a hick and his farm become covered in grass from outer space.

The third episode, "Something to Tide You Over," is almost perfectly in the EC spirit. Sardonic, sarcastic Vickers (Leslie

Nielsen) takes Wentworth (Ted Danson) at gunpoint to a beach and buries him up to his neck below the high tide line, then plants a TV set in the sand nearby, so Wentworth must watch Vicker's wife, with whom he was having an affair; she's also buried, a bit closer to the ocean, so Wentworth has to watch her drown before he goes himself. Of course, when Vickers returns later, both bodies are gone—but come back to get him. This story could have come directly from an EC comic, capturing as it does many of their themes and using a variation on THE POSTMAN ALWAYS RINGS TWICE, on one of their favorite plots. Except for the pointlessly protracted advance of the walking corpses at the climax—we know why they have come back and we *want* them to grab Vickers—the episode works very well indeed. It's sardonic, creepy, and contains a rich and amusing portrayal of utter, self-obsessed nastiness from Leslie Nielsen, one of the best actors for this kind of thing you could find anywhere, at his best when he can use his own ripe humor in his roles.

"The Crate" is the longest and most elaborate *Creepshow* episode, with a great Tom Savini monster suggested by the Tasmanian Devil of the Warner Bros. cartoons. Overall it's the best episode, partly because it is enough *un*like EC comics to be unexpected. The cast is good, although Adrienne Barbeau's incredibly shrewish Billie is a bit beyond belief; we not only cannot understand why Hal Holbrook never left her, but why he ever married her in the first place. Holbrook is outstanding, especially in his satanic stifled merriment just before he feeds Billie to the monster in the crate. The two fantasy scenes of Holbrook killing Barbeau are intrusive, unnecessary, actually brutal. Does she deserve death for being a bitch? The only real mistake in plotting is in having Billie trapped by a generous impulse—she comes to the college building where the crate is because Holbrook has told her a young woman student needs help. Billie should have been trapped by greed or vanity, solely to keep us a bit more on Holbrook's side. But few viewers regret when Billie is gobbled up by the fanged, hairy thing in the box.

"They're Creeping Up on You" is rather poky, and not much like an EC story; if the millionaire industrialist battling the cockroaches also owned vermin-infested tenements, it would pay off better. The story is predictable, so we become impatient to reach the end. Shots of innumerable cockroaches crawling all over computer terminals and clean white floors may be creepy at first, but soon grown old. The final shot of E.G. Marshall's dead body with cockroaches erupting out of it, is unnerving, despite one of the worst dummies in recent screen history. Marshall himself is a delight, having a great time in a rare comedy role.

Creepshow was popular enough that it ultimately generated *Creepshow II*, a complete box office disaster, coming and going so fast in Los Angeles that I was unable to see it. George Romero wrote the script, working from one published story and two screen ideas by King. Romero's company still has the rights to the film THE STAND and PET SEMATARY, but he really isn't a good enough director for the complexities of the first, although he should be able to handle the second well enough.

To date, King has written three of the De Laurentiis films and directed one. None did well at the box office, and it's possible that the sixth may never be made. By the time *Stephen King's Cat's Eye* was released, he was considered prominent enough that his name was made an official part of the title; therefore, moviegoers semi-reasoned, Stephen King must be responsible for these humdrum movies. Although major flaws in them lie elsewhere, they are further indications that Stephen King is not the best possible person to adapt Stephen King to the screen.

The best of the three was *Stephen King's Cat's Eye* (a title subject to several interpretations), a lightweight trio of stories perfectly suited to scare kids at scout camp, directed well but not enthusiastically by Lewis Teague, starring several attractive performers. The many references to Stephen King himself are indications that we're not supposed to take anything in the film very seriously. As a result, despite being nicely made and reasonably entertaining, *Stephen King's Cat's Eye* lacks any dramatic punch, and is forgotten almost as soon as it is seen.

The first story, "Quitters, Inc.," is a comedy based on a serious story from NIGHT SHIFT. It's the ultimate stop-smoking clinic—if you don't stop, they torture your wife or other loved one before your eyes. The major virtue of the segment is James Woods' impish but earnest performance as the man who tries to quit smoking; he is tense, jittery, scared, but never lets us really share these emotions—this is not the story's intent. Woods is an eccentric actor who often appears in eccentric films (*Videodrome*, *Salvador*), and rarely in comedy; he's fine here, however, and he keeps the segment going even when it momentarily jumps the tracks in an overstated but funny nightmare sequence of smokers gone berserk.

What seriously damages the segment, however, are the scenes of the electric grid shocking first the cat, then Woods' wife. Over the scene of the cat (the film's unnecessary linking element) leaping about in pain, we hear "Twist and Shout," but no matter how jokey the music, we can't get past the idea that we're seeing an innocent animal being tortured. It stops the segment dead. Woods gets it back on track, until the wife is tortured. After that, however, both the story and the movie have a serious flaw: we cannot believe that the wife would smile, hug her hubby, and say how nice it is that he found a way to stop smoking. *All he had to do was fry his wife.* But the segment is quickly over, boppity pow, and we're on to the next.

"The Ledge" is about as simple as a story can be: a bad guy makes a good guy walk around the top of a tall building on a narrow ledge. Cinematically, the sequence is stunning, with vertiginous matte paintings helping us suspend our disbelief that Robert Hays—who is fine—is really up that high. Though simple, it is the simpleness of elegance, not of thinness, a respectable filming of a good short story. Kenneth McMillan is nicely rotten as a vulgar millionaire gambler and all-round bad guy.

The last segment, which has been referred to as "The General," was written by King directly for the screen, his best screen writing to date. Although all of *Stephen King's Cat's Eye* seems to have been written by someone who *has* cats but *hates* them, at least in this segment the cat is unquestionably the hero. There's a nasty little jester-clad troll living in the wall of a family's house, waiting to suck the breath of little Drew Barrymore.

The cat knows this, but the girl's mommy, Candy Clark, who doesn't like cats, keeps tossing the pussy out of the house. In the nick of time, the cat returns from the brink of death to wipe out the troll and save our little heroine.

"The General" is especially impressive for the immense, over-sized sets built to make the actor in the troll suit seem six inches high; the special effects putting the normal-sized cat into the scenes with the tiny troll are very well done. Carlo Rambaldi's troll is of an uninteresting design, looking like a fist with needle teeth, but the actor (or actors) playing the troll are excellent mimes, working with a witty sound track to give the critter an endearingly nasty personality.

Although well done for an anthology film, *Stephen King's Cat's Eye* is placid and unexciting; neither King at his best nor worst, watchable but hardly memorable. Yet it is better than the next film.

In a way, it's a shame that King did not make his directorial debut with *Stephen King's Silver Bullet*; it's a better script and better concept, no matter how many werewolf movies there have been, than *Maximum Overdrive*. He seems to have worked on the characters with some care in *Stephen King's Silver Bullet*, trying for, if not something definitive, at least something respectable. But again, it is not a good script overall: the identity of the werewolf—the local reverend—is reasonably obvious to anyone who's seen many of these films; everything seems cut and dried. Also, Daniel Attias is an unimaginative director, and the werewolf is badly done, looking more like a bear; with the astounding transformation scenes in *An American Werewolf in London* and *The Howling* still relatively fresh in the memory, similar scenes here are third rate.

Paradoxically, two of the principal strengths of *Stephen King's Silver Bullet* are among its weaknesses. In an apparent nod to *To Kill a Mockingbird*, King has the film narrated by the grown sister of our hero (Corey Haim), remembering the summer when they discovered they actually loved each other. Haim is confined to a wheelchair, but he's still a kid, inclined to tease his older sister (Megan Follows), who resents the attention his infirmity brings him from their parents. The relationship between them is warm, touching: both children are good actors. But by having her narrate, we know that she (and probably he) will survive the story, reducing the suspense. Also, if this whole story is supposedly being told by her, we are improperly shown scenes she could not possibly know about.

The greatest strength of the film, Gary Busey's intensely warm, amusing and well-observed performance as Uncle Red, the kids' favorite relative, is in fact so strong that the film suffers when he's not around. In a way, Busey is the perfect Stephen King actor; he's broad yet real, in touch with his emotions, expressive, unusual and funny—elements often found in King's own fiction. Such a marriage of material and actor is rare in horror movies and, in fact, it's odd to find Busey in such a film. The scenes between him and Haim are so strong that you may find yourself wishing that this wasn't just another werewolf movie.

But it is. The attacks are conventional, the behavior of the werewolf while in human form is conventional. Everett McGill as the werewolf reverend is acceptable, but he's just another tortured soul suffering the curse of lycanthropy. The one odd thing is that he tries to justify his werewolfery as working the will of God. We never know how he became a werewolf (very unusual for such a movie), nor how long he's been one, but the chances seem good he got this way rather recently. King's original draft gave the werewolf—in wolfy form—some funny lines, but these were removed. They should have been retained, because a joking werewolf would have helped make the movie a bit different from all the other werewolf films.

David Cronenberg says King was not happy about having the child at the climax of *The Dead Zone* be Sarah's son, claiming it was too pat. Few movies are as pat as *Stephen King's Silver Bullet*. Everyone who turns up has something to do with the story, as if there isn't anyone in town except werewolf fodder. People are introduced, sometimes very awkwardly, only to turn up later killed by the werewolf.

In this film King tried a technique he uses in his novels, of having sideline characters talk at length about something marginal to the story. In the novels, it usually works because it provides color. In a film, things need far more to be directed to one end. The worst of several instances in *Silver Bullet* is when the father of a boy killed by the werewolf stalks into a bar and delivers a lengthy harangue about personal justice; we never saw him before, we hardly see him again, but he takes center stage for a long speech and stops the film cold.

King's script needed a heavy rewrite; there's much that's good in it, but also too much repetition, some bad laughs (the dream of werewolves in a church starts well but goes on too long, getting silly), and overly-tidy coincidences. But even this script deserved a better director than Attias, who has no new ideas and doesn't know how to deliver old-fashioned shocks. Even when they look like they should work, the numerous sudden-shock scenes fall flat because of Attias's lack of understanding of the crucial importance of timing and camera angle. A better director—even a slightly better director—would have made a much better film.

On the other hand, it's not likely that a better director could have improved *Maximum Overdrive* very much. King directing a King script is a stunt, like William Castle's Percepto, just a gimmick to get audiences into the theater. Once there, they probably didn't have a good time—but it's not all due to King the director; it's also due to King the writer. He made a mistake in choosing his short story "Trucks" to turn into a film. What is disturbing and full of implications in a short story—and it's not one of his best in the first place—is merely silly in the film. Trucks endlessly circle a diner somewhere in the Carolinas, menacing the uninteresting people within. King made his story longer in the worst possibly way—he just made it longer. *More* of everything, not a rethinking of everything. The film simply is not very interesting, and even a better director couldn't have improved things much.

I hope King directs again; this is partly personal—I have a passion for what he does, and will read and see anything his name is connected with. But also he is an intelligent man and can learn from his mistakes, which are many in *Maximum Overdrive*. It's grotesquely vulgar, for one thing. In King's fiction, this is like a dash of pepper sauce, spicy, over with quickly.

In *Maximum Overdrive*, there's a scene of a character on a toilet, taking a crap; his dialogue is punctuated with farts. This isn't earthy, it's little-boy kaka-poopoo humor.

The actors are either over the top, like Pat Hingle, or frozen, like Emilio Estevez; reactions often are overdone or inappropriate. There's little sense of pacing or timing, or of a growing sense of danger. Events simply happen, then they happen again. King wanted a very violent film, and made one so bloody it had to be cut several times simply to get approval from the Motion Picture Association of America. He did not provide enough "coverage" in many scenes (shots from different angles, or more takes of the same scene), so many are puzzlingly incomplete. But as with his performance in *Creepshow*, no one really should complain about the lack of finesse of Stephen King, Movie Director. That he took on this daunting challenge at all is a tribute to him; it was worth trying—even if the film isn't any good. There are worse sins than making a bad movie, or daring something different.

However, we can legitimately criticize King's script. First, his rationalization for why the machines are rebelling is foggy at best. The earth is passing through the tail of a comet—*and* aliens are doing it. Come again? Do the aliens follow the comet around, waiting for an inhabited, mechanized planet to drift through the tail so they can come down and take over? If they *send* the comet around, why not park it over the earth for longer than the eight plus days it stays? If this is going on all over the world, why are we stuck with these boring people in the Dixie Boy truck stop? What about missiles? Ships? Computers? Atomic power plants? Surely something more interesting happens elsewhere. The dialogue plays as if it was written by a Northerner who thinks Southerners are funny, and got all his ideas about them from movies and TV shows. For instance, in this film (and elsewhere) King uses the exclamation "Jesus Palomino," apparently unaware that it was (allegedly) invented for Steven Spielberg's movie *1941*. Hingle's character is particularly unbelievable and repellent.

The movie invites comparisons with *Duel* and fails the test.

We've seen all of this before and better. There's no freshness or vitality to the movie; it's a plodding, boring mess. But in all honesty, I am not sorry it was made. Perhaps King did learn from it.

I suspect *Stand By Me* was a more powerful lesson to him. Not only an outstanding film on its own merits, of all King adaptations, it is the one truest to its source. Set in a small town, dealing with friendship among children, it's suffused with references to contemporary mass culture, and it's a journey to understanding. I hope King loved it; it was made with love.

The film stunned many critics and movie audiences, who apparently knew King solely from the films based on his work; those familiar with his writing could have been surprised only by how good the film is, for it is pure Stephen King, based on the best thing I have read by him, his DIFFERENT SEASONS novella, "The Body."

Unexpectedly, Rob Reiner, ol' Meathead of "All in the Family," has shown promise of becoming one of Hollywood's best directors. *Stand By Me* is a sweet, gentle and touching coming-of-age story set in Oregon in 1959. (The original story, of course, was set in Maine; though both states have Portlands, more minor dialogue changes should have been done to make it thoroughly Oregonian. But this is not important.) The fine adaptation is by Raynold Gideon and Bruce A. Evans.

The story is more than a comedy-drama about a couple of groups of kids sauntering through gorgeous Oregon scenery; it's about a loss of innocence, a journey to understanding, the meaning of friendship. The lines are drawn simply and quickly at the very beginning; Gordie, played as an adult by Richard Dreyfuss, is seen brooding over the death of the adult Chris. At 12, Chris is Gordie's best friend, and the best among them. Chris is a thoughtful, sensitive boy, devoted to Gordie and to Gordie's promise as a writer, Chris looks out for the other boys, too, giddy, impulsive Teddy and pudgy, gabby Vern. These children are not realistic, but are the fond memories of children the writer knew when he was young.

The film is always well observed, amusing and touching,

filled with characters so well-drawn they might come out of your own childhood. Reiner's direction is subtle, unobtrusive, dealing primarily with the performers (all of whom are good), but does add a haunting touch in the very last moment we see Chris: as the writer tells us how Chris died, the young Chris literally vanishes. This kind of direction is the hardest to praise because, in a real sense, it's the hardest to see: it seems smooth, effortless, natural—as it must.

As with *The Dead Zone*, one of the film's few rivals to the Best Stephen King Movie honors, the changes from the original are improvements. King has told interviewers that the three friends he depicted in this autobiographical tale really did die, and so their deaths are reported in the story. But in the film, only Chris dies; the others live ordinary lives. In "The Body," it's Chris who brandishes the gun he brought, chasing off Ace and his buddy; in the film, it's Gordie—as it should be, since it is his story. But the core of the story is intact and treated with affection.

Stand By Me is a funny, stirring, emotionally moving and handsome film; it isn't a dream of childhood, as most such movies are; it really is about the things we learn and, in fact, the things most of us forget. We may be at our best at 12, and Stephen King, Rob Reiner and the others involved know that well. They make us remember.

Though overkill and indifferent adaptations changed Stephen King from one of the hottest movie properties to a stale commodity, the movies clearly aren't through with Stephen King, nor he with them. *Stand By Me* and *The Dead Zone* show how well King can be presented on the big screen, when care and intelligence are applied, "Apt Pupil," from DIFFERENT SEASONS, has been announced; *The Running Man*, from a "Richard Bachman" novel, will be out anyday now; *It* has been announced as a TV miniseries; George Romero keeps promising *The Stand* and *Pet Sematary*; Steven Spielberg at one point said he would film THE TALISMAN, King's collaboration with Peter Straub; *Training Exercise*, from an outline by King, has been announced by De Laurentiis, although it may not be made. And I have not discussed the *short* films for TV based on King, including "The Woman in the Room," "The Boogeyman," "The Word Processor of the Gods" and "Gramma."

King recently has taken a hiatus from writing, but will no doubt return in time. And so will the movies.

"COME OUT HERE AND TAKE YOUR MEDICINE!" KING AND DRUGS

by Ben P. Indick, R. Ph.

*T*he down-home side of Stephen King, whose books are sold in the millions because he can scare the Calvin Kleins off his readers, is that he peppers his writing with familiar product names. It isn't necessarily because he likes Big Macs, Whoppers, Plymouths and Camels so much as that they root his writing in recognizable down-to-earth reality. Rarely does anyone light up a mere cigarette, which was good enough for most writers in the past: it will be a Winston, a Carlton, or a Kool; and the popular reputation which adheres to particular brands may indicate the nature of the character inhaling, perhaps a snob, a machismo guy, a truck-driver, a woman. Likewise, his people seldom drink "beer;" it is Rolling Rock, Coors, or Budweiser. If they eat too much they chew Di-Gel or Rolaids. For colds they wipe their noses with Kleenex. On occasion they even read Stephen King novels.

The technique is not original with him. James Jones filled his busy pages with brand names. Ray Bradbury, who certainly influenced King, used it now and then, but King, whether naming gas stations, toys or pharmaceuticals, sprinkles his text like raisins in Raisin Bran with brands that dot our daily landscape. The horror which ensues in the story is easier to accept when the reader is in comfortable, everyday surroundings. Thanks to an increasingly homogenous civilization they are familiar to readers around the nation, and even around the world. This is no esoteric writer off in some ivory tower, but a regular guy who sets the reader down in his own turf, and then delivers his shock—an essential part of a style which has made him a publishing phenomenon.

What is remarkable about his use of familiar names is the range of his observation; for a writer just barely forty years old, he has apparently seen every horror flick, read most horror stories, listened to all the rock and roll, and yet somehow has managed to spend innumerable hours in supermarkets, bars and—yes—pharmacies where no label has escaped him. King's numerous pharmaceutical references include those items which might be purchased over the counter or by prescription within any community pharmacy, not only the colossi in which the prescription department is buried within a supermarket-city, but an average and well-stocked store, say one of those Rexalls his characters discover now and then along their route. Here you can buy cosmetics, hair sprays, deodorants, cigarettes, occasional sundries and can find the Rx counter without a road map. Some of his usages are quite good for a layman, if King is indeed a layman in anything, and his first prescription appears to be for a junior high school girl, overweight, shy and somewhat sluggish. She has been left woefully unprepared for certain facts of life by a neurotic mother. Her name is Carrie White.

The heroine of CARRIE is introduced in a post-gym shower having her first, belated menstrual flow. She is derided by her classmates for her failure to understand what is happening to her. Tampons and sanitary napkins are recommended to her, even *thrown* at her, but without brand name identification. Perhaps, in his first published novel, written in the period when he was writing the novels he would publish later under his "Richard Bachman" pseudonym, King was unaware of the immediacy of an actual trade name. Such familiar names are uncommon in the Bachman books as well.

Labels are not entirely absent in CARRIE: Rheingold is the favorite beer of Carrie's classmates, Schlitz of some of the older men; music is played on a Webcor phonograph; the boys drive

VWs, Dodge Chargers and Javelins. When a popular pharmacy product is at last mentioned by name, its effect is startling. Christine Hargensen is moved by apparent aphrodisiac power in the combined odors of Billy Nolan's cigarette breath, his sweat and the *Brylcreem* on his hair. Later, after making love upstairs at The Cavalier, the two sleep while below the band is wiping sweat and Vitalis from its brows. King also initiates the use of "Kleenex" as a generic term for facial tissues. In general, he has not discovered the marvels of the pharmacy. As his writing richened in subsequent books, he would do so.

The Bachman books are among King's most pessimistic, two involved with people very preoccupied with themselves and two set in the near future. In consequence, there is little opportunity for King to visit the corner drugstore. However, the cigarettes the kids of RAGE pick up indicate their personalities. Charlie smokes Kents; his dad smokes Pall Malls. His classmate Sylvia Ragan prefers Camels. This brand is often considered strong, a man's cigarette; King is probably inferring that Sylvia is wilful and independent, an impression confirmed later when she lights up, drops the match on the floor and stretches out her legs, unconcerned about the skirt line.

In ROADWORK when Vinnie Mason smokes Player's Navy Cut, an unusual brand, Bart Dawes thinks it is a "dipshit" cigarette; he believes Vinnie's the kind who would smoke "King Sano, Murads, English Ovals or Twists." For such exotic brands as these, however, we must leave the drugstore and go to the smoke shop down the block. (Ironically, in his short story "Quitters, Inc.," devoted to persuading people to quit smoking, no brand is mentioned at all, save for the hero's laconic description of himself as a "Marlboro Man.")

Bart Dawes suffers, along with his stubbornness, some gas while in Harvey's Gun Shop. The proprietor sees he needs relief, spells it ROLAIDS. Alone, Bart wants to call his wife, doesn't, commits an onanistic act instead, and climaxes as the TV announcer states that Anacin "has the highest pain-relief of any brand." Bart also likes Pepto-Bismol, uses it, as do several other King characters, in preference to Kaopectate for diarrhea. Not unexpectedly, Charmin is also on his mind. For tension headache, Bart uses Pepto-Bismol to wash down an Excedrin. If you were blowing up bulldozers you might also be tense.

THE RUNNING MAN like THE LONG WALK is a tale of the future. A few fast food places have familiar names, but pharmacy products are unmentioned. By 2021, when even the monetary system is different, our brand names of today would nearly all have undergone change except as museum pieces. In spite of all the glowing words the public is given about miracle drugs even they have only their moment in the sun, and are gone. The uses to which pharmacopoeias of a century ago put various herbs and drugs sometimes seem laughable today; however, the reaction to the drugs of our own chemotherapeutically-minded era by a future generation may be one of equal and mirthful disbelief.

THINNER is King's final Bachman book, and should have given him adequate opportunity to play his name-the-product game, in view of the problems the characters have with body weight and skin ulcerations; however, "Bachman" does not share King's medical expertise. Bill Halleck's physician uses a Q-tip on his patient's nose, and suggests Num-Zit for oral problems (having nothing, however, to do with the unusual sexual driving tastes of Billy's wife); he does nothing for Halleck's diminishing girth. Billy might have at least alleviated his weight loss problem by consulting his neighborhood pharmacist, and buying, as many barebones teenagers do, some therapeutic strength multivitamins or even Wate-On, a high calorie vitamin supplement.

Billy's friend Cary Rossington, the judge who had incurred the gypsy's wrath by letting Billy off easy in the hearing, finds his skin growing increasingly scaly. He uses Nivea Skin Cream, fine for soothing dry skin, but scarcely therapeutic for serious skin problems. The judge should have consulted a dermatologist at once, or at least his pharmacist. The latter would have suggested 0.5% Hydrocortisone Cream, the strength available over the counter, and Cary might well have nipped the fatal condition in the bud. When he finally talks to his dermatologist the condition is too far gone, and so is he.

After all the hesitation, King finally nudges "Bachman" aside and calls in a doctor to prescribe some potent medicine. Unfortunately, it is an antibiotic named Aureomycin which Dr. Houston, quite possibly the "cocaine-sniffing old gasbag" Billy suspects him to be, prescribes. Bill would, in 1985 (although the book was probably written much earlier), have had great difficulty obtaining the capsules as they had been discontinued for some years in favor of a derivative, Achromycin-V. Dr. Houston warns him about potassium depletion and recommends he buy some potassium pills in the vitamin section of the drugstore. That would surely have been adequate for a minor imbalance, but considering Billy's alarming state, he might well have done better to write Billy a prescription for a potassium of proper strength, whether Slow-K, K-Lor, K-Lyte, Klotrix *etc.*

The doctor, however, is called on to prescribe for Bill's pain as well. He considers but rejects "Darvon or Darvocet" each propoxyphene or a compound of it. (We shall hear more about a misnamed Darvon derivative in several other novels.) Either is an excellent pain-reliever, albeit classified under federal narcotic regulations due to a possible habituating tendency; this fear, as well as the danger of coma in Billy's debilitated state, induces the physician to prescribe instead some "fairly strong Empirin." Empirin originally consisted of the traditional A-P-C formula, aspirin, phenacetin and caffeine (and was known as Empirin Compound); when phenacetin was frowned upon by the FDA, the tablet was reformulated, and labeled simply "Empirin," consisting of aspirin alone. The only stronger form at any time would have been Empirin (Compound or plain) with Codeine, most of whose strengths would have been stronger than the propoxyphenes—and would indeed have been hazardous inasmuch as Billy later took three tablets at one time. Having shown him the ropes, King retires in favor of "Bachman," whose final and desperate therapy is not a drug at all, but rather some pastry.

'SALEM'S LOT, a novel of the vampire-ridden small town of that name, is not rich in pharmaceutical terms, inasmuch as the usual cures for vampirism lie more within folk remedies or religious items. It does, however, lead to interesting speculation of a practical nature for folk living in such a state of hazard. While in retreat in Mexico from the horrors they have experienced, Ben and Mark read in a newspaper that the small town is now deserted, not one business remaining open. The last to go, they read, was "Spencer's Pharmacy." I wonder, since he was not mentioned as having succumbed to Barlow, did the ingenious pharmacist make an anti-vampire medicine? Sprigs of garlic, placed over windows and doorways, are the traditional safety factor against the intrusion of vampires. No pharmacopeia mentions such a use for the herb, however, so did Spencer perhaps take garlic tablets orally? (They are usually used, again an old remedy, for mild relief of hypertension or gastric distress.) Did he perhaps develop a garlic aerosol? In 'Salem's Lot (or Transylvania, for that matter, where the market would be large) that could have been carried on one's person at all times, to be sprayed directly upon one's body, like 6-12 or Off insect repellents. Holy water, another traditional weapon in the armamentarium against evil, also might be used in aerosol form for spraying upon the vampire.

The explanation is more mundane. We learn later that Spencer had sold his shop to LeVerdiere, the huge Maine chain, which subsequently shut the branch down. Apparently the news release which Mark and Ben saw a continent away was not up to date, or, unaccountably, in view of their usual procedure, LaVerdiere had continued to use the Spencer name.

The author has one interesting and logical medication used by no prior writers in such a tale: tetanus vaccine. It is, of course, not used within a pharmacy, but is frequently supplied by pharmacies to physicians. The vampire, after all, having rested within earth could well have picked up, as might a dog or a rusty nail, the deadly germ. The shot will not be efficacious against the vampire's actual bite, but the victim is in trouble enough without having to worry about lockjaw.

Just as "Kleenex" is King's invariable synonym for tissues, "Band-Aid" and "Red Cross tape" cover adhesive tapes. In 'SALEM'S LOT, a rude cross is formed using two tongue depressors bound by Red Cross tape. Several other drugstore items mentioned include Supp-Hose for elastic support hose and Sterno, the familiar little red can used as a source of heat for cooking, but used here, as often in fact, for the ethyl alcohol which winos squeeze from its gelid substance.

A terrifying litany punctuates the nightmares of young Danny Torrance of King's brilliant THE SHINING. In these dreams he sees his father, driven mad by the horror inherent in the Overlook Hotel, screaming at him to "Come out here and take your medicine!" The prescient youngster realizes that Jack is using the expression metaphorically, for something indescribably worse than the most vile-tasting of medicines.

The actual medicines encountered in THE SHINING are far less fearful than Danny's nightmare. Jack's favorite is Excedrin, a compound analgesic. Jack's belief is that it is good for hangovers, and he pops it regularly through the book. Once, when he actually has a headache, and asks his wife Wendy if she has aspirins in her bag, she hands him a tin of Anacin. He asks teasingly "What, no Excedrin?" The name is a sore point with her, because it reminds her of his alcoholism. Once, early in the novel, when he has gone to a local Rexall to get Danny a Baby Ruth candy bar, he thinks back to the past, how after a bender, he would "chew four Excedrins." (In MISERY, Paul Sheldon recalls when he would try to counteract "long, muddled nights spent bar-hopping" by drinking coffee, orange juice and gobbling vitamin-B tablets.) King's characters *do* tend to chew tablets, which is unpleasant when they contain bitter substances, although it does not stop them. (The Baby Ruth is only incidental to THE SHINING but in THE STAND, Harold Lawlor's Payday candy bar wrappers form a trail for Larry to follow as surely as the signs Harold scrawls.)

The author's preoccupation with drugs forms part of the hotel's history, one of whose shadowy residents was a woman who killed herself by taking "about thirty sleeping pills [name unidentified] on top of all the booze." A less drastic pharmacy item is part of a classic chapter, when Jack enters the bathroom of the long dead but fearfully present apparition in Room 217. Instead of the usual hotel-size bars of Camay or Ivory Soap, he thinks he smells Lowilla Soap. This is a soap often recommended by dermatologists and pharmacists for skins allergic to ordinary soaps.

In the horrendous climax of the story, as Wendy seeks to escape her by now mad and murderous husband and his mallet, she looks desperately into the medicine cabinet for razor blades with which she might defend herself. Bottles are falling as she claws, "cough syrup, Vaseline, Clairol Herbal Essence Shampoo, hydrogen peroxide, benzocaine." It is but a sampling, however, of the collection which will be amassed later in IT by Eddie Kaspbrak.

The disastrous plague, "Captain Trips," released accidentally from a government biological laboratory in THE STAND, is probably a viral analogue of influenza. Virus illnesses are not susceptible to antibiotics or other medications. The use of antibiotics is intended to treat or prevent secondary infections which would complicate the primary illness. Vaccines have been successfully used to prevent, but not to cure, such virus infections as poliomyelitis. "Trips" is a reflection of the terrible influenza epidemic which racked the country after World War I and, although the author could not know it, is a frightening precursor of today's growing virus infection, AIDS. The world was unprepared for Captain Trips, and did not have time to develop a vaccine. The only survivors had a natural immunity. No such hope exists for AIDS, which by definition leaves its victims with no immunity at all, so that they cannot withstand such deadly diseases as pneumonia, the cause of most AIDS-related deaths.

King wisely eschews prescribing against his virus, but there are other pharmacy references in THE STAND. To her surprise Fran discovers she is pregnant, although she has been taking "Orvil." It is possibly a mere typographical error, for "Ovral," similar to the misspelling in MISERY of Motrin as "Motrim." Before burying her father, Fran does not merely powder him; she uses a brand, Johnson's baby powder (the last two words properly uncapitalized by the observant author). Larry Underwood is told by Rita, the New York refugee who briefly accompanies him, that her husband had been at a luncheon "with one of those Arabs who always look as if they have rubbed all the visible areas of their skin with Brylcreem."

Rita, a nervous woman, has brought with her on her exodus with Larry all her pills, including Darvon and Quaalude. The latter has subsequently been frowned upon by authorities for regular use, but at the time of writing was a commonly prescribed sleeping tablet. She has also some "reds and yellowjackets," as Larry terms them, colloquial names on the illegal market. Larry's "West Coast" terminology refers to the potent barbiturates Seconal Sodium as "reds" and Nembutal Sodium as "yellowjackets," although he is mistaken in describing the latter, a small all-yellow capsule as "a large red and yellow" capsule.

Nick Andros and Tom Cullen discover a deserted Rexall in an empty town. Nick picks up a bottle of Pepto-Bismol for Tom, who has diarrhea after eating too many raw apples. In Boulder, residents do not treat poison ivy with mere itch lotions; they have found Caladryl in their own Rexall. On a surgical pharmacy level, a court-appointed lawyer who had once represented the punk Lloyd had come "into court lugging a colostomy bag." An operation on the colon, whether for cancer or a lesser dysfunction, may require the closing, temporary or permanent, of the lower bowel, and the use of a tube and colostomy bag to collect wastes for later disposal. It is worn, of course, beneath the clothing so as not to be visible.

In the latter half of THE STAND, concerned with survival and the moral battle surrounding the survivors, today's trademarks, however, seem petty, and King swings to generic terminology. Glen produces some "arthritis pills," otherwise unlabeled, although subsequently we learn they are morphine-based, so that they are actually straight pain-killers. Tom also comes up with "penicillin and ampicillin." Flagg's protege, Trashcan Man, helps himself to some morphine syrettes and Vaseline for burns. Once, in prison, he had learned about "morphine and Elavil and Darvon Complex." Elavil is a mood elevator, but "Darvon Complex" must await discussion later, along with a sedative picked up by Harold Lawlor from a deserted pharmacy.

King will on occasion use ordinary drugstore items in a sardonic way. In THE DEAD ZONE he refers to the gynecological "D & C" operation as a "Band-Aid." When editor Warren Richardson threatens to blow the whistle on Greg Stillson and ruin his political plans, the latter's strong-arm man grinds his thumb into Richardson's ear, sarcastically advising him to use Q-tips on his ear wax. Later, to nail down his threat should the article appear, the thug says simply "Q-tips." A harmless, useful household item becomes a powerful symbol.

Stillson attempts to ingratiate himself with small town voters by telling them their tax dollars should not support methadone programs in New York City. Methadone is, of course, used to wean addicts from heroin; its actual usefulness is a matter of opinion, but no doubt voters who are quite uninvolved with any use of that drug would be swayed against politicians who vote funds for its use in large cities.

When King abandons brand-name drugs, such as Johnny Smith's being given only a "blue sleeping pill," it lacks the impact, the sense of identification with an actual name. The mother of Frank Dodd, the rapist/murderer, suffers from "hypertension, thyroid and a semidiabetic condition" but no drugs are named. However, the unidentified medication she takes for what she calls her "heart" after Johnny grasps her wrist is probably nitroglycerin. King does not mention it as such, perhaps because the lay reader may see in it the implication of nitroglycerine as an explosive; however, as a sublingual tablet (dissolved under the tongue for rapid absorption into the blood stream), it is administered in very minute doses and is quickly effective in dilating the blood vessels and bringing relief from the constricting chest pains. Dodd, meanwhile, is busy slashing his wrists with Wilkinson Sword Blades.

Some of King's novels have little or no need for pharmaceutical references. FIRESTARTER, a tense novel basically concerned with individual freedom and governmental secrecy, has no time for fun and games; CHRISTINE's teenagers care only about girls and cars. In the course of CUJO, King's claustrophobic *tour de force* of a woman and her child trapped in a car by the rapid Cujo, he comments that Gillette Foamy (aerosol) was used on a dog in the film *To Kill A Mockingbird* to produce the appearance of rabies. Cujo needs no make-up. (In his discussion of horror films in DANSE MACABRE, when Michael Landon changes to a werewolf in *I Was A Teenage Werewolf* King writes that he "begins to drool a substance that looks suspiciously like Burma Shave." King also amusingly describes Ray Milland's unique ocular problem in *The Man With the X-Ray Eyes* as the result of the eyedrops he has developed, "a kind of super-Murine, if you will".)

In *Creepshow* poor Jordy of "The Lonesome Death of Jordy Verrill" is another King character who would have benefited from a visit to his pharmacist; a tube of tolnaftate cream, an excellent fungicide, might have stopped his extraterrestrially derived fungus infection.

PET SEMETARY has as hero a college dispensary physician, who becomes more involved in magic than science. One of King's coldest, most frightening novels, it refers infrequently to pharmaceuticals. This may seem odd, inasmuch as the young doctor is soundly educated in scientific technique; however, he is capable of accepting the most incredible happenings without question, such as the return to life of a very dead cat. Mundane drugs and prescriptions can hardly compete with the power of the "Wendigo." The few drugs which do occur are fairly drastic. Once, when Dr. Creed is distraught after a student's terrible, fatal accident, he takes Tuinal to relax. Creed probably wanted its powerful hypnotic effect, instead of the milder action of a tranquilizer such as Valium or Ativan. Later, however, when his wife Rachel recalls the awful, lingering death of her sister Zelda, and the ever present smell of Smith Brothers Wild Cherry Cough Drops, Louis gives her Valium.

THE EYES OF THE DRAGON is a fairy tale, set in the past; one of the author's most engaging stories, it cannot use current pharmacy, but Flagg's concoctions refer to its ancestral science, alchemy. He prepares for aging King Roland an aphrodisiac, a drink both "green and foaming." It is not uncommon for today's physician and pharmacist to receive like requests. While they will each caution the client that impotency is frequently a question of the mental state, the doctor may prescribe methyltestosterone, if the hormone is lacking in the man's endocrine system. This is in truth uncommon. The pharmacist cannot offer Flagg's brew, and advertised products are usually vitamin/mineral supplements, of which the latter may mildly irritate or stimulate the genito-urinary area. This could be interpreted by the mind as a sexual impulse. As for the deadly poison which Flagg concocts, that is beyond the purview of a pharmacist, better the property of a toxicologist.

In THE TALISMAN young Jack searches in alternative universes for the magical talisman to cure his cancer-ridden mother and her alter ego, Laura DeLoessian, the Queen of the Territories. Jack passes between the two worlds with the aid of an elixir Speedy Parker has given him, but no earthbound pharmacologist has yet devised such a potion, other than Imagination, the domain of the writer. At one point Wolf prepares an infusion from various herbs to help cure Jack of a momentary illness. Jack figures it contains "ragweed, poison oak and bitter vetch"; the taste is awful, as medicines often taste, but it helps, as medicines should. Several other references are amusing. Stuart Ullman, that "officious little prick" of THE SHINING had used English Leather cologne, which Jack Torrance clearly regarded as effete; here Sunlight Gardiner's son, as bad an apple as his father, smelled like "rancid English Leather." In California, Speedy tells Jack to go to the Point Venuti drugstore and get him a bottle of "Lydia Pinkham's Ointment," an unusual request inasmuch as Pinkham's is a traditional remedy used by some women for menstrual difficulties and also as a tonic; it is available in liquid or tablet form, but not ointment. Speedy is no doubt just teasing Jack to work faster to obtain the talisman. Jack finally succeeds, and with it cures both his mother and her twinner, Laura. In a third universe, our own, we must make do with far less perfect cancer cures; radiation therapy, surgery and dangerous, body-wracking chemotherapeutic drugs.

A number of King's short stories also include pharmaceuticals. Ingeniously, in "The Mangler," he manages to work an ancient magic spell requiring belladonna, which would be uncommon in the area, by having one of the men take an antacid tablet, E-Z Gel (possibly fictitious or a private brand). It contains a bit of the drug, whose action relaxes the smooth muscle of the intestine. When the package of pills falls into the machine, the final ingredient of the spell brings it to fearful life. "Rita Hayworth and the Shawshank Redemption" takes place in a prison, where a guard describes his power: "If she ate her way through a boxcar of Ex-Lax she wouldn't dare fart unless I gave her the nod." In "Apt Pupil" Dussander's apartment "has a stinky medicinal smell of Vicks and Mentholatum." The narrator of "The Body" recalls being "the child of two Geritol-chuggers." The supermarket of "The Mist" has a section of proprietaries; the fright causes sleeplessness and the trapped customers use up the Sominex and Nytol. And what could have happened to the people hiding within the drugstore next door? "They're sure not over there eating Dristan and Stayfree Mini-pads." Burma Shave, Rolaids, Vitalis and Wildroot Cream Oil are used characteristically in various short stories as well.

King's most recent novels, IT, MISERY and THE DRAWING OF THE THREE are strong in pharmaceutical and medical elements. Eddie Kaspbrak is one of the great hypochondriacs of all time. No reader will soon forget Nurse Annie Wilkes, who is to nursing as Sweeney Todd is to barbering. And the efforts of Roland, "the last gunslinger," to obtain his Keflex lead directly to a tumultuous and thrilling climax.

IT's wealth of references to medicines, both proprietary and prescription drugs, are due almost wholly to one character, Eddie Kaspbrak. Through him King also offers a view of the inside of a pharmacy and the nature of one pharmacist.

There are, however, the usual other references to popular drugstore items: Stanley Uris, afraid to face again a nightmare he had fought in his childhood, commits suicide, slashing his wrists with Gillette Platinum Plus razor blades. Rich Tozier, a funny man and impersonator is nervous, would like a cigarette but settles for Mylanta, an antacid. Ben Hanscomb's small town includes that mainstay of old-time America, a Rexall pharmacy. Beverly Marsh requires a Band-Aid for a cut sustained while fleeing her brutish husband. Would "adhesive bandage" or even a competitor, such as Curads, have worked as well? It is unlikely in either case. Kay McCall, who helps Beverly escape her husband, is beaten by him and requires Valium and Darvon. Dick Clark's Bandstand program, advertising Stri-Dex, a still-popular medicated pad for cleansing the skins of young acne patients, is the banal background on the TV for the young Beverly's moment of horror when she hears menacing voices coming from the plumbing. All these are, however, pharmaceutically incidental to Eddie Kaspbrak.

Joyfully recalling his famous line from THE SHINING, King takes commercial pharmacy and its familiar advertising for an hilarious and satirical joy-ride in the chapter headed "Eddie Kaspbrak Takes His Medicine." (The line will enjoy a reprise, in THE DRAWING OF THE THREE, when "Roland Takes His Medicine.")

Eddie is a pharmacist's delight, since he obviously tries everything. His medicine cabinet is a pharmacopoeial cornucopia. It includes such popular pain-killers as Anacin, Excedrin and Tylenol. Cold relief aids and remedies commence with Contac and a "large blue jar of Vicks (Vap-O-Rub)." There are also antacids including Gelusil and large bottles of Tums, Rolaids and "orange-flavored Di-Gel tablets." His laxatives include "two bottles of Phillips Milk of Magnesia, the regular, which tastes like liquid chalk, and the new mint flavor, which tastes like mint-flavored liquid chalk." Taking no chances, Eddie stocks a bottle of Serutan, a laxative he remembers being advertised in his childhood on Lawrence Welk's show as "Nature's spelled backwards." And this is only the top shelf!

On the second shelf is Eddie's vitamin supply. Eddie has clearly sought economy by buying generic packagings, perhaps at a discount pharmacy or even a health food shop. Here he has his "E, C, C with rosehips, B simple and B-Complex and B-12." (There is really no "B simple;" individual components of what is called B-Complex would include Thiamine, or B-1; Riboflavin, or B-2; Pyridoxine, B-6; cyanocobalamin, B-12, Niacin, Folic

Acid, *etc*.) Eddie also stocks some amino acid derivatives which, as King explains properly, are used by many individuals for self-identified needs and cures, Eddie's including "L-Lysine, which is supposed to do something about those embarrassing skin problems, and lecithin, which is supposed to do something about that embarrassing cholesterol buildup in and around the Big Pump." Eddie, taking no chances, also has iron, calcium and perhaps hearkening back to childhood days and a zealous mother with a ready tablespoonful, he has his A and D in Cod Liver Oil.

Eddie is, however, in no imminent danger of A and D deprivation, because this marvelous shelf contains as well an assortment of multivitamin tablets, from the basic One-A-Day to the therapeutic strength Myadec and Centrum. Just to be absolutely certain, there is alongside these a "gigantic bottle of Geritol."

Eddie's private Rexall continues on the third shelf, with such "utility infielders of the patent-medicine world" as Ex-Lax and Carter's Little Pills, "which keep Eddie moving the mail." Then, "in case the mail moves too fast or too painfully," Kaopectate, Pepto-Bismol and Preparation H are on hand. Eddie even maintains a supply of Tucks, a moist, impregnated wipe "to keep everything tidy after the mail has gone through."

The locus of Eddie's armaments against the common cold and the flu are on the crowded third shelf. Formula 44, Nyquil and Dristan, as well as a large bottle of castor oil. King has not misplaced this apparently incongruous item; tradition has it that this tasteless but unpleasantly oily laxative is good for "cleaning out the blood." Eddie also has Sucrets lozenges plus antiseptic mouthwashes: Chloraseptic, Cepacol, Cepestat and, King adds jovially, "good old Listerine, often imitated but never duplicated." Thanks to an obdurate governmental decree, Listerine is no longer allowed to advertise that it kills millions of germs, but Eddie's faith is shared by many still.

The same shelf also contains Visine and Murine eyedrops and Cortaid and Neosporin ointments "for the skin (the second line of defense if the L-Lysine doesn't live up to expectations)." Cortaid is an anti-inflammatory, a hydrocortisone cream, which at 0.5% is sold without prescription. Neosporin Ointment contains several antibiotics and is an anti-infective. Eddie washes his hair with any of his three bottles of coal-tar shampoo (perhaps Zetar or Packer's but for once King does not say). For occasional "zits" Eddie has Oxy-5 and Oxy-wash, which like nearly all anti-acne preparations contain Benzyl Peroxide.

Eddie keeps his hard stuff, prescription drugs and even some illegals, on the bottom shelf of this almost inexhaustible private pharmacy. The anti-depressant, Elavil; the legal narcotic Percodan for severe pain; some Quaaludes, already illegal, a sleeping tablet when first marketed, but later a junkie's delight, these within a Sucrets tin. And, that misnamed analgesic we shall discuss later. To top it off, Eddie's wife Myra even adds some Midol, the anti-menstrual pain tablet, and a tube of Blistex for cold sores. Withal, a magnificent display of total faith in advertising, and, while the author is—not without some justification—having his fun with the whole business of bottled health, any pharmacist must envy the owner of the store where Eddie does his business.

If Eddie has become the complete hypochondriac, it probably stems back to his childhood, to an overbearing mother, and to one item upon which he depended then and still does, his aspirator for relief of asthmatic attacks. Ironically, it is at the same time the most important and the least biologically useful of his medications. His mother, convinced of his weakness, had prevented him from taking Phys Ed, although a school physical had shown him to be normal, a fact confirmed by his own family physician. All too quickly the boy was conditioned by this argument into a total acceptance as well as a complete dependence upon the spray.

He would get the spray in what King describes as a "Windex-like spray bottle" at the Center Street Drugstore. The owner, Mr. Keene, is one of two pharmacists to play active—if minor—roles in King's writings, and is first encountered when young Eddie's friend Bill Denbrough rushes to the pharmacy to refill Eddie's desperately needed spray. The druggist, Keene, does not appear "exactly kind" to Bill, but he seems "patient enough" when the boy, a bad stutterer, writes a message about Eddie's "bad ass-mar attack." Keene brings him the medicine, and when Bill blurts out that he has no money, the man tells him he will charge it to Mrs. Kaspbrak's account. He grins sourly after Bill. Perhaps he is not, as the boys believe, entirely a kind man, but neither is he unfair. He charges very little for the preparation, on which he types a name which sounds real enough: "HydrOx Mist," but is nothing more than water with a dash of camphor. He knows he "could have soaked her, and there were times when he was tempted . . . but why should he make himself a party to the woman's foolishness?"

What Eddie is receiving is, as King explains later, a placebo, an apparent medicine whose effect is merely psychological, though giving the *appearance* of being real. In a sense the physician who had originally prescribed it for the boy was giving it as well for his mother, since she would not be content until he was using something for what she perceived to be his ailment. One might frown on such prescribing, but the physician must make his decision based on the facts before him. Perhaps he entertained a hope that the mother might in time realize the fatuity of her demand, and the boy might even realize he had no true need of it.

In fairness, the importance of such "medication" should not be denied. Placebos are used in testing new medications, wherein one group receives an actual drug while another receives a placebo. Thus, the actual effects of the drug may be ascertained. On an individual level, I have on occasion filled prescriptions in which the physician directed that a readily identified capsule containing a barbituate be emptied and re-packed with a harmless drug; in all likelihood, the patient, who was known to have suicidal tendencies, would sleep as well from the inert filler substance, merely magnesium oxide or lactose, and if he or she were to take the entire contents of the bottle, would not be injured.

The creature that the children label "It" is less kindly than the dour pharmacist. It presents balloons stamped "ASTHMA MEDICINE GIVES YOU CANCER," a statement as frightening as it is untrue. Eddie is understandably upset when he sees the balloons. He had only recently been in the pharmacy for his medicine, a scene in which King presents a fine portrait of an old store which has not appreciably changed as it reached the late 1950s. Wooden fans turn beneath the pressed-tin ceiling, and a smell of "mixed powders and nostrums" pervades. (The author displays a fine sense of nostalgia in using the evocative old term for medicines, "nostrums.") Instead of giving Eddie his HydrOx Mist and a bill, Keene takes the boy into the back and offers him an ice cream soda "on the house." (King does not mention the fountain, once an invariable part of the local pharmacy, but one can picture the old marble top bar, the soda syrup, seltzer and water spigots, the bent wire chairs, even the shaped Coca-Cola glasses in their metal cups. In so small a town as Derry, it is unlikely Keene would have spent the considerable sum of money required for modernization of his old fixtures.)

Eddie stares open-eyed at the paraphernalia on the pharmacy counter, the mortar and pestle, scales and gleaming brass weights. Keene points out the "fishbowl full of capsules" into which he shall place medicine, sometimes "head-medicine" as he explains to the boy the meaning of the term placebo. It is an excellent explanation, but is lost on a little boy who is frightened by the pharmacist and his reputation as a cold, even mean person, and is convinced moreover that not only is he a true asthmatic, but that his medicine is both good and useful. "My medicine does so work," he insists, suspecting incorrectly that he is being accused of being mentally unbalanced. He escapes as quickly as he can with his spray, while behind him the druggist stands "smiling that dry desert smile."

Eddie's faith is momentarily shaken, but quickly enough resumes, and is strangely justified many years later in his second and final encounter with the monster, fatal for Eddie, but not before he shoves his atomizer into the creature's maw and, screaming in fury, sprays as though it were a weapon. In his adulthood, he would not be still using his old camphor and water spray. More likely he has a compact metered isoproteranol or epinephrine spray, genuine medications safe for humans, perhaps less so for alien creatures. It is noteworthy that Eddie's encyclopedic medicine chest held no asthma sprays or even tablets; however, it is likely that he would have carried the spray on his person at all times, or on his bedside table when sleeping.

Keene makes one final appearance, in an "Interlude" from Michael Hanlon's history of the town. The druggist is now retired, and his grandson is operating the store; the old man insists on doing his books for him. He offers Hanlon an account of some gangsters and their great shooting match with the State Police and the FBI. He had also seen, he thought, the ghostly, shadowless figure of Pennywise the clown. He remains a laconic if somewhat mellowed man.

King's second scene involving an actual pharmacy occurs near the climax of THE DRAWING OF THE THREE when Roland, desperate for the antibiotic Keflex, enters a pharmacy to obtain some. He is expecting an alchemist's cubicle and is unprepared for the contemporary store with its multitude of products for sale. King has his fun with Katz, the owner, and his telephone conversation with a customer, Mrs. Rathbun, as Roland approaches. The lady, not unlike many customers a pharmacist encounters, is demanding a refill of her prescription for Valium, which the prescribing physician had not authorized. The druggist becomes so exasperated that he gives in and allows her a partial refill until she brings in a new prescription. King's perception of a pharmacy scores again when Roland gets it in mind that the more significant medications available are called "Rexes," interesting inasmuch as usually only pharmacists will use such a term, derived from the classic symbol for a prescription. (Its origins lost in history, "Rx" generally is interpreted to stand for a physician's order to the compounding pharmacist: "Take thou of . . ." such and such ingredients such and such an amount.)

Scenes such as these convince me that King must have put in hours as a youth working in his local pharmacy, observing the customers and the pharmacist! Just as possibly, King, in that presumed youthful employment, may have seen the wrong end of a gun pointed at him, as have too many pharmacists, except for here the burglary is transmuted into a demand for

Keflex, not money. When Roland asks, "How many pills in that bottle?" the pharmacist's clerk quite properly corrects him by explaining that Keflex is a *capsule* and not a pill. As Roland leaves, the bemused aide, astonished by a robbery for antibiotics alone, mumbles, "The guy didn't even seem to have the sniffles." The scene is amusing as well as honest, including the author's satire of inflated claims made by non-prescription medications, cosmetics and the variety of goods that constitute a pharmacy located in midtown New York City.

King's pictures of Keene and Katz as representative pharmacists are fair enough to the image most people would entertain of the typical man behind the pill counter. However, as an alumni editor for my college pharmacy magazine for a decade and a half, I have seen pharmacists who were spare time athletes, sulky drivers in harness races, actors, playwrights, mathematical philosophers, one a musician playing a euphonium, another a prospector for gold in the hills of darkest Ohio, and one even a commentator on writers of fantasy and science fiction!

If Eddie Kaspbrak's life revolved in many ways around the drugstore, writer Paul Sheldon in MISERY is forced against his will be concerned with a nurse and her unprofessional ways. Although Annie Wilkes no longer practices her profession, she retains a goodly supply of pharmaceuticals in her home. Her favorite drug is one King admittedly has created for the story, "Novril." Paul discovers that the habit-forming opiate Codeine is its active ingredient. "Maybe," Paul thinks, "you spell *relief* R-O-L-A-I-D-S, but you spelled Novril C-O-D-E-I-N-E." His addiction is quite intentional on the part of Annie, his fan/captor, to keep her favorite author docile.

There are, of course, other pharmaceutical references. Annie, inveterate reader of the stories of Misery Chastain, buys her paperbacks at Wilson's Drug Center. When Paul manages to manipulate himself to her pantry he discovers her motherlode, physicians sample packets from Upjohn, Lilly and other companies. "No shampoo, no Avon samples" for Annie, just drugs; Lopressor (for heart pressure, not one of Annie's problems, but she has removed the sample packages indiscriminately from her hospitals); Keflex and ampicillin, which she gives to Paul when an infection has run up his temperature; Darvon, Darvocet, Darvon Compound (finally King has the name right!), Librium and Valium; and numerous boxes of "Novril."

When the story turns to *guignol*, and quite truly *grand* it is, King provides the details to make it linger. After wielding her electric knife where it will do the most harm, fastidious nurse that she is, Annie applies Betadine (an antiseptic solution) to the wound. The "maroon droplets" of the povidine-iodine solution, splattering from the knife, contrast to the "much redder droplets" also spraying into the air. Annie injects scopolamine into the hapless author, but that will be discussed later.

As the newspapers remind us daily, the word "drugs" refers to more than the medications sold in pharmacies. *Illegal* drugs have become a major element in Society, and certainly loom large in King's writing. In his Afterword to THE DARK TOWER, Vol. I, King states simply and directly, "I have gone on drugs and gone off them." As a young man in a generation which was fascinated by a new culture of mind-expanding and perception-affecting drugs and chemicals, he could not help but be aware of them. Fortunately for himself, his family and millions of readers, he escaped the terrible grasp and deadly effect of such drugs. He does not dwell on his personal involvement, and a reader may assume it was slight. However, he clearly knows the territory, and most of his stories have at least a mention of illegal drugs, usually without much ado, less an indicator of King's own tastes than a clue to those of the particular character.

When Mike Ryerson of 'SALEM'S LOT is looking bad, Matt Burke asks him "what kind of shit" he is on. "Dope," he explains to Mike, "Bennies? Reds? Coke?" Mike confesses that "grass," marijuana, was the worst he had ever used, and not for four months. "Bennies" refer to Benzedrine, an amphetamine; "reds" to Seconal, a barbiturate; "coke," of course, is cocaine, now supplanted on the street by its derivative, "crack." Aside from crack, each has at one time or another been available legally, and with strong restrictions, still is.

Steve Dubay in IT is described as the guy who took "a red

pill . . . maybe it was even legal." Later on Steve is "high on something and looking for trouble." He finds it, as well a fifteen year sentence for first-degree manslaughter.

The school counselor of that "Apt Pupil," Todd Bowden, is relieved that the boy is not taking "speed, mescaline or PCP." Only speed (methamphetamine) would have been legal, albeit restricted. The others are illegal.

Bart Dawes, of ROADWORK, does take some mescaline. This plant derivative is used in THE DARK TOWER by Roland to gain awareness for a session with an oracle. The latter tells him three persons will be of great significance to him, of whom the first is "infested" by a demon, "HEROIN" (sic). The prophecy is confirmed in THE DRAWING OF THE THREE, in the person of Eddie Dean, a junkie.

It is ironic that the realism of Eddie's dependency is so strong that it works against the sense of mystery and the mythic which made THE GUNSLINGER so memorable. No addict will share, or care to share, Eddie's fantastic and melodramatic adventure; all will understand his desperate craving. It is an honest portrait of addiction. The novel's mythic quality returns only when Roland finally assumes an active role.

LSD plays a part in "Survivor Type," an especially grisly short story. A surgeon is washed up on a barren island and satisfies his hunger by amputating and eating parts of his own body. Heroin helps allay pain. (In his notes to the story in his collection SKELETON CREW, still brand-minded, the playful King describes his muse as moving him by evacuating its "magic bowels" upon his head, and says he would feed it Ex-Lax if necessary.)

"The Ballad of the Flexible Bullet" mentions "heroin and 'ludes" in a metaphor for writers comparing notes as junkies would compare drugs.

A cheated husband, a criminal as well, in "The Ledge" plants heroin in the cheater's car to force him to accept a hazardous wager.

Young Jack, in THE TALISMAN, is falsely accused of having and selling "Coke, hash, PCP and angel-dust." Morgan Sloat, having popped a Di-Gel into his mouth, snorts cocaine, and encourages Jack's sick mother to do the same. "Everybody does coke now," he tells her; she is not interested.

It goes on. In CUJO, Steve Kemp, who had been for a time the lover of the heroine, is a restless bum who carries about with him in his van "a very nice little pharmacy," consisting of such items as "marijuana, some cocaine in an Anacin bottle, three Amyl Nitrate poppers and two speedy combinations of the type known as Black Beauties." Amyl Nitrate, a small gauze-covered glass tube is popped apart and inhaled. Legitimately it is used for relief of angina pectoris; illegally it is combined with other drugs such as Quaalude to heighten sexual experience and get a peculiar high. Black Beauties refers to Biphetamine, an amphetamine (hence the "speedy"), restricted but available.

Whether or not King ever did stock drugstore shelves, stocking his own mind meanwhile with nuggets for future use, he is bound on occasion to trip up on facts. Those few errors are really quite insignificant compared to his very high batting average, which does so much to enhance the credibility of the stories. However, just as Annie Wilkes, who felt only boundless admiration for her favorite writer, could be merciless, the pharmacist-admirer of Stephen King too must with reluctance discover and detail these occasional *faux pas*.

His most persistent error, in three separate stories, is a drug which is intended to be a popularly prescribed pain-killer, Darvon Compound. Until he at last corrected the error in MISERY, it remained stubbornly misnamed "Darvon Complex." In THE STAND Trashcan Man had learned of it while in prison. It reappears in "The Woman in the Room," a short story from NIGHT SHIFT, as well as on the lowest shelf of Eddie Kaspbrak's private drug store in IT.

Darvon Compound is of the most importance in the short story, a moving vignette of a loving son who cannot watch his aged mother dying painfully of cancer; in an act of euthanasia he overdoses her with the pain-killer. The story is well told, and free of any didactic intent. The lay reader will not object to its scientific aspects, surgical or pharmaceutical. Few readers will be equipped to do so. Nevertheless, it would appear that a bit of research or a visit to Mr. Keene in his Center Street Drugstore King would have avoided errors, in name and in strength.

Darvon Compound, manufactured by the Eli Lilly Co. is a non-narcotic analgesic (albeit still classified under addicting drug laws). It is available in either of two strengths, 32mg or 65mg of Darvon HC1, plain or with aspirin. King writes in the short story that the capsule differs from "regular Darvon only in that they are gray gelatin capsules." The strength, he relates, is "350gr of aspirin" and "100gr of Darvon." Later he figures out what should be a fatal dose: "three or four [capsules] would be enough. Fourteen hundred grains of aspirin and four hundred grains of Darvon."

The figures are wrong, but the errors do not hurt the story; indeed, the high numbers probably lend to the dramatic effect. However, not to nitpick but simply to emphasize the value of research, Darvon Compound consists of 65 *milligrams* of Darvon and 389 *milligrams* of aspirin. Milligrams. Not grains. The term "grains" is part of the ancient Apothecary system of weights; "milligrams" is, of course, part of the more modern Metric system. It takes 64 milligrams to make *one* grain. The quantities King speaks of would fill much of a cup with powder. In addition, no form of Darvon is simply gray. Darvon Plain is all pink; the compound is either pink/gray or red/gray. Finally, the son plans to have his mother *chew* the four capsules with her food. This would be very difficult since the ingredients are very bitter; any reader who has incompletely swallowed an aspirin can attest to this. When he came to write MISERY, King was aware of this and has Sheldon complain about the terrible bitterness of the drug.

Another goof which sets the specialist chuckling occurs in King's screenplay *Silver Bullet*, the dramatization of his short novel CYCLE OF THE WEREWOLF. To flesh out the brief vignettes of the book for film purposes, King has added characters and conversations. In the book as well as the film, young Marty escapes the rampaging beast by hurling a firecracker into its eyes. In the published screenplay, when Father Lowe appears later wearing an eyepatch over one eye, the boy is certain that he must be the werewolf. He tells his Uncle Al of his suspicions, but Al is annoyed by the very concept of a werewolf being the culprit behind the murders. He announces triumphantly to Marty how foolish his suspicion is anyway: he tells the boy that the priest was observed going into a drugstore "two days ago for a bottle of otic solution. That is a fancy way of saying eyewash. He's got a corneal inflammation."

Unfortunately, an otic solution might well further inflame the priest's eyes inasmuch as "otic" refers to a preparation for the *ears*. Marty, in addition, is wise enough to know that the killer did not have a prescription for medicine because he would have had to see a doctor for that, something he would not have dared to do, fearing explanations. In the end Marty shoots the werewolf in its other eye with a silver bullet; neither otic nor *ophthalmic* solution would save it now.

In THINNER, Aureomycin, several years out of date, was used as an antibiotic. THE STAND goes it many decades better when Fran looks at the men in their sleeping bags on the road with her and muses "Take Sominex and sleep." Actually, the men are not on Sominex, but on "half a grain of Veronal apiece." The heavy drugging is the idea of Harold Lawler, who had suggested they try a whole grain of Veronal, "available at any drugstore." It is an interesting notion, but the stores that would stock Veronal exist only in the pharmacies of King's mind, possibly from some ancient story he has read. Veronal was a brand name (also called Barbital) for dimethyl barbituric acid in the days nearly a century ago when the somnifacient powers of the drug were first discovered and exploited. It was replaced for reasons of safety and efficacy by phenobarbital, phenylethyl barbituric acid, which has remained a very important drug, both as hypnotic and in the control of epilepsy. It is a safe drug taken properly, although slow in onset with a long half-life in the body.

When King wrote MISERY he decided to avoid errors by getting help from health professionals, including a physician and a registered nurse. Their advice is evident in the fine medical details of the book. Furthermore, to avoid error King states clearly in a foreword that a drug crucial to the story, "Novril," is fictitious. *It is not alone.* Within Nurse Wilkes' cabinet of drugs and samples, are "Morphose" and "Morphose Complex," which remain unknown to the Red Book, the compendium of available pharmaceuticals.

Annie herself is guilty of an error as well, when she prepares an injection for the helpless Paul. "I wish you'd relax," she tells the cowering writer. "That's scopolamine, which is a morphine-based drug." Annie is confused. She no doubt recalls her hospital days when she gave scopolamine together with morphine to produce "twilight sleep." While it has some hypnotic action, (and has been used in many spy stories as a "truth serum") it is unrelated to morphine. The latter is an alkaloid from the opium plant, whereas scopolamine is an alkaloid from Atropa Belladonna. It dilates the pupil; morphine causes the famous "pin-point pupils." In any event, Annie's intent is not bad. She has little morphine, and wants to sedate Paul; the injection will do that.

Why should such easily-checked errors occur? The Greeks would perhaps accuse so self-confident a writer of *hubris*. The popular Yiddish "chutzpah" is also feasible. A King character, one of those truck-drivers or beer-drinkers, might call it "balls." A quick visit to Mr. Keene or Mr. Katz would have given the author any information he required. However, while I do not exonerate King of these charges, it is only fair to add that he is not alone in his pharmaceutical miscalculations.

Those same proofreaders King hires to edit out such errors in his text apparently also work for Ken Follett, a comparably successful creator of international thrillers. In his LIE DOWN WITH LIONS (the New American Library edition of 1986, pg. 111) the traitorous physician Jean-Pierre treats an Afghanistani child's skin problem with "thirty 250-gram capsules of griseofulvin." This is literally seven and one-half kilograms, several pounds of powder!—surely enough to take care of the ringworm, and the child as well. It is, of course, *milligrams* the usually careful doctor had in mind.

Not all physicians and pharmacists will find these errors amusing. Once noticed by the professional, they jar the reality of the story. This pharmacist-collector of King goofs enjoys a small laugh on King, whom he admires as man and author, while still appreciating his general grasp on drugs and their application. He appreciates too King's attitude toward illegal drugs, which, without preaching, usually associates them with less admirable characters. He also admits that if druggists could write like this ex-high school teacher they would not be standing around counting capsules and tablets.

HORROR WITHOUT LIMITS: LOOKING INTO *THE MIST*

by Dennis Rickard

*"So what happened? Huh? What happened? What is that
damned mist?"*

You can't fault Stephen King for variety. He has resurrected vampires, dusted off werewolves, dabbled in science fiction, and tried his hand at psychological terror, post-apocalyp-
tic epic, surreal western, fairy-tale adventure, "mainstream,"
and of course, plenty of straightforward, go-for-the-throat horror. All this with varying degrees of literary success, but with
legendary commercial appeal.

Having read most of the panoply that King has published,
THE MIST, from SKELETON CREW, strikes me as his single
most memorable work. This is not because it is "essential"
King, nor because it is a radical departure from the rest of his
fiction—though a good case could be made for both. Dualities
abound. In what is ostensibly his most hopeless tale, hope in
the face of complete (and literal) pandemonium is a keynote. In
structure, the story contrasts a cross-section of everyday
people, surrounded by the trappings of "civilization," with the
absolute unknown. And for a story in which the magnitude of
horror is so overwhelming, there is a balancing restraint and
reliance on *atmosphere* that propel THE MIST to the front rank
of King's fiction.

177

The story is told by artist David Drayton, who lives with his wife and son at Long Lake in southern Maine. A sudden violent storm forces the family to seek safety in the cellar. When they survey the damage the next morning, they see an ominously dense bank of fog moving toward them, against the breeze. Despite misgivings, Drayton leaves his wife behind when he goes into town with his son and a neighbor to buy supplies. The fog moves into the town while they are in the supermarket. Several customers leave to investigate; only one man staggers back into the store, yelling that "something in the fog took John Lee and I heard him screaming!"

Little by little, the remaining shoppers realize that inimical things lurk in the mist. Most believe that the storm has damaged a nearby secret government facility, the Arrowhead Project, which apparently had been conducting experimentation on a momentous scale. Held prisoners over that day and night, the microcosm of society inside react to the denizens of the mist—and the awesome implications they represent—by degenerating swiftly into madness and hysteria. Drayton and a handful of others who have resisted these impulses decide to flee the market when they realize that there is a more immediate danger posed by their terror-crazed community than by the unknown horrors in the mist.

Critical regard for this short novel has been almost universally positive since its first appearance in Kirby McCauley's superb 1980 anthology, DARK FORCES. Efforts to pigeonhole THE MIST, though, usually have seized upon peripheral aspects, leading to incomplete understanding. Douglas E. Winter, who has written extensively on King, considers THE MIST to be a parable warning against the danger of unchecked scientific and military experimentation: "this short novel is a paradigm of the complicated metaphors of Faustian experimentation and technological horror consistently woven into the fiction of Stephen King." Winter argues that this message is framed in a context borrowed from the ubiquitous 1950s "technohorror" films (such as *Them!*, *The Beginning of the End*, *Tarantula*, *Attack of the Giant* _____), and the more recent films of George Romero, particularly *Night of the Living Dead* (1968) and *Dawn of the Dead* (1979).

There is no question that these ideas and influences permeate THE MIST. King himself said that "you're supposed to visualize the story in grainy black and white." And the parallels between King's characters taking refuge in the supermarket and Romero's survivors holing up against armies of the undead in a farmhouse (in *Night of the Living Dead*), a shopping mall (in *Dawn of the Dead*), or a military bunker (in the post-MIST *Day of the Dead*) are obvious. The King novel and the Romero trilogy even share a grim, absurdist humor derived from the juxtaposition of the familiar with the unimaginable.

If we view THE MIST primarily as a caution against technology and its dangers, however, we limit the story. It is both more and less than technohorror. Less, in that we are too far removed from the source of the catastrophe, from any conception of its nature, and from any of the central participants in the nebulous experimentation to consider this primarily as an indictment of technology. The mist is no mere toxic leak or nuclear accident. The fact that King gives us so little data from which to extrapolate so inexplicable an event would indicate that he deliberately sped through dealing with the *cause* of the awful fog in order to glory in its *effect*.

THE MIST is also much *more* than a technological horror tract. Much of the story is given over to purely human horror. The breakdown of values and retreat into madness and mob dynamics in the face of the cataclysm are almost as unsettling as the monsters in the fog. But the fullest appreciation of the story comes from a consideration of the dizzying brush with infinity that is central to the tale. There is an open-endedness, an immensity and a finality to THE MIST that is found nowhere else in King's work. He has delivered a chilling and apparently irremediable apocalypse, with an admirably sympathetic human counterpoint.

Much in THE MIST, of course, ties it to the rest of King's work. Critic Michael Collings refers to this story as "archetypal Stephen King," in that it "represents in miniature the essence of what makes Stephen King's narratives unique." It is set in his native Maine, in a town where King lived for a time. The writing is his trademark colloquial style which King peppers with a veritable shopping list of brand names (Pepsi, Cricket lighters, McCullough chain saws, Ragu spaghetti sauce, Naragansett beer, Special K, Purina Puppy Chow), drawing us into the world of his characters.

The common denominator that brings King's characters together is food—they came to the supermarket to get it, and stay to avoid becoming food themselves. Many of the characterizations are familiar to King's readers. *The narrator*, trying to do what he can for his family. *The child*, clinging desperately to one parent when the husband and wife are separated. *The contentious neighbor*, another "officious little prick" in King's fiction. *The elderly grade-school teacher*, solid and unflappable. *The quiet, unassuming man*, who rises to the extraordinary situation. And one of King's more exaggerated "types"—*the crazy old broad*, Mrs. Carmody, echoed in other works, as Sylvia Pittman in THE DARK TOWER, Vera Smith in THE DEAD ZONE, and recently as Annie Wilkes in MISERY. Formerly only a dotty local harbinger of doom and purveyor of folk remedies, Mrs. Carmody quickly emerges as a raving prophetess, calling for blood sacrifice to atone for man's tampering in God's realm. Initially shunned by everyone in the store, she slowly assembles a band of spellbound "converts." This character, probably the least believable in the story, serves as the embodiment of superstition and misdirected religious fanaticism, a symbol of religion as a negative force, a monster on the inside to match those lurking outside.

Coming events are foreshadowed, as is common in King's work. When Drayton's family is forced into their cellar by the freak storm, he has a dream—an actual dream of King's, in fact, that was the genesis of THE MIST—that symbolically reveals the coming holocaust.

> I had a dream that I saw God walking across Harrison on the far side of the lake, a God so gigantic that above the waist He was lost in a clear blue sky. In the dream I could hear the rending crack and

splinter of breaking trees as God stamped the woods into the shape of His footsteps. He was circling the lake, coming toward the Bridgton side, toward us, and behind Him everything that had been green turned a bad gray and all the houses and cottages and summer places were bursting into purple-white flame like lightning, and soon the smoke covered everything. The smoke covered everything like a mist.

The family trapped in the cellar on the night of the storm is reprised on a larger scale when the townspeople take refuge in the supermarket. Later, after escaping the store, a more family-sized unit again huddles claustrophobically in Drayton's Scout.

The weather itself, before the coming of the fog, is a precursor of disaster. Mrs. Carmody has been telling anyone within earshot that the "Black Spring" in the area boded evil. The combination of hard winter, late spring, and sweltering summer had people talking about "the long-range results of the fifties A-bomb tests again. That, and of course, the end of the world. The oldest chestnut of them all."

On a more personal level, Drayton experiences fears for his wife, when he leaves her behind to put things back together in the wake of the storm; fears which have little actual ground until the fog's deadly threat is revealed. Word choices indicate what is about to transpire: Drayton refers to the "mist of disquiet" that had settled over him before the fog rolled into town. Mrs. Carmody too shows a smattering of precognition when she sees the mist and shouts, "It's death! I feel that it's death out there!"

In King's fiction, the story that most resembles THE MIST is "The Raft." Four teenagers swim out to a raft in an out-of-the-way lake, where they are trapped by an amorphous floating blob that eventually engulfs them one by one—most dramatically by sucking one of the boys through a small crack between two boards of the raft. In both tales a small group, held prisoner in a confined refuge with no hope of outside help, is forced to make difficult decisions... or decide not to make decisions. Reference is again made horror movies ("The last time I saw anything like that was the Halloween Shock-Show down at the Rialto when I was twelve"), and similarities to 1958's *The Blob* are obvious. But most significantly, the menace they face is absolutely inexplicable. There is no precedent, no accepted set of rules for dealing with the situation—it's a whole new ballgame. The last survivor on the raft realizes that the rational explanations are simply beside the point:

> Maybe it was an oil slick, after all . . . or had been, until something had happened to it. Maybe cosmic rays had hit it in a certain way. Or maybe Arthur Godfrey had pissed atomic Bisquick all over it, who knew? Who could know?

In these two stories, King is more concerned with his characters than with the mechanism of the horror. The larger number of people in the supermarket, of course, gives a wider range of actions and reactions in the two days and two nights that both groups spend trapped. The shoppers quickly polarize into factions. Drayton dubs one group, led by his neighbor, the "Flat-Earth Society" for their steadfast refusal to accept that four people saw a tentacled monstrosity pluck a bag-boy from the loading dock. The Flat-Earthers, nevertheless, are reluctant to act on their conventions—at first. Later, their contingent feels compelled to seek help, with predictable results.

Others in the store react differently. Tough-talking skeptics who egg on the bag-boy suddenly turn coward when they see the octopoid entity. Many choose to remove themselves through drink; others retreat into a catatonia of denial or madness. The store manager busies himself by toting up items that customers are eating and drinking, as if the situation is merely a disturbing but transitory episode. Two young soldiers, on the other hand, go off to hang themselves in a storeroom. They were stationed at the Arrowhead Project, and their suicides seem to offer confirmation not only of the source of the fog, but that it is unlikely to be a survivable phenomenon. King easily could have had the soldiers allude to what was Really Behind All This—the course they took was far more eloquent.

The "better" side of human nature is shown, too, as another contingent busies itself barricading windows and mounting guards. The inadequacy of their preparations is pathetically evident, but the greater value comes from their sense of doing something to help themselves.

Despite ennobling incidents of bravery, the helplessness of their predicament wears down even the narrator. Drayton sneaks off to an empty office to make love to the *attractive woman* type, so they can both escape the horror briefly; a couple in "The Raft" deal with their fear in the same diverting way.

Scores of creatures buzz and shamble through the mist to terrify the characters, but the real horror comes from the mist itself. It is a tailor-made device for allowing, even enforcing, restraint. It blunts the senses of sight and sound, and forces those in the store to strain for hints and glimpses of the things that it harbors—an anticipation as numbing as the fog's progeny.

> It wasn't so much the monstrous creatures that lurked in the mist... It was the mist itself that sapped the strength and robbed the will. *Just to see the sun again*... That alone would be worth going through a hell of a lot.

The fog is more than just a veil that covers, then selectively reveals, the horrors. It can be seen—almost too easily—as symbolic of return to the dark ages, presaged by the swift loss of vaunted human values as the veneer of civilization is peeled from the characters. It is a false night harboring very real nightmares.

There have been other fogs in the literature of the macabre. In THE GREAT FOG by H. F. Heard, a freak mold creates its own protective cloud of mist that quickly blankets the planet and leads to the collapse of civilization. John Carpenter's film, *The Fog*, and Dennis Etchison's novelization from the screenplay, employ an uncanny fogbank as a cloak for a shipload of ghost lepers that seeks revenge on the descendants of their persecutors. Donald Wandrei's short story, "The Black Fog," has the Earth pass briefly through an inky, stinging fog that closes a chapter of life on the planet, and opens a strange new one.

Of all the works in the genre in which a mist is central to the story, the one that probably had the most direct influence on King is James Herbert's THE FOG (1975). A better candidate for the label "technohorror," Herbert's novel deals with the accidental release of a military-developed bacteria that forms a sickly yellow mist to surround a sentient, glowing core. Exposure to the fog engenders madness in humans and animals alike, and THE FOG glories in showing the fruits of the madness. A herd of cows methodically stomps a farmer to death. A 747 pilot plows his plane into a skyscraper just to kill his wife's lover. The mass suicide of nearly 150,000 inhabitants of Bournemouth, England is a staggering scene.

King devoted several pages of his 1981 study of horror in print and film, DANSE MACABRE, to this, Herbert's first novel. Though King's analysis appeared the year after THE MIST saw print, it seems likely that he was familiar with THE FOG before writing his variation on the theme. Other than a deadly fog, and a common military/scientific origin for the mist, there might not seem to be a great deal of kinship between the two novels. As horrendous as Herbert's calamity is, it's something that can be studied, understood (to a degree), and battled. A strong similarity, though, is that both have a markedly cinematic approach. King points this out in his appreciation of Herbert's novel:

> In its construction, THE FOG shows the effect of those apocalyptic Big Bug movies of the late fifties and sixties. All the ingredients are there: we have a mad scientist who was screwing around with something he didn't understand and was killed by the mycoplasma he invented; the military testing secret weapons and unleashing the horror; the "young scientist" hero, John Holman, who we first meet bravely rescuing a little girl from the fissure that has Unleashed the Fog on an Unsuspecting World; the beautiful girlfriend, Casey...

If the tone here sounds somewhat derogatory, King elevates THE FOG above the stereotype:

> We will recognize these obligatory trappings of science fiction from such movies as *Tarantula*, *The Deadly Mantis*, *Them!*, and a dozen

others; yet we will also recognize that trappings are all they are, and the heart of Herbert's novel lies not in the fog's origin or composition, but in its decidedly Dionysian effects—murder, suicide, sexual aberrations, and all manner of deviant behavior. Holman, the hero, is our representative from a saner Apollonian world.

The duality of Apollonian versus Dionysian is illustrated powerfully inside THE MIST's Federal Market. Here, too, is attempted murder (in the form of ritual sacrifice), a double suicide, a sexual encounter, and a wide range of deviant behavior. Holman, Herbert's "whole man," is not untouched by the fog. But direct exposure to it, and recovery from it, strengthen him. Drayton's brief encounter with the woman in the story, while not admirable, does not drag him down to the level to which most of the other shoppers have sunk. In his realistic approach to the mist, he serves as this novel's representative from the Apollonian world.

Much of King's commentary on THE FOG, then, applies to THE MIST as well. It too borrows the format of the "Big Bug" movies, but rises above being a pastiche.

The cinematic flavor of THE MIST is vivid. The mist outside, as well as the absence inside of artificial light, almost force us to see things in black and white. Drayton bolsters this connection with Fifties science fiction films by referring to the creatures in the fog as something you'd expect to see in a horror movie. Michael Collings in THE SHORTER WORKS OF STEPHEN KING, notes other filmic aspects of the novel:

Coming from a writer whose stock-in-trade is the visual image, frequently drawn from contemporary film, THE MIST carries that sense to an extreme, building scene after scene on the scaffolding left by filmmakers of the 1950s on. . . . Individual touches also seem directed toward particular films. It is hard not to think that several scenes grew out of King's memories of *The Crawling Eye* and countless other B-movie masterpieces starring revenant pterosaurs, slugs, multi-limbed monsters, and giant spiders; while the battle against the tentacles early in the story translates visually as a land-locked version of the giant squid in Disney's *Twenty Thousand Leagues Under the Sea*.

The novel seems eminently adaptable to other media also. Apart from cinematic possibilities, THE MIST already has been recorded as an audio tape and turned into a computer game. The story could, with relatively little difficulty, be adapted to the theater: the action takes place in a few tight locations, much of the emphasis is on the interplay between a small number of people, a good deal of the horror is hinted at, rather than hauled before us and spotlighted—a stage version is a viable and intriguing possibility.

Although THE MIST may be viewed in contexts that follow the traditional structure of introduction, then rising action and resolution, the most remarkable aspect of this story is that there is *no tying up of loose ends*. This is usual for King, and perhaps it tends to go against the grain for most storytellers, but the tale is far more chilling for being left open and unresolved. Two interrelated factors contribute to this success: cosmicism and ambiguity.

In his career, King has written a handful of stories, notably "Jerusalem's Lot" and "Crouch End," that intentionally borrow elements and ideas developed by H. P. Lovecraft. More so than any of these stories, however, THE MIST echoes Lovecraft's underlying fictional philosophy. King is well aware of Lovecraft; the two, for perhaps quite different reasons, could be considered the century's most influential writers of horror. Lovecraft is best known for stories and short novels written for various amateur and pulp magazines in the '20s and '30s, *Weird Tales* being the usual market. Much of his fiction relies in part on a framework or background he developed to give added depth to his tales of horror. It was built upon a grim and decidedly non-anthropomorphic concept of the cosmos and man's place in it, and a pantheon of "gods" of an awful sort. This construct and the stories Lovecraft wrote that employ it have come to be called, somewhat misleadingly, the "Cthulhu Mythos," after his tentacled monstrosity Cthulhu, sleeping in the sunken city of R'lyeh under the waters of the Pacific. The Mythos, however, for whatever power, credence and atmosphere it gave to his fiction, was not Lovecraft's essential message.

For Lovecraft, horror was more than just the monsters. As E. F. Bleiler notes in THE GUIDE TO SUPERNATURAL FICTION,

> His fiction, while stylistically that of a technical writer working according to smash-ending formulas of the period, has been considered important in stating in clearest form one of the alienation myths of the mid-20th century: the precarious aloneness of man, surrounded by concealed horrors emergent from both the inner world of his psyche and the cosmos, beyond phenomenality.

Add to this what Lovecraft's friend and fellow writer of cosmic horror, Donald Wandrei, says of his stories:

> Lovecraft often expressed . . . his conviction that the most effective horror stories progressed from that which is known in every detail to that which is unknown in any detail; which, starting from the familiar, ended on a plane of such cosmic departure from all things human as to leave the reader darkly adrift from all this moorings and imbued with terrors for which there could be no name.

Both statements are pertinent also to THE MIST; both help to explain how the novel succeeds. While not writing to the "smash-ending formulas" of Lovecraft's time, King can be said to often write to his own formulas. Winter, for example, has found in King's fiction the recurring "night journey" theme—literal and figuratively quests and rites of passage—in works from THE STAND on. THE MIST is a prime example. Yet in this novel, King superbly handles, as did Lovecraft, man's aloneness against horrors from within and without. THE MIST, too, fulfills Wandrei's progression from the familiar to the absolute unknown. No other work of King's could be said to so "leave the reader darkly adrift from all his moorings" as does this one.

Well, perhaps the monumental IT *might* be nominated. This novel is monumental both in length and in the sense that IT is a monument—"a summation of everything I have learned and done in my whole life to this point." As grand an undertaking as IT may have been, King's longest novel nevertheless is a far less satisfying example of cosmic horror than THE MIST. "Cosmic" is the operative word. Both quotes regarding Lovecraft use the term as meaning that, in the vastness of the cosmos, powers of such enormity and strangeness exist that man is utterly dwarfed, his ability to comprehend less than inadequate. Lovecraft's cosmos impinging on our world, and King's in THE MIST, show the terrible indifference with which the universe regards mankind.

"It" is not indifferent. In 1958, a group of kids in Maine do battle with a malevolent, godlike creature that has been laying seige to their small town for centuries. They subdue this thing, which can take a number of forms borrowed from '50s B-movies, but it is then driven from their memories until the next go-round in the 27-year cycle. This time the grown-up kids fight It in its true guise as a huge spider. In both IT and THE MIST, we see an apparent rent in the so-called "fabric of reality." Something, somehow, intrudes into the world we know from the Outside. Whether the intrusion comes about through some doing of the spider-thing or by scientific accident is of little moment. All that really matters is that we have some hardcore unreality with which to come to terms. Yet the mindless, impersonal, all-encompassing threat in THE MIST rings far truer than the strangely personal vendetta waged by It. The eventual defeat of the monster in IT by the children (described by the reviewer in *Newsday* as "a bunch of junior G-Men") strains credulity in contrast.

The things that lurk in the mist also bear comparison with Lovecraft, who in "The Festival" (the first story to mention his arcane volume, THE NECRONOMICON) describes

> a horde of tame, trained, hybrid winged things that no sound eye could ever wholly grasp, or sound brain every wholly remember. They were not altogether crows, nor moles, nor buzzards, nor ants, nor vampire bats, nor decomposed human beings . . .

The creatures of the mist are not of this earth, so King tries to convey this strangeness by creating beasts that are bizarre variations on normal creatures. Sometimes it's just a matter of size; the oversized squid at the loading dock, or the huge red lobster that bisects a man in the parking lot are, in addition to being out of their expected element, extremely large. A foray that Drayton and some others take from the supermarket to the adjoining pharmacy in Chapter 9 brings the party into a nest of arachnids:

> One of the spiders had come out of the mist from behind us. It was the size of a big dog. It was black with yellow piping. *Racing stripes*, I thought crazily. Its eyes were reddish-purple, like pomegranates. It strutted busily towards us on what might have been as many as twelve or fourteen many-jointed legs—it was no ordinary earthly spider blown up to horror-movie size; it was something totally different, perhaps not really a spider at all. . . .

These spiders also spin ropy, corrosive webs that cut through flesh as if it were warm butter. Another obscene parody of pre-mist lifeforms shows up on the store's windows:

> It was maybe two feet long, segmented, the pinkish color of burned flesh that has healed over. Bulbous eyes peered in two different directions at once from the ends of short, limber stalks. It clung to the window on fat sucker-pads. From the opposite end there protruded something that was either a sexual organ or a stinger. And from its back there sprouted oversized, membranous wings, like the wings of a housefly.

By far the most appalling creature encountered is never fully seen. After Drayton, his son, the school teacher and the Attractive Woman flee the market in Drayton's car, they are nearly crushed by "something so big it defied the imagination." All they really see are two cyclopean legs ascending until they are lost in the mist; each track it leaves is "big enough to drop the Scout into." This, of course, is a twisted reprise of Drayton's dream of "God" walking across the lake. But the wrathful Jehovah has been transmogrified into a colossal beast, indifferent to the inconsequential beings in the car below. This "god" points out an even more disquieting question: since the evolution of horrors seems incredibly speeded up, what else is to come . . . or is already out there?

We're back in Lovecraft territory here; even the phrasing is reminiscent, as when we are told that "there are certain things that your brain simply disallows. There are things of such darkness and horror—just I suppose, as there are things of such great beauty—that they will not fit through the puny human doors of perception."

To be sure, not all of the creatures smack of the supernatural in the way that Lovecraft's do. Drayton even comes right out and says that "they were no Lovecraftian horrors with immortal life but only organic creatures with their own vulnerabilities." One of the bug-things entering the store is brought down by a two-fisted attack by the teacher, shooting cans of Raid. (Later she switches to Black Flag to assault one of the pharmacy spiders). An albino pterodactyl ("a bit like the paintings of pterodactyls you may have seen in the dinosaur books, more like something out of a lunatic's nightmare") is ignited by a make-shift torch and flames out in the spaghetti sauce section. These things, seeming recombinations and mutations of present or past earth creatures, are more terrestrially oriented than most of Lovecraft's, though he too created variations on fauna with which we're familiar—not altogether crows nor moles. . . .

King may have learned another lesson from Lovecraft, on the matter of what not to do. The tendency to over-describe in this kind of fiction, to do all the work for the reader, is often irresistible. Writing of Lovecraft in DANSE MACABRE, King says:

> "I cannot describe it," protagonist after protagonist tells us. "If I did, you would go mad with fear." But somehow I doubt that. I think . . . Lovecraft . . . understood that to open the door, in ninety-nine cases out of a hundred, is to destroy the unified, dreamlike effect of the best horror. "I can deal with that," the audience says to itself, settling back, and bang! you just lost the ballgame in the bottom of the ninth.

There is a thin line here—atmosphere and restraint are good; confusion and uncertainty about where the story is going are not good. In Kirby McCauley's introduction to DARK FORCES, he tells of the origin of THE MIST. What was to be a short story of around fifteen thousand words grew, over the weeks of writing, to a novella of forty thousand. (King, for his part, claims that McCauley pulled it out of him "with a chain fall.") This does not mean that King simply didn't know where to stop; closing at the point he did before revealing more seems a wise decision. But it is possible that King might not have been completely comfortable ending the story in the way he did. At the novel's conclusion, he seems to anticipate criticism.

> It is, I suppose, what my father always frowningly called "an Alfred Hitchcock ending," by which he meant a conclusion in ambiguity that allowed the reader or viewer to make up his own mind about how things ended. My father had nothing but contempt for such stories, saying there were "cheap shots."

If King meant that remark in self-reproach, he needn't worry. Horror writer Clive Barker, in his essay on King, "Surviving the Ride," contrasts him with Poe. Barker feels that while the "plunge into the subconscious" that Poe took cost him a certain amount of accessibility, King's usual careful buildup of detail in order to make the horror acceptable and plausible, on the other hand, has resulted in a loss of ambiguity.

But Barker applauds King's achievement of that kind of ambiguity in THE MIST. Although he regards King as a masterful writer of stories dealing with "domestic demons"—stories with familiar settings and commonplace particulars that give a believable context for horror—Barker expresses a preference for the nightmare voyages that take you out of any recognizable context into

> things vast; contradictory; mythological. King can conjure such stuff with the best of them; I only regret that his brilliance as a creator of domestic demons has claimed him from writing more of that other region. When he turns his hand on it, the effect is stunning. THE MIST, for example, is a story that begins in familiar King territory, and moves through a variety of modes—including scenes which, in their mingling of the monstrous and commonplace work as high, grim comedy—towards a world lost to humanity, a world that echoes in the imagination long after the book has been closed.

Barker defines the kind of ambiguity to which he refers in

terms of yet another duality. Even in the moment of horror, we may feel awe and fascination, "wanting an encounter with forces that will change our lives—that will deliver us once and for all into the regions of the gods...yet fearful that we are negligible things and so far beneath the concern of such powers that any confrontation will simply kill us."

The hope held out at the conclusion of THE MIST is minimal; it may have been a final lagniappe to temper the bleak outlook for humanity. We don't know how far the fog has spread or will spread, but it is difficult to believe that it is containable. Something we can't fathom or control has burst into our existence. Drayton thinks that he might have heard the word "Hartford" emerge from a radio's static as his small group goes to ground in a roadside Howard Johnson's. There might be an outside perimeter of the mist...or there might be a growing enclave of people in Hartford trying to fight the fog...or it might be wishful thinking.

Mankind may have reached its outer limits. The horror hasn't.

FEAR AND THE FUTURE: STEPHEN KING AS A SCIENCE FICTION WRITER

by Darrell Schweitzer

*O*ne of the numerous what-ifs in Stephen King's career is this: what if he had become a science fiction writer? While some of his fans may find it hard to imagine King on the same shelf with Isaac Asimov or Robert Heinlein, or perhaps writing lead novelets for *Analog*, his career could have turned out that way. King has clearly been aware of science fiction from earliest childhood. According to the chronological chart in Doug Winter's STEPHEN KING: THE ART OF DARKNESS, King was submitting stories to the science fiction magazines as a teenager, around 1960. King's acquaintance with the field goes further back. He can remember hearing a radio adaption of Ray Bradbury's "Mars Is Heaven" in 1953, when he was six years old. In 1957, King saw *Earth vs. the Flying Saucers* at a showing memorably interrupted by the theater manager's announcement that something very science fictional indeed had happened — Russia had orbited the first Sputnik.

The science fiction movies of the 1950s seem to have exerted a more lasting influence on King than any books he read, for all he shows himself to be familiar enough with the field and cites John Wyndham, author of THE DAY OF THE TRIFFIDS, as his personal favorite. DANSE MACABRE is peppered with references to '50s sf films. His first "published" story, "The Star Invaders" (a 1964 "book" typewritten, carbon-reproduced, stapled, and circulated to fellow high-school students; only one copy is known to exist) sounds, from available summaries, like a juvenile pastiche of *Earth vs. the Flying Saucers*. Among his mature works, we can easily point to "The Raft," an updated, more psychologically grueling version of *The Blob* and to "The Mist" with its vast array of B-movie monsters.

Two of the four early novels published under the "Richard Bachman" pseudonym, THE LONG WALK and THE RUNNING MAN, are clearly science fiction. Had these and other fledgling efforts been bought when King first submitted them...who knows?

On one level, the whole idea is a chimera. When the Bachman secret was revealed and King told all to reporter Steve Brown, he speculated on what might have happened if his early "straight" novel RAGE had been published at the time. Might he have gone in *that* direction, and not into horror? (Or, similarly, science fiction?) "...it really wouldn't have changed anything; because in the long run, the monster would have come out."

In other words, no matter what his books were labeled, they would have turned out the same because they would be books by Stephen King, whose mind is rich with monsters.

At the same time, King has never been one to rule out science fictional monsters. In DANSE MACABRE he tells us, "Horror doesn't have to be nonscientific," then goes on to argue that the precise definition of science fiction is a trap anyway. There is a borderline between science fiction and fantasy (of which horror fantasy, what King mostly writes, is a subset) but "it's a squiggly border indeed."

Maybe we can't define the border, but we *can* define the countries on either side of it. Robert Heinlein, surely the leading science fiction writer of this century, declares that science fiction is a form of *realism*. It differs from fantasy in that it deals with the "imaginary-but-possible." It takes place in the real, physical universe. The past history of the world is assumed to have happened (as opposed to imaginary-scene fantasy, including King's own THE EYES OF THE DRAGON, which takes place in a non-historical setting). Scientific discoveries and scientific laws are assumed to be valid. The fantastic element in the story is something which, while not yet known to be possible, can't be ruled out either, and from this starting point the author develops the consequences in a realistic, logical manner.

By this broad definition, Stephen King has written quite a lot of science fiction, some of it quite far from that squiggly borderland, falling into the categories of:

1) The two relevant Bachman books and other future-scene stories.

2) Stories of psionic powers.

3) Non-supernatural monsters.

Let's discuss them, then conclude with the true, squiggly borderline case, THE STAND.

In 1984 the world learned what some devotees had suspected all along, that bestseller Stephen King was also the little-known Richard Bachman, alleged recluse, of whose novel THINNER a Literary Guild reader reported, "This is what Stephen King would write like if Stephen King could really write." THINNER, clearly supernatural horror, involving a Gypsy curse that makes the hero lose weight uncontrollably, along with RAGE and ROADWORK (which lack any fantastic element), can be dismissed from the present discussion as irrelevant. But the other two of "Dick's" books are a different matter.

THE LONG WALK was apparently the first novel King actually completed, in 1967, when he was twenty. He submitted it to Bennett Cerf for the Random House first novel contest and got it back with a form rejection. The manuscript was then consigned to the proverbial writer's trunk.

While the manuscript may have seen some polishing before actual publication (1979), it is still an astonishing effort for so young a writer by virtue of its intensity, grasp of character, and, paradoxically, the very *narrowness* of its action.

The story concerns a hundred boys who take part in a brutal sporting event. They start walking southwest along a highway in Maine. Soldiers follow in armored vehicles, shooting anyone who falls below four miles per hour for more than two minutes. There are no pauses, even for the call of nature, and there is no finish line. The winner is the last boy alive.

The entire book consists of this walk, with virtually no extraneous material, flashbacks, and the like. Just kids, walking, talking, dying.

Most first novels have vast amount of action and movement, quick changes in scenery, and ideas piled on in heaps as the author tries to hide a lack of depth (and sometimes what you might call a lack of authorly attention-span) beneath the razzle-dazzle. Young writers tend to write wild melodrama, even would-be epics. But King, with his cast merely walking along a road, tells a gripping story of people pushed to their ultimate limits. Through dialogue alone we learn about each of the major characters, and, slowly, about their world.

THE LONG WALK takes place in what science fiction fans call an "alternate timeline," a place in which history as we know it *didn't* happen. In a way, we are right back on the science fiction/fantasy border, but still events are handled realistically and logically, without supernaturalism.

Science fiction has long featured time-travelers going back to change some crucial event in history. If they succeed, then the future from that point on is different: an alternate timeline. But the time-travelers are not necessary. Sometimes it suffices merely to set the story in that new timeline. It's an old tradition which has produced such classics as Philip K. Dick's THE MAN IN THE HIGH CASTLE and Keith Roberts' PAVANE, and THE LONG WALK falls squarely into the middle of it.

The time of the action is roughly the present, but not the same present you and I and Stephen King live in. The United States suffers from a dictatorship run by the Major, a homey American fascist with a good sense of showmanship. The Walks are an annual ritual, immensely popular and touted as the ultimate expression of patriotism. Anyone who disagrees vanishes in the night at the hands of the elite Squads.

Through incidental details, we get some idea of how this all came about. World War II seems to have turned out differently.

It isn't clear who won, but the Nazis blitzed the American east coast and had a nuclear base in Santiago, Chile, which was stormed by the Americans in 1953. More than this we never learn, but one can guess that the strain of a long, inconclusive, possibly nuclear war with Nazi Germany pushed America into fascism.

But King's interest is not in the alternate history *per se*, merely in using it as a device to produce a setting in which the Long Walk can take place. It's a story about boys walking along a road, learning about death, losing their illusions one by one. It partakes of an established science fiction tradition in order to get us to that road.

THE RUNNING MAN is another blood-sport story which might be loosely summed up as "The Most Dangerous Game" done as a future TV show. The novel is King's most extensive foray into the future, set in a crumbling, polluted America of the year 2025, when greedy corporations distract the masses from their misery with sadistic FreeVee shows, the most popular of which forms the title and substance of the book. Contestant Ben Richards volunteers for the show out of desperation to get medical help for his dying daughter. All he has to do is stay alive while professional Hunters try to kill him. In theory, at least, every hand is against him, because viewers who report his whereabouts are richly rewarded.

This is another early book, written in a single weekend in 1971. As such, it is another impressive performance for a novice writer, furiously-paced, vivid, and at least superficially plausible.

It is not, however, very original. The future depicted is a conventional one, particularly for the time. In 1971 the Ecology movement was just getting started. The first oil shortages were around the corner. The Vietnam War was grinding on. Cops beat up protesters. Nixon was president and lying every step of the way. Particularly if you were young and politically liberal, like King, the future didn't look bright. Not surprisingly, around the end of the '60s, there were numerous stories about brutal, corrupt capitalistic futures slowly choking in their own auto-exhaust. The best-known ones are Harry Harrison's

MAKE ROOM! MAKE ROOM! (which was filmed as *Soylent Green*) and John Brunner's STAND ON ZANZIBAR. These nasty futures frequently featured gladiatorial-type sports, as in the movie *Rollerball*.

THE RUNNING MAN adds very little to this tradition, but King depicts his future capably enough. For once he is able to write of something other than the present. The brand-names are different. People don't smoke Luckies, for example; they smoke Blams. Aircars lower themselves gently to the curbside when they park. Since all the characters are native to this future world, they act naturally in it. Nobody stops to explain how things work any more than a character in a novel set in 1987 would be expected to stop and explain to another character how his dishwasher works. Such things are just taken for granted.

In this King is using techniques developed in the 1940s, by Robert Heinlein and others. Prior to that, science fiction characters *did* explain . . . and explain . . . and explain. Often a professor would lecture to a reporter for pages, to fill the reader in, or else there would be an obligatory time-traveler from the present, whose chief function was to have everything explained to him.

It was a breakthrough when writers discovered the *lived-in* future as opposed to the future visited by tourists. The future of THE RUNNING MAN is lived-in. The book is no breakthrough, but it does show that King can, if he chooses, write competent, future-scene science fiction.

King's other stories of the future are less successful. "Beachworld," first published in *Weird Tales* in 1984 (the story may be found in SKELETON CREW), is King's only tale set on another planet, and, one hopes, a bit of resurrected juvenilia sold to editors desperate for the King name. It is an unmitigated disaster, harkening back to "The Star Invaders," a B-movie in prose, the old monster-in-the-sand-gobbles-spacemen plot. It notably lacks any sense of the future at all, for all the action is supposed to be taking place *eight thousand* years in the future. The characters land on a sand-world and make jokes about The Beach Boys, which is about as plausible as someone today referring to some popular street singer of ancient Babylon. They use expressions like "Surf city with no surf" and "No shit, Sherlock,"—about as plausible as today's average joe speaking Babylonian. From the evidence in the story, it would seem that *no cultural development at all* has taken place in those eight millennia. Of course the resultant story completely fails to convince the reader. It is easily King's poorest work.

"The Jaunt" (in SKELETON CREW) is a much better story but also seriously flawed by what, to an experienced science fiction reader, would seem like childish mistakes.

We are supposedly three hundred years in the future. People teleport to Mars and Venus routinely. The story opens in New York's Port Authority Terminal, which, in the 23rd century, is still called the Port Authority Terminal. Announcements are made over loudspeakers. The waiting room is a little grungy with "white eggshell" walls hung with "pleasant nonrepresentational prints." There's a "harried businessman" with a newspaper under one arm, who wears "spit-shined shoes."

And once again King's power of observation, the very sense of detail which make his contemporary-scene stories so effective, works against him. He is describing the Port Authority Terminal of the present, not of three centuries hence. All the details are contemporary. Apparently he can observe, but he is unable to *imagine* that sort of thing. He can't make up *different* details.

The science of the story is patently ridiculous: Mars is being developed because of its *oil*. There also seems to be enough oil on Venus to last 20,000 years. But the major export of Mars is . . . water!

This is clearly not the solar system, or even the universe of real life. In *our* universe oil is formed over eons from decayed vegetable matter, something Mars and Venus conspicuously lack. Further, Mars is cold and dry with virtually no atmosphere, more like the Moon than like Earth. Venus is hot enough for lead to run in streams, with an intensely corrosive atmosphere as thick as soup. The toughest Russian space probes to Venus have burned/melted/dissolved within a half an hour of landing.

So maybe it's an alternate universe? No, King is merely being sloppy. Robert Heinlein, after defining the realistic nature of the field, identified something called "wooden-nickel science fiction." A historical novel in which Henry VIII is the son of Queen Elizabeth would be wooden-nickel historical fiction, completely fake. A story about oilfields on Mars is wooden-nickel science fiction.

Yet this is the product of the mature King, who should know better. The actual writing is up to standard. The characterizations are good. There is even a genuine shock when a boy does what he shouldn't during the teleportation and comes out raving mad. The sections set in 1987, dealing with the invention of the teleportation device, are eerie and effective. But here King shows complete incompetence in the specifically science fictional aspects of the story. He does not depict a convincing future. He makes scientific errors a glance into any high-school textbook could have prevented. And he even makes the quaint blunder of having his characters *lecture* one another about the history of teleportation, as if they were 20th century characters in a bus terminal, lecturing one another on the history of the internal-combustion engine.

The obvious conclusion is that King either has little talent for or little interest in the future-scene story. Perhaps THE RUNNING MAN's future works merely because it is so standard. Other writers have worked out the details for him.

Certainly King knows his science fiction—he even cites, in the text of "The Jaunt," Alfred Bester's classic of a baroque, teleporting future, THE STARS MY DESTINATION—but he has simply failed to learn from it.

Science fiction writers have never adhered to Heinlein's rules of realism very strictly. There is always some fudging. For example, two of the staples of science fiction, faster-than-light travel (so that ships can cross interstellar distances in less than a human lifetime; *Star Trek* wouldn't work without faster-than-light) and time-travel into the past, are far less scientifically plausible than werewolves. Yet, by convention, FTL spaceships and time-travel belong in science fiction while werewolves are fantasy. Why? Because the traditional explanation for were-wolves requires supernaturalism, but the sf writer, lying through his teeth about the possibility of time-travel, is at least *pretending* to be scientific.

By another such convention, stories about psychic powers, telepathy, telekinesis, clairvoyance, precognition, *etc.* have been incorporated into science fiction in the past thirty years or so.

Originally such powers were an element of folk superstition, as in the Scottish belief in the "second sight." They formed an important part of the repertoire of 19th century Spiritualists. By the mid-20th century they had become quasi-scientific, particularly after J. B. Rhine's celebrated (but now largely discredited) experiments at Duke University. Rhine tried to get mind readers to send and receive images on cards: stars, wavy lines, *etc.* The fringe-science of parapsychology was born.

The great science fiction editor John W. Campbell took a lively interest in *psionics*, as the belief was now called. His magazine, *Astounding Science Fiction* (later *Analog*) was soon filled with stories of ESPers (i.e. people with E.S.P. or *psi* powers), many of them persecuted for their difference. "Psychic" matters invaded science fiction in a big way, even if real-life science failed to make much progress proving the existence of such "wild talents."

Stephen King's CARRIE, FIRESTARTER, and THE DEAD ZONE are all psionics stories. It is hard to imagine John Campbell publishing any of them. He probably would have found King's work depressing, tasteless, and crypto-Communist (Campbell had his quirks, like most strong-minded people), but he would not have objected to the premises of any of them.

All three books are too well-known to require much plot-synopsis. THE DEAD ZONE is arguably King's very best novel for its perfection of form, its subtle characterizations, and dramatic (as opposed to melodramatic) scenes. CARRIE, of course, launched King's amazing career. It is not top-drawer King by any means, the only one of his novels which is actually *too short*. It is little more than a brief setup for a vivid climax, the whole front end synopsized away in pseudo-scholarly notes.

FIRESTARTER, a much better book which is perhaps less known because it was made into an inferior movie, is to some extent a reworking of CARRIE.

All three are stories of people with psi-powers, and King makes every effort to give these powers a scientific rationale. In CARRIE there is a vast pseudo-documentary apparatus, allegedly put there to pad the story out to book-length, but nevertheless providing much verisimilitude. Carrie White is that old science fictional standby, a *mutant*. An autopsy reveals an abnormal development in her brain. She has inherited her ability genetically, the psi-gene being a recessive which only becomes dominant in females.

Here King's science is better than usual. He provides a perfectly competent explanation of Mendelian genetics using the famous example of hemophilia in the royal families of Europe, before making an oil-on-Mars pratfall by telling us that because so many royal folk were bleeders, this was known as "The King's Evil." (Wrong. "The King's Evil" is *scrofula*, the ancient belief being that the hands of a true king could cure it.)

In FIRESTARTER, the strange powers are awakened by a drug. In THE DEAD ZONE, the hero has an auto accident, goes into a coma for four and a half years. When he awakens, his brain is strangely altered and he is precognitive.

There is no hint of the supernatural in any of these novels. Carrie's mother clearly thinks her daughter's powers come from the Devil, but we, the readers, know better. In *form* these are not typical science fiction novels. King inserts one fantastic — in these instances, science fictional — element into the story, then plays out the human drama for all it's worth. All the psionics novels are essentially about "different" individuals seeking freedom and self-determination.

King works from a different set of assumptions than those of the average science fiction writer. One can imagine CARRIE as by a novelist in *Astounding* circa 1956: there would be a sisterhood of ESPer women, mothers teaching daughters, either completely underground or working hush-hush with the U.S. government. They would have to band together to either save or destroy the rogue ESPer before she wipes out Chamberlain,

Maine, blows the secret, and sets off a hysterical persecution of "wild-talented" people.

That, of course, is not the story Stephen King chose to write. But his subject matter is still pure science fiction.

"Horror fiction doesn't necessarily have to be non-scientific," says King. Indeed, the most famous horror novel of all time, Mary Shelley's FRANKENSTEIN, is thoroughly scientific. British writer Brian Aldiss, in TRILLION YEAR SPREE, has made a good case for FRANKENSTEIN being the first authentic science fiction novel. But it is also a product of the Gothic movement. Horror and science fiction have been intertwined that long. We are back at the squiggly border.

A certain number of King's straight horror stories—stories intended to scare, rather than to develop ideas in a speculatively interesting way—contains monsters or menaces which just happen to be non-supernatural. Otherwise these monsters are unremarkable.

There is the aforementioned "The Raft," an updating of *The Blob.* The story is largely a study of fear and courage. For dramatic purposes it requires a Menace. The black Thing that eats the various swimmers could just as readily have been the undead ghost of somebody drowned in that lake, but it isn't—it's a viscous mass, rather like Theodore Sturgeon's famous "It," an uncleanness come to life, probably jolted with a generous dose of industrial pollution.

"Gray Matter" (in NIGHT SHIFT) likewise uses a non-supernatural menace. It doesn't make much sense, but it's explained by a bad can of beer.

"Graveyard Shift" (also in NIGHT SHIFT) is another story of sheer terror, exploiting our obvious fears of dark, closed places and particularly of meeting rats in such places. Its huge rodents are arguably mutants, or a species unknown to science. The story is science fiction, by default.

"I Am the Doorway" (in NIGHT SHIFT) is more substantially science fiction, with its retired astronaut slowly taken over by alien life. But the thrust here is again toward horror. The story is closer to Ray Bradbury's "Fever Dream" (in which a boy is taken over by germs and one by one, the parts of his body aren't *him* anymore) than to most science fiction. It is a story of pure emotion, an *Outer Limits* or *Twilight Zone* episode in prose.

Much more interestingly, the novella "The Mist" (in SKELE-TON CREW) uses science fictional monsters for King's own purposes. All the classic King trademarks are there: the clean prose, the vividly described, everyday characters and setting, the sudden intrusion of the monstrous into the everyday—and of course, *trademarks*. Only in a Stephen King story would someone dispatch a blood-thirsty, extra-dimensional Thing with two cans of Raid.

The science fictional idea behind "The Mist" is, again, familiar, and fully as impossible as time-travel. Yet other "dimensions" which lead to strange worlds or let even stranger invaders into our world have been a standby of the field for decades. Another convention.

This time King makes striking use of the idea. "The Mist" contains some of his best writing, particularly toward the end where the characters gain a glimpse of a world awesomely and irrevocably transformed.

With THE STAND, King crosses that squiggly border, out of science fiction entirely. This may be a surprise to some readers, a disappointment to some.

Once again, the book begins in a familiar sf situation. Stories of the destruction of mankind have been with us since antiquity. Mary Shelley's THE LAST MAN (1826) set the modern pattern, with the world as the author knew it wiped out by a plague. Other classics of the type include M. P. Shiel's THE PURPLE CLOUD (poison gas does it) and A. Conan Doyle's "The Poison Belt" (only they're not really dead). In all of these, there is much fascination with the empty world, as the handful of survivors, or even a single survivor, wander through the ruins.

THE STAND begins very much in this vein. With a touch that recurs in King's work, the disaster is caused by an accidental release of "superflu" at a government biological weapons installation. Once the magnitude of the catastrophe is clear, the perpetrators deliberately spread the disease to the Chinese and Russians, lest America's rivals "get any ideas." And so 99% of the population of the globe is wiped out in a few weeks.

At first, everything is handled with strict realism with only minor lapses. One wonders how cows survive without milking, or why someone goes to enormous trouble to open the storage tank at a gas station when there is plenty of gas to be siphoned out of the tanks of stalled cars. But for the most part King's holocaust is a convincing one.

Then, halfway through the novel overtly supernatural elements occur, until the book becomes a modern-dress LORD OF THE RINGS and ends with an authentic miracle. At this point King is no longer writing science fiction, but mystical, almost religious fantasy. This is not to criticize, only to define. THE STAND may start like science fiction; it may share many of the concerns of science fiction; but it clearly is *not* science fiction.

A related short story, "Night Surf" (in NIGHT SHIFT) is science fiction. There are no divine miracles, no visions, no embodiments of evil present, just young people, possibly the last survivors of the superflu, waiting for death on the beach, trying to understand themselves and what their lives might have been.

It is all very well to show that Stephen King has written science fiction of various types, with varying degrees of success, but the observation doesn't become interesting without a *purpose*. What does he *do* with science fiction?

King as a science fiction writer is reminiscent of Ray Bradbury, only with better characterizations and a lot less poetry. His actual imagination is second-rate. He uses off-the-shelf ideas and does not extrapolate them very far. He writes purely for emotional effect without much regard for scientific realism. At times this works. At times, as in "The Jaunt" or "Beachworld," it is just plain sloppy. (One thinks of a ridiculous Bradbury story about interplanetary hitch-hikers who use magnets to attach themselves to the outsides of spaceships.) But if we look at his science fiction as a whole, some interesting patterns recur.

The Bachman books are angry books, science fictional or

otherwise. RAGE, the title of the first, could sum up the lot. THE LONG WALK is about the horror and fury of the victims/contestants, and their anger at the society which has made such a travesty possible. THE RUNNING MAN is about a malcontent determined to rip down the whole facade of the world he lives in. And you know that it's right . . . as the rock song has it.

King's science fiction often contains a strong element of social protest. Its genesis is more readily understood with the knowledge that the author was twenty years old in 1967. He came to manhood protesting the Vietnam War, in a time when the "Evil Empire" was in the White House and everything the government said was taken by many to be an obscene lie.

In King's sf, the U.S. government is always evil. He isn't against *law*—there are several sympathetic portrayals of small-town sheriffs—but the Powers That Be are always brutal, reckless scum. In both THE STAND and "The Mist," the world as we know it is destroyed because the U.S. military has an accident. In THE STAND the government denies everything until the end, then, out of spite, deliberately spreads the plague to the rest of the world and sends an assassin to kill Stu Redman, one of the few immune Americans. In "The Mist" the perpetrators, who have opened a dimensional gate and flooded the world with monsters, realize what they've done and commit suicide—which is small help to the survivors. In FIRESTARTER the secret agency called The Shop consists of absolute and utter sleaze, vicious, hypocritical murderers who regard people as things. (And the story may have been partially inspired by the revelation that the U.S. government *did* conduct a variety of unethical biochemical tests on civilians in the 1950s. But no one developed pyrokinesis, fortunately.) In both of the Bachman science fiction novels, the government is mere tyranny, in THE LONG WALK a military dictatorship, in THE RUNNING MAN an unscrupulous and uncontrolled network of corporations which are deliberately polluting the environment for profit and suppressing all information on the subject while keeping the masses in hand with lethal games. In CARRIE the government is at least no help, and can only suggest that the

Carrie White phenomenon either be ignored or all future teleki-netics be shot at birth. And in THE DEAD ZONE a psychotic is well on his way to being elected president.

Clearly King is not a believer in the innate goodness of big government.

King's science fiction stories — except for a few like "Grave-yard Shift" which are just coincidentally non-supernatural methods of saying "Boo!" — deal with real-world issues. They are often the most didactic of his works. "I am always going to be a social novelist," Winter quotes him as saying in THE ART OF DARKNESS.

The ultimate question raised is King's attitude toward science itself.

He is not blindly anti-scientific. He is sophisticated enough to realize that the same laser technology which brings us space weapons also works in everything from eye surgery to compact discs. He knows that without highways to transport food, fac-tories to make the trucks, mines to produce the metal, *etc.*, the whole technological ball of wax, most of the world's population would simply and very quickly starve.

But at the same time he clearly doesn't trust high technology in the hands of big government. For all its mystical elements, THE STAND is the most explicit about this. The depopulated world doesn't devolve into some post-holocaust Eden. Instead the survivors rapidly get their hands on the nuclear "toys" left lying around. The book ends with the realization that all the horrors visited on the world could happen again. *All any of us can buy is time* Stu Redman thinks. Men being what they are can create or destroy. There is no answer.

King remarks in DANSE MACABRE: "My lesson in writing THE STAND was that cutting the Gordian Knot simply destroys the riddle instead of solving it, and the book's last line is an admission that the riddle still remains."

The last line is an answer to the question, *Do you think people will ever learn anything?*

And it is, *I don't know.*

THE SUMMATION

by Don Herron

M: But a lot of people think you are great.
SK: I know, from letters I get, that there are people who believe that.
But the other thing that goes along with that is that you have to
evaluate the critical reaction to your work and decide from that
what you're doing. You see, I don't think writers are very good
judges of their own work. Maybe they're not bad judges, but they're
no better judges than anyone else. Everybody has an opinion, but
nobody's opinion is better than anybody else's.
> — Stephen King, interviewed in *Mystery*, March 1981.

Prologue: The Year That Was and the Great Escape

I've been a published Stephen King critic for about as long as anyone else regularly punching the clock in this cottage industry, longer than most. The job is fairly lucrative for part-time work, some fun, and overall I can recommend it. Still, I felt honest relief as I watched the year 1986 roll through with the prospect of a satisfactory retirement. I'm certainly among those people who experience the greatest sense of freedom the moment the words "I quit" hit the wind.

Back in 1980-81 when I initially began putting together an essay on King's writing, the subject was full of potentialities. THE DEAD ZONE had been the first of his novels to reach the top of the bestseller lists, with CUJO and FIRESTARTER, then recent releases, following it up the charts. In these books King avoided some of the crudities of his admittedly more energetic early novels, and it looked as if he might get just the right grip on the word processor, blow out the doors of perception—taking horror readers places *no one* would want to go. Already King was the all-time bestselling writer of horror, about to enter serious competition with Clavell, Michener, and other authors who sit right at the top of the sales lists; and I suppose at that moment in history perhaps as many as fifty people may have read the first paperbacks by "Richard Bachman," RAGE and THE LONG WALK.

By the time I came to write further King essays it seemed clear that he had reached a plateau; moreover, I suspected that we had seen the true peaks of his career in THE SHINING, "Apt Pupil," THE DEAD ZONE, "The Body," and a handful of other works. When I got the assignment to write the entry on King for the PENGUIN ENCYCLOPEDIA OF HORROR AND THE SUPERNATURAL I felt it *was* possible to give his *oeuvre* a reasonable assessment, though I did load the concluding sentence, where I noted, ". . .King certainly is meeting the needs of his public, and he seems likely to remain without any serious challengers in the horror field as master of the good read." King is a master of the Good Read, and I did not think then and do not think now that any truly serious writer of horror will ever rival his popularity.

Yet even as I wrote that entry rumors were abroad of IT, said to be King's *magnum opus*, his longest, scariest, *best* novel of horror, a book King declared would be a "monster rally—everything is in the book, every monster you could think of." And King's debut as a film director loomed, with his fans talking about how terrifying MAXIMUM OVERDRIVE was going to be, with the director himself quoted in *Newsweek* for June 10, 1985 as saying, "I want to get a Stephen King feeling—a kind of spirit—into a movie."

The world of Stephen King criticism, paused on the brink of 1986, *still* seemed pregnant with vast, dark potentialities, much larger than life, at least ten times as hairy, maybe twice as mean. . . .

And then 1986 rolled through and I sensed my impending escape from yet another job, with the first key to freedom coming in the form of IT: two tons of crap in a five-ton crate.

I. A Monstrous Big Fairy Tale

In 1958 in the city of Derry, Maine, a gang of seven kids called The Losers battled a supernatural creature they call "It" to a standstill. Afterwards, the families of all but one leave the area, and The Losers forget all about their childhoods, forget the threat of It, and enter a fairyland version of the American Dream. It comes from Outside, the place H. P. Lovecraft got most of his monsters back in the 1920s, and It is a virtual god, who weaves a mystic spell. As adults, The Losers become very successful—one grows up to be a bestselling horror writer. Only the boy who stayed behind in the blighted town remained poor, and only he remembers. When the monster returns in a twenty-seven year cycle of child murdering, he calls the far-flung members of the club back for the final confrontation, "through the fairytale door, and into the lair of It."

Such is the framework of IT, which totals 1138 pages and weighs three and a half pounds, a novel which bulldozed into America's bookstores with an 800,000 copy first print run backed by one of the largest advertising budgets ever for a hardcover release. A guaranteed critic-proof bestseller, IT instantly gave the vast audience of Stephen King horror fans what they presumably want: *more—much* more—of the same old same.

King makes no effort to hide the origins of this work in earlier tales, in superior stories such as "The Body," which portrays a boy's gang of 1960 facing the reality of death and their growth toward adulthood, or "The Bogeyman," where King wrote, "Maybe all the monsters we were scared of when we were kids, Frankenstein and Wolfman and Mummy, maybe they were real. Real enough to kill the kids who were supposed to have fallen into gravel pits or drowned in lakes. . . ." The city of Derry is only another version of 'Salem's Lot, that ill-reputed Maine village haunted by vampires, or Castle Rock and environs, home of rabid dogs and rapist-cops—whereas Derry's lurking fear is IT, sometimes known as Robert Gray or Bob Gray, sometimes seen in the guise of the evil Pennywise the Clown, sometimes as the Mummy, the Creature from the Black Lagoon, the Crawling Eye. The press release accompanying review copies of the novel quotes King as saying: "I put in every monster I could think of, and I took every childhood incident I had ever written of before, and tried to integrate the two."

It was a shock to encounter the salacious hobo who offers the boy Todd in "Apt Pupil" a cheap blow-job—another milestone on Todd's highway to hell, as he is driven toward madness by adolescent sexual frustration and visions of Nazi torture gardens. When Todd returns to the hobo hangout later with a hammer and, under strange compulsions, begins his own career as a mass murderer, the reader feels the impact. It is not a throwaway scene in a thousand plus pages of "monster rally" as it is in IT, where Pennywise *aka* Teenage Werewolf *aka* Abbott and Costello Meet Frankenstein reprises the scene at one point, appearing as a hobo with the same offer. Other than just another "horror" effect, what *impact* does this incident, so integral to the movement in "Apt Pupil," have in terms of the story? Why, none at all—there are too many pages ahead and too many monsters and recycled childhood incidents to be tabulated into the tale to waste much time with this one, so the scene shifts, It shapeshifts, and we're off!

I'm sorry to say that I found the short story "The Bogeyman," where the initial kernel of this novel crops up in King's writing, a much scarier, much more satisfying work of horrific art than IT. Terror, apparently, does not come by the pound.

Of course, *more* may be at stake in IT than a few hundred pages of cheap thrills, since the author once stated that this novel would be "a summation of everything I have learned and done in my whole life to this point." So, how much has he learned?

In a quest for topicality King brings in the big new bugaboo of AIDS *via* some stereotyped gay bashers and the stereotyped gays they bash. (*All* characters in this novel come off as stereotypes: The Losers comprise a fat kid, a sick kid, a stuttering kid, a wisemouth kid, a Jewish kid, a Negro kid, and a female kid; and, hey, guess which ones are *expendable*, you know, the ones who actually die or get seriously trashed by the Forces of Evil.) King reveals his own small-town origins when he pictures a bartender—supposedly not a dimwit—whose unsuccessful tavern becomes a thriving gay bar, and who for *five years* does not realize that the saloon he is operating is a gay bar! How could anybody over the age of twenty-one whose mommy lets him cross the street alone be expected to believe that?

King postulates that, "Like the man with the cheating wife, he was practically the last to know. . . ." which at least offers *some* kind of explanation, even if it is for a completely different set of circumstances. Everyone *else* could see what was happening, you see, but not the guy standing behind the bar for hours every day.

I did give King the courtesy of checking my opinion with a gay man, easy enough to find in San Francisco: Would it be possible, I asked, for someone to run a gay bar for *five years* without realizing it? "Well, no," he said, "it wouldn't be." Then, deciding to give a break to the author who could conceive such a notion, he added, "I mean, it would have to be a *very* dull place.'

When *Playboy* interviewed King a few years ago he was asked if Chelsea Quinn Yarbro's observation that he could not "develop a believable woman character between the ages of 17 and 60" was a fair criticism. "Yes, unfortunately," King responded, "I think it is probably the most justifiable of all those leveled at me. In fact, I'd extend her criticism to include my handling of black characters." If we add owners of gay bars to that list, still King has a lot of leeway in the material he might work with direct knowledge—boyhood, the history of horror movies and horror novels, husband, father, life in small town U.S.A.: the elements which have always made up the significant parts of his work.

But a professional and prolific fiction writer is expected to know (or be able to fake convincingly) many other aspects of the world than the ones he or she may know *best*. It's part of the job description, being a know-it-all, trotting out all manner of *expertise* on a moment's notice (when, for example, James Bond needs to express an opinion on a liquor or a firearm; or Travis

Magee decides to let the readers know what *really* goes into planning, financing, and building a condominium on the Gold Coast). I like to think that at one time in history, from the creation of Sherlock Holmes to shortly before the beginning of World War I, it was possible for a writer in English to knock out a so-called "realistic" story filled with the acceptable character types and racial stereotypes and send it unquestioned into print, happy readers, by and large, being none the wiser. More recently, readers have occasionally demanded that a realistic writer have *some* idea of what he's writing about, and that's the school of thought I attend, although I know there will always be a market for the fake and even the unintentionally but utterly ridiculous.

Obviously King's readership has no problems with his cobbled-together explanations of the unlikely, and this recalls an observation Virginia Woolf made in A WRITER'S DIARY, published in 1954, with her diary entry dated April 11, 1939: "I am reading Dickens; by way of a refresher. How he lives: not writes: both a virtue and a fault. Like seeing something emerge; without containing mind." (It recalls too Fritz Leiber's observation that King aims at convincing the *senses and feelings* instead of the intellect.)

In Dickens' time I'm sure he carried off a great deal a writer couldn't get away with today, when the concept of the Renaissance Man or even the know-it-all has given way before the *vastness* of potential knowledge, and even highly intelligent and ambitious people have been forced into specialization. It's interesting to think of King, who in the past has worked in a laundry, taught high school and college, but who has for most of his adult life worked at the fiction trade; who says he usually writes 362 days of the year, sitting home virtually *all the time*, living life vicariously by writing.

Yet I wonder how *meaningful* this sort of exercise is today, without life experience behind it—how much *can* King have learned and done when he has made it clear (and turned out the product that *proves*) he has been pounding on a keyboard all day, nearly every day, for *years*. I almost feel sorry for a guy who *has* to write about gay bars and AIDS to keep in step, because he's writing about "real life" and people in the real world are talking and talking about AIDS.

With IT King has developed a new approach to handling black characters. Now he doesn't tell us they're black. We follow scene after scene with the black kid without knowing he's black—cleverly done, worth taking note of if you're in a creative writing class. I believe I got the message about the point where Dick Hallorann, the Overlook Hotel's psychic cook from THE SHINING, does his cameo appearance (and a *fine* cameo it is: "I know it!"). King doesn't mention that Hallorann is black, but I remembered he is. Of course, Elmore Leonard, probably the best dialogue writer going, never has to tell you a character is black, either; you know it after reading a couple lines of speech, the nuances of language are so superb. Here it takes a long time and suddenly you say, "Hey, this Loser is black." What a shocker.

When he worked this same thematic territory in "The Body" King left out the multitude of monsters and limited his gang of kids to white males, tactics which abetted the believability of that short novel. I suspect the ethnic mix here is prompted by much the same concern that creates mention of gay bars and AIDS: topicality = commercialism.

Integration *a la* IT is a current response to an old set of problems, very 1980s, and will date IT as such—just as seeing Burt Reynolds playing second string to Jim Brown in *100 Rifles* dates that movie as late 1960s, the era of blaxploitation film. We all know that Burt went on to the big time, and for topicality, who hasn't heard the rumor that Burt has AIDS? Does anyone suggest that Jim Brown might have AIDS? No. He's not topical. After that brief landslide of *Shaft*, *Superfly*, *Blacula*, *Black Belt Jones*, etc., Hollywood largely dropped starring vehicles for black actors for over a decade—and while *The Color Purple* got eleven well-deserved Oscar nominations, it won none, which says something by default. Now blacks and other minorities are predictably, routinely fitted into the program: the Lando Calrissian syndrome.

Integration in IT is worth mentioning precisely because it is so trendy. One would think a serious novelist, if we wish to consider King a serious novelist for a moment, would at least try to get ahead of the game. The ethnic mix among the boys doesn't present much of a problem in the story; we don't even need to know that one of the gang is black, and this is supposed to be 1958. For any actual difference it makes, the boys could all be WASPS, and the cliched rationale that comes to mind, along the lines of *the husband is always the last to know*, is that *boys will be boys*.

But The Losers are not exclusively male (they couldn't be in the 1980s, could they?), so the male-bonding and steps toward adulthood that occurred in "The Body" as the four boys went out overnight in search of the corpse of young Ray Brower are not quite enough here. In IT you have a girl, and if you have a girl, well, what options open up? Does anyone recall years ago in *Spiderman* comics, I guess it was close to the hundredth issue, when the guys at Marvel killed off Peter Parker's girl-friend? Afterwards they said in an editorial that they felt that had to kill her off—it was either death or she and Spiderman would have had to get married, and Spidey just was not ready for marriage. *Some choice*, but the same primitive kind of thinking operates in this novel, so what option could King possibly pursue except *sex*?

If you like to consider women *en masse* as a minority, including a girl in the gang pretty much rounds out the current topical list of downtrodden, with this character set up to be the object of sexual abuse. The girl is the key to why The Losers as adults cannot remember their first fearful encounter with It. She takes the author in a direction he has never traveled before, since even in the stories where King's characters have sex, it doesn't seem as if they've *really* had sex.

To give it all away, as the seven kids flee that fairytale lair of It, the girl realizes that the *only way* they'll be able to escape, to somehow make the magical jump into adulthood (wow!) and safety (for 27 years, anyhow) is for her to offer some nooky around to her friends. What follows is perhaps the most utterly *polite* gangbang I ever expect to read, an event so patently false it's almost as if you didn't read it. *What* was that?! They need *sex* to become adults? In "The Body" they only had to stay out all night, swear a little, stand up to some bullies and look at a dead kid. . . . *Now* they need *sex*?

It does seem a bit much to read a thousand pages of flashbacks and flashforwards made necessary because the kids can't remember shit, only to find that the *reason* they can't remember is because the author had them take part in some mild kiddie porn, and wants to save this Big Surprise for real late in the book. Won't that be a shocker.

The novel is much too long for the amount of creative energy King can put into IT. Sure, he continues his evocation of American life by means of quoted rock 'n' roll lyrics, brand name products, and other trademarks of his fiction. His colloquial style remains easy to read, with occasional nice, simple moments, such as when one of the boys smiles "a dopey, dizzy, and absolutely beautiful grin." But over the course of a thousand pages he runs out of drive, and you can see him almost realizing it as he putters along.

Take Henry Bowers, the young thug who acts as the major human bully (and ultimately as a pawn of IT), making day-to-day life in little Old Derry miserable for The Losers. He and his pals slam the good guys around some, get in a few licks, but then The Losers begin to strike back. One of them kicks him in the balls. Later another one kicks him in the balls. Let's try for three. You begin to lose count of the humiliation this character has to take: he can't catch The Losers without falling off a cliff or something. By page 980 King sees that his human henchman for the evil monster is a complete klutz, and has The Losers raze him with the term "banana-heels." When Bowers returns for his big showdown you wonder what he'll fall over this time.

IT falters because the major excuse for the story is unmaintainable for 1000 pages, "the eternal fascination of the fairy story: would the monster be bested . . . or would it feed?" When the monster appears looking like Michael Landon in *I Was a Teenage Werewolf* or another of those drearily unscary films of King's '50s childhood (whose hackneyed images seem to be the greatest influence on his imagination), I think It will go hungry. We have here a creature as powerful as an Antichrist, which has preyed on an entire town in 27-year cycles for centuries, but one which cannot take out a bunch of horny Junior G-Men. When King tries to tie this plot into the real world about halfway through by suggesting that something like the Atlanta child murders may occur because of some cyclical cosmic monster like It, all I can say is "bullshit." Real people are mean enough.

One feature of the novel might have been great, if King knew how to develop it in a more reasonably sized work: Pennywise the Clown. Robert Bloch, author of PSYCHO, once wrote an article entitled "What Is Horror?" which gives an answer to the title question by Lon Chaney, Sr., the Man of 1000 Faces. *Chaney said*, Imagine you are alone in your living room, reading, and are startled by a loud knocking at the door. The house is empty. The town is asleep. The knock sounds again. You hesitate, then move toward the door. The knock comes again. You open the door. On your porch, its face bleached and gleaming in the moonlight, is a clown, in full costume and make-up, smiling at you. *Would you laugh?*

Bloch summed up his article with this image and suggested that the quintessence of all horror is The Clown at Midnight, and clearly King plays with this idea in It, and may have had it in mind when he came up with Pennywise, for all I know different. The many roles It assumes in the novel might then even be a sort of tribute to Chaney, master of makeup, but I doubt it. Chaney, of *The Phantom of the Opera*, *He Who Gets Slapped*, and so many other films, was a genius at encapsulating horror. He spoke of The Clown at Midnight, not The Clown Lurking Down in The Sewers, Ready to Turn Into Teenage Werewolf, Rodan, King Kong, and Dracula. If King was influenced by Chaney's notion, he got carried away.

The big battle with It ranks among the dumbest episodes I have ever read, with It in its last and most cliched form (you know: black, hairy, eight legs, but big, *very* big—the *invention* here is almost chilling). King, in a bad marriage of Lovecraft with Kurt Vonnegut, takes The Losers beyond Time and Space into a flight of "cosmic absurdity," where they bite It's metaphysical tongue (no kidding) and think very nasty thoughts about It. I guess the more dedicated King fans may find this sequence a religious experience. At least it is an attempt on King's part to go further with his horror material than he ever has before, to show terror on a cosmic plane—and now that we've seen what he can do with cosmic horror, I'll be happy when he just blows up the town and kills everyone, no Afterlife, no Out of Body Experiences desired, thank you.

Reviewing IT in the *Wall Street Journal* for October 13, 1986, Amanda Bennett found the very last part of the book one of the dumbest things *she* had ever read: "What's more, the final scene, in which the wife of one character is rescued from her It-induced catatonia by a breakneck ride on her husband's childhood bike that takes her back to simple, innocent, childish things is stupid beyond belief." It is that, but like most other aspects of the book, is very trendy; like the flying bike ride of the narrator's kid brother in King's recent short story "The End of the Whole Mess," this scene has one name written on it: Spielberg. Who knows, maybe Spielberg (or more likely one of his proteges) will direct the film, so a fancy bike ride would be nice—he does them so well. Try the rides in IT against *E.T.* and "Whole Mess" against *Young Sherlock Holmes*; King is fairly successful at recapturing the Spielbergian feeling of such scenes.

In retrospect, I'd say the cameo by Hallorann was my favorite moment in IT, which means I had more fun playing find-the-name games than waiting for It to turn into the Mummy. You could read this novel strictly for in-jokes and come away happy, if that's your pleasure: King's radio station WZON gets a mention; there is a brief appearance by Christine or one of her sister Furies; a blurb for Dennis Etchison; more of King's usual reference to Shirley Jackson's THE HAUNTING OF HILL HOUSE, on pages 901 and 943; an allusion on page 70 to one of my favorite King stories, "Sometimes They Come Back." And, as they say, *more*. This aspect of King's writing is an important part of his appeal to his large fan following, but of course it is something else H. P. Lovecraft did first, making cross-references between stories and tossing out lots of in-jokes way back in the 1920s, one of the reasons Lovecraft became the first cult American horror writer of this century.

Critics have a name for what King is doing when he drops in-jokes *a la* Lovecraft, makes bikes fly like Spielberg, or borrows as many 1950s movie monsters as he can squeeze into 1138 pages to threaten The Losers. Jeremiah Creedon neatly presented the argument in his article "Stolen Moments: Recombinant Culture and the Art of Appropriation," *In These Times*, May 13, 1987, beginning:

> Look anywhere these days and you'll find an example of what the art crowd is calling "appropriation." The term signifies a trend among artists toward borrowing (or stealing) images from earlier art works, often from the "icons" of their various disciplines. Once limited to painters and photographers, this postmodern tic is spreading beyond them, mutating as it goes into a contagious metaphor. Now pop writers and critics are using the term, perhaps because the concept behind it seems so familiar to us.

Everyone is doing it, perhaps because nothing new remains to say or paint or draw or play. Creedon quotes art critic Kay Larson as stating, "the Great Appropriator must have no style; he is merely a vehicle for the rearrangement of images, a kind of auteurish director who splices from the collective eye of his cameramen."

King certainly is one of the Greatest Appropriators, a postmodern end-product of this trend, a Great Regurgitator, swallowing literature, pop literature, film, culture, and pop culture whole. After brief digestion, he spews it forth again, and apparently feels he is giving his readers the benefit of his life experience, for such seems to be his life experience.

Appropriations pervade his work, and most are obvious enough. You'd have to be pretty stupid or very much uninformed to think King created the notion of killer cars, vampires, psychics, mad dogs, werewolves or even Teenage Werewolves. I sometimes think that almost *every* element of his writing could be traced, if a person had the time and the results were worth the bother. Take King's statement that he likes to give his readers "good weight." It sounds good, democratic, generous, and the statement in full comes from his afterword to DIFFERENT SEASONS:

Subtract elegance from the novelist's craft and one finds himself left with only one strong leg to stand on, and that leg is good weight. As a result, I've tried as hard as I can, always, to give good weight.

In her diary for April 28th, 1933, Virginia Woolf noted, "Oh I could only stand the voyage by writing. I've written 3 or 4 books. I like to give the public full weight. Books should be sold by the pound."

King loves Jackson's THE HAUNTING OF HILL HOUSE; he drops mentions of it all the time throughout his writing. Do you recall the scene in CARRIE where Carrie White, three years of age, sees a neighbor girl sun-bathing and ask her *what* her breasts are? The fanatically religious Margaret White discovers her child with the half-naked teenager and goes berserk, and the trauma apparently triggers Carrie's telekinetic abilities. A shower of ice chunks rains on the White residence. Later come stones, "whistling and screaming like bombs." In the Jackson novel the heroine "Eleanor Vance was thirty-two years old when she came to Hill House. . . .

Her name had turned up on Dr. Montague's list because one day, when she was twelve years old and her sister was eighteen, and their father had been dead for not quite a month, showers of stones had fallen on their house, without any indication of purpose or reason, dropping from the ceilings, rolling loudly down the walls. . . . The stones continued intermittently for three days, during which time Eleanor and her sister were less unnerved by the stones than by the neighbors and sight-seers . . . , and by their mother's blind, hysterical insistence that all of this was due to malicious, backbiting people on the block. . . .

If this incident and the reaction of Eleanor Vance's mother seem quite familiar to readers of King's first published novel, the name of Eleanor's sister should be familiar as well: Carrie.

In his early story "Strawberry Spring" from NIGHT SHIFT King portrays a college campus terrorized by a Jack-the-Ripper style killer. The narrator of the tale notices police cars parked near a dormitory where a murdered girl had lived. "On my way past there to my ten o'clock class I was asked to show my student I.D. I was clever. I showed him the one without the fangs."

That's a Chandlerism. At the beginning of Raymond Chandler's THE LADY IN THE LAKE private detective Philip Marlowe enters an office and goes over to the secretary. "I put my plain card, the one without the tommy gun in the corner, on her desk and asked to see Mr. Derace Kingsley." A ripper killer has a card without fangs, a detective has one without a tommy gun: the tone is identical. But Chandler demands more of his readers. Where King stops and explains to his audience that his Chandler-like joke is "clever" *before* he springs it, Chandler just hooks it in and assumes his readers are alert enough to weave, duck or roll with the punch.

In the 100th anniversary issue of *The Writer*, April 1987, King has a piece called "How IT Happened," where he discusses the origin of the novel in "The Three Billy-Goats Gruff" with the troll under the bridge — a bridge today runs over *sewers*, sewers are also tunnels, and as a kid in Strafford, Connecticut, the library King went to had a corridor (or tunnel or bridge) that lead from the *children's* section to the *adult* section. "I sensed something worse than a symbol; I sensed a THEME, and this made me nervous. I'm not a bright novelist, no Graham Greene or Paul Bowles. If I wrote a book with a conscious theme I would end up with a bunch of sound and fury." From the guy who has told us repeatedly what every one of his books is *Really About* for years now, that's pretty cute. Does he mean there might be *sub-texts* in IT? No, do go on now.

What is this novel really about, if it is not about recycling the recycled, throwing all the appropriated old bones in a bigger pot of stew? Back in the good old days of 1981 I liked to comment on how King typically ended his books by 1) burning the evil town or bad building down, or 2) blowing the town or bad building up. In IT he *sinks* the evil town and then drowns it like a dog, but when it comes to special effects, I vote for fires and explosions. Gosh, why couldn't King have blown Derry off the fucking map, just for old times' sake?

I wonder who exactly is supposed to find this book scary. Little kids usually go in for more compact fairy tales, ones without fairy bars and fairy murders in them; teenagers can see James Cameron's great film *Aliens* at a fraction of the cost and see a far better job done with (coincidentally) the same themes; and I'd think that all those years of "Little House on the Prairie" long ago exorcised the last traces of fear from the mind of those adults who originally saw Mike Landon in *I Was a Teenage Werewolf*, if they weren't laughing through the movie in the first place.

The only truly good thing that came out of reading IT was that I decided to reread the short story from which King appropriated the title, "It" by Theodore Sturgeon, published seven years before King was born. I regret to think that because of the massive advertising push given to the novel the public will come to think of the word "It" as a Stephen King title, because he doesn't deserve the honor. Sturgeon created an *original* modern fairy tale, at once charming and incredibly brutal, told in the simple language of the fairy story, set in the real world, and he did his IT with economy. As far as I'm concerned there is only one story worthy of the title, and IT isn't the one that weighs three and a half pounds. I cannot rate fiction by weight.

Those dark creative forces that first made THE SHINING so terrifying and later molded THE DEAD ZONE into such a *believable* narrative are like weak ghosts here, a run-down engine, mama, as ineffectual as this ultimate cosmic monster against a gang of determined kids.

At the self-proclaimed end of the first stage of his career (drum roll, anyone?), IT proves only that King is still one very fast, persistent typist.

II. On the Highway to Hell

In the chapter "King and the Critics" from THE STEPHEN KING PHENOMENON (no less than his fifth book about you-know-who), Michael R. Collings noticed that some of the popular criticism of King in newsprint "tends to ignore the works themselves and concentrates on *King* as personality—generally to his detriment." Collings specifically cites some of the articles about King's film *Maximum Overdrive* to support this point, but I say give these poor newspaper interviewers a break: you can't expect anyone to pay genuine attention to some dog movie, and working reporters have copy to turn in.

Collings does have a point, of course. These guys trash King. My favorite of the lot is Glenn Lovell, whose article "King Wants Them to Say Film Was Fun" was syndicated by the Knight-Ridder Newspapers. Lovell notes that King looks "at age 38 like a cross between Jerry Lewis and Li'l Abner," that he arches "Cro-Magnon eyebrows," and that he says things like: "God, save me from people who have no imagination because they're the most dangerous—belch—people in the world."

What's going on here?

What's going on is this: one day you're sipping fine wine and the next day you're stomping the grapes.

King is one of the most commercially successful writers in the world today, knocking down five million dollars in advance for new novels, but he has just now slipped a directorial foot into the door in Hollywood (or Wilmington, North Carolina, as the case may be), where Dino De Laurentiis paid him $70,000 to direct *Maximum Overdrive*. He's hot stuff in B. Dalton, Crown, and Waldenbooks, but his name really doesn't mean much to that much larger audience of horror-moviegoers, who would rather see Freddy Krueger than Stephen King. As Lovell said in his article, "After 11 motion pictures based on his novels and original screenplays . . . King's stock in Hollywood is down. His name no longer assures box office success. There hasn't been a hit King movie since *Carrie* and Stanley Kubrick's *The Shining*."

With *Maximum Overdrive* the thought seemed to be that if King actually *directed* the movie, got that old "Stephen King feeling" into the thing, then it might take off. The tag line on the ad was *Stephen King's masterpiece of terror directed by the Master himself.* But since King shows little talent for directing, much less mastery, few people bothered checking their brains at the box office.

If IT was the first key to my freedom as a King critic, *Maximum Overdrive* certainly was the second, a movie that lived up to every expectation I had for it.

Not that my expectations were high. By no means. I figured

it would suck, and it did. Almost everyone who saw it agrees with me; I find this refreshing. All I can say to people who haven't seen King's directorial debut is to save your money, maybe you'll find the videocassette in the middle of the street someday.

I knew *Maximum Overdrive* was going to be bad, simply because every time King makes a statement about the art of film he sounds like a moronic twelve-year-old. My favorite of many such comments is the one from vol. 2, no. 2 of PLAYBOY GUIDE: ELECTRONIC ENTERTAINMENT, where King says, "Movies are great fun—but I do mean 'movies,' not 'films.' I don't want to know about Fellini and what he was doing in his film that I didn't know he was doing. I like the kind of movies where you check your brain at the box office so the movies can wash over you with a lot of energy and color. I'm totally uninterested in pictures where people sit around in dingy hotel rooms talking about their wives' affairs with Nietzsche. I don't like Woody Allen movies." If you happened to see *Maximum Overdrive*, remember that it came out the same year as *Hannah and Her Sisters*, and drop me a note about which one of the two you figure really deserved the Oscar for best screenplay and best director of 1986, King or The Woodman.

In media statements about *Maximum Overdrive* King seems to apologize for his movie being so stupid by saying it was *meant* to be "a moron movie." You figure Dino didn't give King enough money to take a scary movie and he didn't want to invest any of his own millions, so he had to make a dumb movie instead. What the hell. Maybe King will do better next time.

I wouldn't bet on it. In the *Datebook* section of the *San Francisco Chronicle*, July 27, 1986, the new director repeated his statement that *Maximum Overdrive* is a moron movie, but added, "I don't say that to be mean. *Splash* is a moron movie unless you believe in mermaids. *Dracula* is one, unless you believe in vampires. The idea is"—here goes that twelve-year-old movie critic again—"you check your brains at the box office and pick 'em up again on the way out." If King actually thinks his movie is as good as *Splash* or *Dracula* because they are *all* "moron movies," then could he (*could* he?) possibly think it's on an even higher level of accomplishment? Could it be equal to a Tobe Hooper movie, a John Carpenter movie? Could it be equal to Hitchcock?

In the *Chronicle* interview reporter Calvin Ahlgren describes the scene early in *Maximum Overdrive* where King, "as a nerdy tourist," goes up to an ATM at a bank. We know something is going wrong, because the time-temperature display starts printing out "Fuck you . . . Fuck you" over and over. When King starts to withdraw some money, the computer screen flashes the message: "You are an asshole." As far as I'm concerned, that scene was the highlight of the movie. But King told Ahlgren:

> "Most of the critical raps I'm gonna take on this movie . . . are gonna have to do with that cameo." He was afraid critics would accuse him of pretentious self-comparison with the late Alfred Hitchcock. "It wasn't an *hommage* to Hitchcock," he said, "it was just a goof."

Whew! I'm glad King told us all that he wasn't "pulling a Hitchcock," he was just pulling "a goof." As soon as I saw the cameo I was sure I was in for a roller-coaster ride like *North By Northwest*, *Strangers on a Train*, possibly *The Lady Vanishes*, and if you believe that, you'll believe anything.

Is it any wonder that reporters got a little hostile, with King carefully explaining to them (would anyone have thought of it on his own) that he was not out to compare himself with Hitchcock? He told Ahlgren that "part of the package that went with script-writing and directing the film" was a publicity tour, with King agreeing to do media stopovers in seven cities. The De Laurentiis Entertainment Group scheduled King for nine stops, instead; King said—"I called my agent—the reason I didn't call DEG, was, I was p—ed and didn't want to say things I'd regret later." Some of King's unhappiness with the tour obviously transferred to the reporters given interview assignments, reflected in the "Li'l Abner"-style coverage many of them in turn gave him.

Essentially, King, used to sipping fine wine as a #1 bestselling writer, has climbed out of that beginner's rut where you have to get out and push the books by traveling endlessly cross-country. He's done it, he has done it for years, and like the big ape in another of Dino's big releases for 1986, *King Kong Lives*, "he's back — and he isn't happy." King doesn't seem to appreciate the point that in film circles he's nothing but another of a multitude of new kids on the set who may or may not make it to the top, and they expect him to get out there and stomp those grapes. When *Ishtar* appeared with the screaming whine of a very big bomb, Warren Beatty took it on himself to do a media blitz, appearing on talk show after talk show, trying to save that turkey. Beatty is better looking than King, and you know, I bet he's even *richer* than King, and he didn't seem to be complaining about the facts of life in filmland.

The movie itself isn't worth talking about, though one appropriation may rate a mention. The meanest tractor-trailer rig besieging the people in the roadside diner and gas station has as hood ornament the immense leering face of Spiderman's arch-foe, the Green Goblin, duly acknowledged as the property of Marvel Comics in the end credits. I kept wondering, Why doesn't one of these characters mention that the face belongs to the Green Goblin? Don't they recognize it? Stupid stereotypes like these people are *supposed* to read comic books. Does this mean they don't even read comic books?!

After thinking about it for a few minutes, I've come to the conclusion that the best piece of film which involves King is the commercial he made for American Express — he always *Carries* his American Express card, hoo-hoo-hoo. It's campy, fun, and his obvious peak as an actor. Next to the bank machine calling King an asshole, the best moment in *Maximum Overdrive* comes as endless lines of trucks pull into the gas station for refueling and hero Emilio Estevez says, "I hope they remembered their American Express cards." Like the in-jokes in *IT*, that moment provides *some* relief for the seriously bored.

I'd be curious to know what percentage of the audience caught the reference. Perhaps as many as caught some of the in-jokes in King's earlier screenplay for DEG, *Cat's Eye*, which begins with cameos by Cujo and Christine, and has a woman reading PET SEMATARY in bed in the last of the three episodes.

Surely everyone who was awake got those. A *lot* of people working in movies do this sort of thing, with Joe Dante one example of a modern master of the in-joke (in *The Howling*, to name just one of his films, among countless allusions and nods this way and that, Dante sets a scene in an occult bookshop, with *Famous Monsters of Filmland* editor Forrest J. Ackerman browsing the stock while holding the very issue of *Famous Monsters* in which Dante had his first publication). My favorite in-joke in *Cat's Eye*, by the way, occurred in the second episode, "The Ledge," in which Kenneth McMillan (as the bad guy) tells Robert Hays (as the hero) that if he manages to walk around the ledge of his penthouse apartment, then "You'll get the girl, the gold watch and everything"—a nod toward John D. MacDonald by King. MacDonald wrote the novel THE GIRL, THE GOLD WATCH AND EVERYTHING, and of course Robert Hays starred in the TV movie made from the book.

If only in-jokes could *make* a movie, King would have Hollywood by the short hairs, but it doesn't work that way. I understand why he wants to go on into film work, both for reasons of money and artistic ambition—if King is big, then someone like Spielberg is bigger, and new frontiers do beckon. But given his attitudes, I readily understand why reporters give King the movie-maker snotty write-ups.

I even can understand why commentators like Michael Collings feel it is necessary to cover junk like *Maximum Overdrive* in their studies, as if a "moron movie" was literature or something pretty close to it, deserving serious consideration. Jack Williamson, longtime writer of science fiction and fantasy, in the 25th anniversary issue of *Extrapolation* set up the basic explanation for the phenomenon of someone taking *Maximum Overdrive* seriously:

> Recently absorbed in the history of the old Incas and their fatal encounter with Francisco Pizarro, I've been struck with an image of the science fiction critic as a bloodless conquistador. His classic haunts had become as bare and poor as Pizarro's native Spain, the golden lodes of Shakespeare and Milton and Chaucer all worked out, the remaining minor poets yielding more pyrites than ore. In science fiction, he found a rich new empire, perhaps sadly given to

primitive simplicities and regrettable barbarisms, yet defenseless and ripe for the looting.

Add fantasy, horror, and mystery fiction to the new territory where literary strip-mining has begun, and end the explanation with a comment made by John Updike in his collection HUGGING THE SHORE, as he reviews the published version of one of Boswell's less interesting diaries: "The academic literature mill, having ground all the grain it can find, will grind chaff rather than shut down."

Chaff is all I'd expect to find on location in Wilmington, North Carolina. To find the true grain in Stephen King's 1986 crop look northwest to

III. Salem Rock, *Oregon*

No one truly expects quality work to come out of DEG studios in Wilmington, North Carolina; it is a perfect place for someone with King's expressed cinematic goals to write and direct. When you get right down to it, not that many people expect genuine *quality* to come out of Bangor, Maine, either. Sheila Benson of the *L.A. Times* said it best in her review of the other 1986 film based on King's writing:

> It should not turn anyone away from STAND BY ME to learn that it is based on a novella by Stephen King, written with that acuity that feels like autobiography. What the movie may do is send readers back to some of King's less celebrated, less cranked-out stories to see if they can possibly match up to this one (which was called "The Body"). Whoa! Come back here. It really is not that kind of Stephen King story.

Initially I didn't realize *Stand By Me* came from King. I heard a couple of radio ads for it, then another where Vern the fat kid says, "You guys want to go see a dead body?" *Hey*, that sounds like "The Body," thought I. But the promos kept saying it was *a Rob Reiner film. . . .*

It's easy to understand why someone making a serious film might ease King's name out of the pre-release publicity, kind of keep it quiet that another of his stories is about to project across the screen. Other stories to hit theatres have been *Children of the Corn*, *Firestarter*, *Cujo*, *The Dead Zone*, a list which goes from utter junk to the okay, but not a blockbuster, category. None of these had a screenplay by King, but *Creepshow*, *Cat's Eye*, and *Silver Bullet* did, and about the same may be said for them, despite King's personal involvement. Perhaps designers of the ad campaign wished to forestall the possibility that King would be extensively interviewed before *Stand By Me* had a chance to establish itself in the marketplace; what would have become of it if America had thought it was just another "moron movie"?

So it's easy to see why King was short-changed in the ads, why his name does not appear until the end credits. I think in a large sense *Stand By Me* is a Rob Reiner film more than it's a Stephen King film, though paradoxically most of its parts derive directly from King's plotline and dialogue. The movie is brilliant in the facets of King's work it omits, in subtle adaptations of story elements actually used.

Before now I've gone on record as admiring "The Body," certainly one of King's best stories. I said the sections with the boys out on their adventure are wonderful, and so they are: they make the story memorable. But most of the sections with the adult narrator, the kid who has grown up to be a writer whose successes sound much like King's own—those sections are kind of weepy, at times self-pitying. If it's possible to be a millionaire and still sing the blues, King comes close to it in a lot of these passages.

He also indulges himself to an extent that could have ruined the story, if not for the freedom to skim a reader always has available, by using complete "early" stories within his narrative to show how Gordie LaChance developed as a writer. The section called *The Revenge of Lard-Ass Hogan* is okay, and makes a great sequence in the movie. The filmmakers add a nice flourish when young Gordie concludes his tale by describing the epic pie-eating contest and puke-out engineered by the put-upon Lard-Ass as a "*BARF-O-RAMA*." This one needed touch makes the story roll on in the mind; in "The Body" King just lets it drop flat.

The section called *Stud City* is excess baggage in "The Body." When I first read it I skimmed around a lot, and still it was so tedious that I later recalled King using *two or three* stories like it within his narrative. It is so halting he may as well have inserted the 400 expurgated pages of THE STAND. *Stud City* supposedly is the first story the adult Gordie feels is really alive, his own beginning voice, and he tells us all about it in a supreme case of Author Intrusion, sidetracking the *real* story about the boys.

Rob Reiner and company know exactly what to do with *Stud City*. They drop it. They know what to do with the grown-up Gordie LaChance. They cut his ruminations way back to a reasonable level, just a voice-over here and there and Richard Dreyfuss appearing as The Writer at the opening and closing of the movie. Notice they resist any impulse to identify the narrator with King; he is not The Horror Writer.

The film also cuts a lot of unneeded melodrama out of the original plot. When King sets the scene for the boys locating the dead kid, a storm is stirring, and hailstones soon fill up Ray Brower's open unseeing eyes; in *Stand By Me* the kid simply is dead and there's not a storm in sight, and that's *fine*. In "The Body" not only does Chris Chambers die to kick off the author's ruminations, closely followed by the movie, but we learn at the end of the tale that Vern Tessio and Teddy Duchamp have preceeded him in death, one in a tenement fire, the other in a car crash. I'm happy to say that in the film they both end up in dead-end jobs, quiet, desperate, just like real life.

The only omission from King's story that bothered me in the film was the *consequence* of the boys standing up to the gang of older boys which also shows up to claim the Brower kid as their discovery; the Gordie LaChance mob wins that confrontation, but later on our heroes get stomped bad. That consequence is highly believable, but what a downer ending it would have made for the movie. . . .

Keyed off by the very West Coast names of young actors in *Stand By Me* River Phoenix and Kiefer Sutherland, I'm tempted to think of the artistic separation between "The Body" and the film, or King and Reiner, as one of Maine vs. California sensibilities. But then this whole business of King as a Maine and only-Maine writer is overblown. Reiner switches the action from King's well-used Castle Rock, Maine, to a Castle Rock he locates in Oregon, and it is quite acceptable, and even more believable for not having the unwieldy baggage of King's references to Cujo, Frank Dodd, and Shawshank Prison. The story doesn't need those in-jokes; unlike IT, it is interesting enough without them, *stronger* without them. Castle Rock, Oregon, is now a more believable place than Castle Rock, Maine, any day of the year with the possible exception of Halloween.

King impresses me not so much as a Maine writer but as a *small town writer*, Anywhere Except a Big City, U.S.A. After he shows the kids getting their lumps he segues to the end of his narrative, as the adult Gordie happens to see the gang leader, played by Donald Sutherland's son in the movie, exit a factory and enter a bar, where Gordie realizes the guy surely sits on his fat ass everyday, except Sunday. The whole adventure winds down to one guy of the four still living and the main bad guy living a life *he* probably enjoys—I doubt that a guy like that worries about any of his dead friends at great length while sitting in the bar. He's probably *happier* than the narrator, who has just bled hearts and horrors for 144 pages. What sanctuary has Gordie reached if this asshole gets the last scene?

In a sense I believe this down and disgusted attitude toward the unfairness and outright brutality of life is one of King's most important *literary* qualities; the sort of thing you have to take seriously, life being as it is. In a writer such as Jim Thompson, one of King's favorites, the quality of disgust reaches a fever pitch and pervades *everything* he writes, so today people are beginning to take Thompson as seriously as they take someone like Kafka. I doubt that King will ever reach comparable critical acclaim on that basis because it's hard to see *what* he should be disgusted about. Thompson wrote novel after novel and never made it big, but King did far better than the national average with his first book. However lowly his beginnings, the world-weariness and despair of a millionaire are hard to credit.

It's easier to see this stance as just another tool of the pro writer, and in fact you can find this facet of King's work encapsulated in a line describing a shopping mall from super-pro John D. MacDonald's CINNAMON SKIN: "Young mothers with tired and ugly expressions whopped their young with a fullarm swing, eliciting bellows of heartbreak." That's it, no?

Just enough of that bleakness is captured in *Stand By Me* to give it backbone and make it real; the overkill never made it as far as the cutting room floor. Reiner and company did King one better and did him a favor by forgetting the way he ended "The Body" and instead taking his conclusion to the 11th section, only a third of the way into the narrative, as their own: "I never had any friends later on like the ones I had when I was twelve. Jesus, did you?'

Stand By Me is the third key toward making a final statement as a King critic: proof that fine and even serious film *can* be brought out of his writing—but in some fifteen years of a very active career as a published novelist, it is appalling to realize how little material of the quality of the boys' quest in "The Body" King has provided for filmmakers to draw upon. Most of his writing so far transfers incredibly well into "moron movies," and one sees claustrophobic *tour de force* novels such as CUJO and MISERY as *primo* Movies of the Week for TV. Without a director like Reiner with piercing clarity to mirror King's best aspects and edit out his padded indulgences, I doubt that *Stand By Me* would have been better than *Cat's Eye* or *Firestarter*. It's legitimately a "Rob Reiner film." A "Stephen King movie," as now we all know, looks just like *Maximum Overdrive*.

IV. The King Watch

When King made the cover article in *Time*, October 6, 1986, he responded to the question "When are you going to write something serious?" by saying, "My answer is that I'm serious as I can be every time I sit down at a typewriter." He also stated: "I get upset about being compared with certain brand-name writers who sell megabillions of copies. Michener is one. I can't read him. Ludlum is another one. I was paid to review one of his books. He's the clumsiest, most awful writer. No style." The last keys turn in the lock.

I sometimes ponder how a man can sit down and one day write a story as good as "Apt Pupil" or the kids' section of "The Body," and later write the screenplay for *Maximum Overdrive*, where a presumed highlight occurs when a truck filled with boxes of toilet paper explodes, dropping smoldering squeezable rolls all over the tarmac. King *says* he's putting *everything* he's got into every story he does; he's been saying so for a long time now. I wonder if he's subject to astral influences?

In the afterword to DIFFERENT SEASONS King noted that he wrote "The Body." upon completing the first draft of 'SALEM'S LOT and "Apt Pupil" upon finishing the initial draft of his next novel, THE SHINING, "and following *Apt Pupil* I wrote nothing for three months—I was pooped." Whatever flaws it might have, THE SHINING is King's scariest novel, and I think "Apt Pupil" his best story. Maybe the stars *were* right from "The Body" through "Apt Pupil," and other highpoints in his career have been sheer professionalism winning through, or the rare personal story exemplified by "The Woman in the Room," where King in a burst of emotional release tried harder.

Whatever the explanation, it's clear that King does not want to think of himself as providing a certain kind of commercial fodder for the bestseller marketplace, not like a Michener or a Ludlum, even though that's precisely what he has been doing for the last few years. Frankly, my major interest in King today is in following his sales position on the *New York Times* bestseller list, since beginning with IT in 1986 we are in the midst of what one of his publishers termed "a Stephen King firestorm," as he releases four novels in only fifteen months, instead of the traditional one hardcover per year of major bestsellers such as Michener, Ludlum, or pre-IT King.

A King fan once told me that King was one of the best writers of all time because he is the bestselling writer of all time. I interjected, You mean he's the bestselling *horror* writer of all time. No, this woman said, he's sold more books than *anybody.* I told her I was pretty sure, and I am, that epic romance novelist Danielle Steel has sold about as many books as King; very few people seem to be putting *her* forth as one of the best writers ever. King's sales have not come close to those of the prolific and popular mystery writers Erle Stanley Gardner and Agatha Christie, to name two writers with sales in the hundreds of millions. As King himself suggests, maybe "megabillions" Ludlum and Michener have sold more books than he has. I don't doubt that they have.

There is a phenomenon, seen in such series as the James Bond films or George Lucas's *Star Wars* movies, where each new release in the series sells more tickets and therefore makes more money (even if it's in inflated dollars) than the previous one. When the Bonds first switched from Sean Connery to Roger Moore most critics and hardcore Bond fans thought it was a mistake, but the Moore Bonds did better, grossed more and more with each film up to the last one, and now with Timothy Dalton as 007 the series is doing even better. King had this sort of roll going with PET SEMATARY, which on release did better than previous novels, and I guess that IT sold even better than that.

I suspect that this phenomenon is produced simply because the world population increases every year, and the market for everything, but especially escapist entertainment, is always expanding. As recently as the 1960s, a sale of 2000 copies of a hardcover novel was enough to make the publisher back his advance and production costs; today a 2000 copy press run is symptomatic of a specialty press, aimed at a select audience. The appearances on top ten sales lists of sequels such as Asimov's FOUNDATION'S EDGE or Clarke's 2010 reflect this phenomenon and expanded marketplace.

IT rocketed the King firestorm off, holding the number one slot from its October 1986 release until almost Christmas, when Clavell's WHIRLWIND bumped IT to number two. After a couple of weeks, IT returned to first place and WHIRLWIND sank to second. Overall, IT maintained a position in the top ten about 32 weeks.

When THE EYES OF THE DRAGON appeared, it too instantly hit #1, while IT hovered in third place on the list. After EYES had been top ten for two months, IT was gone, down to that relatively anonymous section of sales from #11 through #20 and lower where novels by writers such as John Updike usually hold their places.

THE EYES OF THE DRAGON was #1 for one week. The next week Sidney Sheldon's WINDMILLS OF THE GODS bumped it to #2. When Danielle Steel's FINE THINGS appeared, EYES dropped to #3. New titles from Dick Francis and others bounced EYES further down the list, but it rallied back up to #3 in its thirteenth week of release, then slowly sank to seventh, eighth place.

When EYES had been out for eighteen weeks the next firestorm burst came: MISERY, instantly #1 on release. That week EYES was in seventh place. The next EYES was ninth. The next it was gone from the top ten, the firestorm showing a distant fizzle. MISERY stayed #1 for seven weeks, got bounced to #2 in its eighth week as Turow's PRESUMED INNOCENT passed it in sales, and the following week dropped to #3 as Tom Clancy's third novel, PATRIOT GAMES, took first place upon publication.

I find the dynamics of this King watch far more interesting than the plots of any of his new novels, and I'm curious to see how future books fare. A science fiction tale called THE TOMMYKNOCKERS is the last "official" release in the four book firestorm. By summer 1988 a couple more titles should be available, however, since King recently sold reprint rights to the two books in his Dark Tower series, THE GUNSLINGER and THE DRAWING OF THE THREE, for nine million dollars; curiously, when THE GUNSLINGER first appeared in a "limited" edition of 10,000 copies in 1982, an afterword by the author explained how he would never allow the book to be reprinted. After those the only other King book on the near horizon is an unexpurgated edition of THE STAND, containing the 400 or so pages excised from the Doubleday first edition.

Or so King told Tyson Blue in an interview in *Twilight Zone*, December 1986; King explained that he was, after this "firestorm," cutting back on releasing books. *Why*? "Because it's *time*," King said. "I mean, you do kind of wear people out after a while and they say, 'Oh well, it's another Stephen King book.

Ayuh. Big deal."' King even may have predicted his fall from the top ten when he indicated to Blue that, "With the publication of IT, King plans to finish his exploration of the theme of horror and children, which has been a mainstay of much of his work to date." That's akin to Ludlum announcing that he has finished his exploration of the theme of espionage and international intrigue.

While the phenomenon of escalating sales certainly exists, the fact remains that people will at some point get sick of anything, as the material reaches some indefinable saturation point. James Bond movies are hot now, but Tarzan movies were hot once too. For years westerns ruled TV, today they are as dead as the dust blowing off Boot Hill.

A few years ago William Peter Blatty sued the *New York Times* for leaving LEGION, his sequel to THE EXORCIST, off their list, saying "so much is tied up with the *Times* bestseller list in terms of increased quantities stocked by bookstores, rights sales to paperback companies and foreign houses, movie adaptations, everything." Pat Holt wrote up this incident in the book section of the *San Francisco Chronicle* for September 18, 1983, quoting Blatty:

> "The TIMES sends out a list of 36 preselected titles which booksellers are supposed to rate according to sales. There is room on the form for people to write in unlisted titles that are selling well, but you know, write-in candidates don't win elections. . . . It's time someone asked what is so 'scientific' about the *Times* 'scientific sampling based on actual sales figures.' Why was it, for example, that Judith Rossner's AUGUST, with 50,000 copies in print, appeared as Number 3 on the list when LEGION, with at least 70,000 copies in print, wasn't even a candidate?"

As Holt said, "Hm. *How delicious.*"

If King was the coming player in the top ten sweeps for a few years, he's being aced out now. Following the King watch I couldn't help but notice how fast and sure Tom Clancy, with only three novels, has become the hot new ticket on the *New York Times* bestseller list, how a wave of Clancy imitations is hitting the bookracks just as that wave of King imitations began their deluge soon after 'SALEM'S LOT and THE SHIN-ING. The superstar phenomenon itself is fascinating. I recall the couple of years when Peter Frampton was the hot number in rock music, and listen with some attention as the partisans of Michael Jackson and Prince argue who's hot, who's not.

The *Time's* list of bestsellers for 1986 put IT in first place and Clancy's second novel, RED STORM RISING, second. King's second published novel, 'SALEM'S LOT, wasn't even in the top *twenty* the year it was published, for those who may be keeping count—but then Clancy has the advantage of the expanded marketplace.

I personally cannot believe that overall IT outsold RED STORM RISING. IT was #1 for a couple of months until WHIRLWIND appeared and they jockeyed for first place, but then RED STORM RISING, an earlier release which had descended the chart, rose again to #1 for several weeks, dropped only to come back up—for almost fifty weeks, compared to IT's thirty. RED STORM RISING was #7 on the top ten hardcover list the week before the paperback edition, typically issued a year after the hardback, hit the stands. Maybe IT *would* have made such a comeback if THE EYES OF THE DRAGON had not drained off sales; maybe King's *magnum opus* would have held at the top through the release of MISERY, too. Who knows?

I doubt that there is any inherent super-sales power in King's *prose* today; it rests with his *brand name*, as honestly and luckily won as Michener's or Ludlum's. The current "firestorm" was started, we've been told, because THINNER was selling so well at the same time as THE TALISMAN, the publishers realized the market for King *could* support more than the usual one hardcover novel a year. Pretty much everyone in the fantasy field had heard the rumors that King was "Richard Bachman," and bought up the copies of the first printing of THINNER as investments, but let's face it, King collectors aren't numerous enough to support a bestseller. THINNER was well promoted when it first appeared under the Bachman by-line, but didn't sell well enough to make top ten competition for THE TALISMAN until *after* King's authorship was revealed to the public in a media blitz that swept newspapers and radio across America; in case anyone did not hear the news, NAL soon put King's name on the cover of the book so copies wouldn't sit unrecognized in stores. The earlier Bachman books were in no fashion competing effectively with King's own titles, and neither was THINNER by "Richard Bachman." Money was not being made at an alarming rate.

I doubt too that super-sales power will adhere in King's brand name attached to an unfamiliar product such as The Dark Tower books or THE TOMMYKNOCKERS, since King is at his worst when he tries to write science fiction. Out of the three firestorm novels in release at this moment, IT, nothing but a rewrite of familiar King themes, did incredibly well; MISERY seems hot too; but THE EYES OF THE DRAGON with only one week at #1 and twenty weeks in the top ten (spectacular enough by ordinary standards) must be something of a disappointment to anyone looking at the profit logs for IT. The audience may indeed be tired of just "another Stephen King book"—or possibly they don't want to read a *children's book* by their "horror writer" anymore than they'd want to read a novel about college life by Ludlum.

I get the feeling that the "firestorm" is just a way of unloading a lot of backed-up material while King is still more hot than not. He told Tyson Blue in *Twilight Zone* magazine that he is making no plans to have other new novels published in the next two or three years, so the firestorm is over. THE GUNSLINGER and THE STAND are both several years old. THE EYES OF THE DRAGON first appeared in a limited edition in 1984. King has been talking about THE TOMMYKNOCKERS for some years, as well. Only MISERY and THE DRAWING OF THE THREE appear to be fairly recent work, though some attempt has been made to make the new releases *look* current. In the back of IT there is a note stating: "This book was begun in Bangor, Maine, on September 9th, 1981, and completed in Bangor, Maine, on December 28th, 1985." Hey, that means IT was finished less than a year before publication! Of course, Doug Winter in his STEPHEN KING: THE ART OF DARKNESS, writes that the first draft of IT was *completed in 1980*, "after a year of writing. . . ." An excerpt from far into the novel appeared in the souvenir book from the 7th World Fantasy Convention held in October 1981. We're reading a novel that goes back in point of creation several years, with possible late additions of AIDS and other hot items, but for fun let's believe the hype that it comes burning off the word processor, just like all the other books in the firestorm, and was barely held back from tearing that big hole right through 1986. . . .

If an unexpurgated THE STAND comes to pass, that is the book I predict will produce a huge counter-burn against the firestorm, if it doesn't damper itself before then. Presumably the book was edited for *reasons* other than sheer length. In an issue of *Whispers* magazine devoted to King I read his prologue to THE SHINING, cut before Doubleday issued the novel. That prologue would have ruined the book for me; it gave away everything, up to and including the dead woman in the tub. I'd have preferred not to have read that prologue at all, if I could have known. Whoever cut it was a wise editor, and I believe the same man at Doubleday edited THE STAND.

A huge number of people already have read THE STAND; will 400 pages more transform the experience, or only make it tedious? I say a fatter STAND will be the 1989, 1990 or 1991 equivalent to Bruce Springsteen's multi-side monster live album of 1986, which got incredibly heavy rotation on radio, huge promotion, and was heralded as one of the fastest-selling records in history. By June 1987 *Spin* magazine would note: "The *coldest* record on the market right now is the Bruce Springsteen live box. Despite the hype and enormous initial orders, Columbia has now been *forced* to refuse returns from stores that *can't sell* the thing."

V. The Summation

In 1986, the year of King's monster-mashed *magnum opus* and directorial debut, his career lost for me that aura of unknown potentialities and resolved into a limitable pattern. From statements he's dropped in the past it's obvious King considers himself the equal or better of "intellectual" writers like Joseph Heller; now it's equally obvious he feels he's a hell of a lot more talented than other blockbuster bestsellers like Michener. If we're given the *possibility* that there are better writers than King who make less money, and poorer writers who may make more money, then what's the call?

Many people today are saying Clive Barker is the next really big name in horror; King himself has said he sees the *future* of horror in Barker's writing. Certainly Barker, less inhibited than King, creates stories that tear at the sensibilities with even more sharply graphic gore, and that is the product modern horror fandom, bred on graphically violent film, *wants* in tales of terror.

I don't find Barker that much more original than King in his storylines, and have no particular enthusiasm (nor dislike) for his work. As an old drinking buddy of mine put it, "The BOOKS OF BLOOD are just print versions of horror-anthology films like the Robert Bloch-scripted *Asylum* — you have a loose framework connecting one story that's kind of funny, one that's average, and one that goes for the throat."

I wouldn't argue that Barker already has usurped King's favored position among inner circles of horror fans. He certainly knows what he's doing, because he's moving over into film work more quickly and with more assurance than King. If you saw *Creepshow II* perhaps you were as embarrassed as I was to see George Kennedy and Dorothy Lamour in the segment about "Old Chief Woodenhead," one of two sequences King plotted just for this film. *At least they're being paid to appear in this crap*, I thought, finding it difficult to believe that this George Romero production actually found its way to the screen. It more than revives the downward spiral of King films; it's worse than *Maximum Overdrive*. Clive Barker has done better with his first film *Hellraiser*.

In film work resides the real potential and major artistry in what we call "modern horror" — not on the shelves of "occult" novels which rewrite DRACULA for the ten-thousandth time. With Hitchcock's *Psycho*, film became equal, if not indeed superior, at presenting modern horror. Surely the book and film of *Rosemary's Baby* and *The Exorcist* run neck-and-neck, cut-and-throat. I'd rate the films *Kwaidan*, *The Saragossa Manu-*

script, and Polanski's *Repulsion* and *The Fearless Vampire Killers* more highly than any horror novels of their decade, and I wouldn't trade *Texas Chainsaw Massacre*, *The Tenant*, *Don't Look Now*, *The Thing*, *Return of the Living Dead*, or James Cameron's action-packed *The Terminator* and *Aliens* for *every horror novel* published since CARRIE, *and* I'll take De Palma's film over King's novel any day of the week. If you want *great* modern horror, go to the theatre not to the bookstore, though for the indiscriminate, lots of junk may be had at either place.

Barker may well move successfully from writing books to directing film, where critics can match him up against Cronenberg and company. But he'll never assume King's position as Bestselling Horror Writer. Barker's stories are too graphic and feature too much aberrant sexuality to sell enough books at the supermarket. They are like unto *The National Enquirer* back in the 1960s when it displayed articles on torso murders and tiger attacks in the Punjab. With that male sex-sweat-and-blood emphasis, which of course is Barker's emphasis, the *Enquirer* peaked at sales of, what was it, eight million? fifteen million? copies a week—a *lot* of copies, to be sure, but not *half* the copies sold when the magazine switched its target audience to women shoppers—that larger audience that buys Stephen King novels, too.

I personally have trouble thinking of all these women *en masse* as a minority, especially when writing about books in general or what is known as modern horror in specific. Statistically, we know women buy the majority of books sold, which accounts for the success of such obvious categories as cookbooks and romance novels, and I have no doubt that women buy more mystery novels than do men. About the only categories that one would limit to male readers anymore might be the *muy macho* men-of-action paperbacks, certain cretinous war novels, and John Norman's Gor books. Even science fiction, if we get right down to simplifications, where writers have been supported for decades by pimply teenage boys, today must have as many female readers as male, and the new sf writers seem split pretty much 50-50 by sex, and I bet editorial positions in New York tip in favor of women.

Horror also gives equal time or better to women, at least if we're talking books sold. The *Chicago Tribune* syndicated an article in October 1986 that listed the ten bestselling horror-occult paperbacks compiled by the Association of American Publishers, presumably for the previous sales year. Two women and one man are on the list, which reads:

1. PET SEMATARY, Stephen King
2. FLOWERS IN THE ATTIC, V. C. Andrews
3. NIGHT SHIFT, King
4. PETALS IN THE WIND, Andrews
5. IF THERE BE THORNS, Andrews
6. MY SWEET AUDRINA, Andrews
7. THE STAND, King
8. INTERVIEW WITH THE VAMPIRE, Anne Rice
9. HEAVEN, Andrews
10. THINNER, King

As the article says, "Surprisingly, however, Andrews, the lesser known of the two, has five books on the list to King's four." It is not a surprise that the late V. C. Andrews would go toe-to-toe with King on sales, or that Anne Rice would be the only writer to crack their stranglehold on the top ten, if you have any idea of who buys these paperbacks. King in MISERY knowingly has a romance writer help captive by a deranged *woman* reader—he *could* have done the novel with a horror writer held captive by a crazed male reader of age 26-42, but that wouldn't have reflected the larger Truth of the marketplace.

Highpoints in novels of "modern horror" may be traced from Shirley Jackson writing in the 1950s, one of the finest stylists to grace the field, the first new horror writer (if we wish to call her that) truly accepted by the mainstream audience, that wider pool of women who buy most of the books. Jackson was just prolific enough to keep the fiction coming and make a real name for herself, instead of quitting after a book or two. Immediately post-Jackson we find Ira Levin with a woman protagonist in ROSEMARY'S BABY, motherhood the big concern; Blatty with a possessed young girl in THE EXORCIST; Tryon playing out basic fertility rites in HARVEST HOME, one of the sexiest horror novels as well as one where the women really kick ass.

King's position in this progression is easy enough to tab — he came onto the scene with CARRIE, after all. Whatever his skills as a storyteller may be, at this point I'd give almost equal weight to *who* King is for his continuing position at the top. He's a devoted family man, loves his children; he's rich, but he hasn't turned his wife over for a golddigger. Because of this stability in his personal life, stereotypical women readers *know* he's a "safe" horror writer to read. I just met one woman who loves King's books, though she tells me she skips over the scary parts. I suspect the vast majority of his readers have no interest in horror as such and never go to see horror movies. The vocal minority of inner circle horror fans may yell in disagreement, saying *they* go to horror movies, but again they do not constitute a large enough audience to carry King's sales out of the horror paperback ghetto where *most* writers of horror find themselves today. If you're part of that majority and are going to read a horror paperback, who could offer a safe read like King? — well, maybe a woman, like V. C. Andrews or Anne Rice.

I now believe, by the way, that CARRIE is King's one anomalous creation, almost like the moment Edgar Rice Burroughs devised Tarzan or Doyle came up with Sherlock Holmes, supercharged concepts that soon became myths of the pop culture. In the movie *Harry and the Hendersons* the teenage girl reacts with horror to the idea that her family will keep a Bigfoot in the house; she shouts that she will lose all her friends and she'll have "pig's blood dumped on me!" Whether the musical play of *Carrie* now being prepared for Broadway eventually does well or bombs, it reinforces the notion that in his first published book, in the figure of Carrie White, bleeding in the locker room and devastating the prom, King came up with a concept that may last, if not in reprintings of his novel, then in the film, the musical, and other adaptations, expanding beyond the parameters of his fiction into a minor myth in the culture.

Otherwise, I do not see any particular lasting power in King's works. If he does take a break in releasing novels for a few years, King's obvious successor as a top ten Bestseller Horror Writer, someone who can titillate but not turn off the bestseller audience, is already on the scene: Dean Koontz, a pro who has been writing longer than King, more slowly working his way up to his current position as one of the highest paid writers in America. The only thing I can see that's keeping Koontz from the very peak is that King is in the way. If King drops out for awhile, I expect Koontz, not Barker, to drop in.

Like King, Koontz is a pro writer who says he writes hours a day, nearly every day. I admit that however much I respect their industry, I've personally read too much of this kind of writer, and I'm retiring. Raymond Chandler, one of my favorites, who said "I write when I can and I don't when I can't," expressed my opinion before I was born, in a 1949 letter:

> I'm always seeing little pieces by writers about how they don't ever wait for inspiration; they just sit down at their little desks every morning at eight, rain or shine, hangover and broken arm and all, and bang out their little stint. However blank their minds or dull their wits, no nonsense about inspiration from them. I offer them my admiration and take care to avoid their books.

Until 1986 I had some hope that King might do something better than his best and generally better than his worst, or else *why* write about him? Appropriating a quote from Nietzsche: "Insects sting, not in malice, but because they want to live. It is the same with critics: they desire our blood, not our pain." I no longer expect anything great to come from King. An appropriated quote from another of my favorites, Flannery O'Connor, sums up my funk: "Everywhere I go I'm asked if I think the universities stifle writers. My opinion is that they don't stifle enough of them. There's many a bestseller that could have been prevented by a good teacher."

So what's the call?

In my opinion, if King keeps writing at a reasonable professional rate, averaging at least one book a year, producing fiction into his sixties, then he will end up in a position highly comparable to that of the late John D. MacDonald, who gave King his approval in his introduction to NIGHT SHIFT fairly early in

King's career. MacDonald didn't take long to recognize a fellow pro, and as I noted in my first essay on King, MacDonald singled out as best story in the collection "The Last Rung"—gimmicky, fake-emotional, a pro-writerly *product*, instead of King's honesty emotional "The Woman in the Room."

On many levels this is a very favorable call. I think it's accurate. MacDonald tried a fair variety of story types, seldom got too pretentious with his work, was a writer immensely admired by his professional peers; all this already applies to King, who now only needs to show comparable staying power. No matter that MacDonald might be classed, inadequately, as a "crime" writer—as a bestseller he has more in common with King the "horror" writer than King has in common with classic terrorists H. P. Lovecraft, Arthur Machen or M. R. James.

King's narrative voice, his sense of humor, his competent nuts-and-bolts handling of action set-pieces all reflect MacDonald, whose writing King has expressed return admiration for. Even King's comment to Tyson Blue in *Twilight Zone* that he is going to take some time off and "just sorta let the well fill back up" is the kind of remark MacDonald's series character Travis Magee makes at the end of a hard salvage operation, as he sets out for a pleasure cruise on the *Busted Flush* to patch his wounds.

Apparently many writers were angry at MacDonald's death, feeling he never got enough recognition. I suppose by this they mean that he never won the Pulitzer or the Nobel nor ever got truly serious consideration against writers such as Hemingway, Faulkner or Steinbeck. Still, like King, he earned a lot of money by his writing. He was a *bestseller*, *recognized* in the marketplace. In *practical* terms, *what could be better?* It's amazing how the concepts of *Honors* and *Literature* do more than survive.

If the Pulitzer and Nobel mean anything, *I* don't think MacDonald deserved either for his work. Certainly enough literary non-entities have won the prizes in the past, and most intelligent readers wouldn't recognize the names of some winners who are kept alive, if at all, *zombie*-like in academia. But I believe in standards, such as not judging books by weight, and do not consider MacDonald's output, or King's, that good overall. I think THE GIRL, THE GOLD WATCH AND EVERYTHING is fun, just as 'SALEM'S LOT is fun, but then I think Edgar Rice Burroughs's THE GODS OF MARS is fun too, and it doesn't deserve a Pulitzer. THE EXECUTIONERS was done better as the film *Cape Fear*: they improved MacDonald's plot as much as Reiner improved "The Body." SLAM THE BIG DOOR, THE BRASS CUPCAKE, and other hard-boiled titles by MacDonald are good books of their kind, but I can name a few dozen others just as good, and disagree with anyone who'd rank MacDonald higher than Hammett, Chandler or Jim Thompson based on those novels—or people who'd place King higher on the lists of horror than William Hope Hodgson, H. P. Lovecraft or Shirley Jackson based on his epic appropriations.

The Travis Magee series, a sales strategy that put MacDonald on the top ten after years of writing, is at best comparable to television, great mindless reading for an airplane flight. If you say MacDonald deserves a Nobel for the series, I'll laugh.

The closest King has come to the Magee books is in talking about a sequel to 'SALEM'S LOT. If he does RETURN TO 'SALEM'S LOT in a few years, in a few years more dare I say we'll see 'SALEM'S LOT III? By then the state of literature may be so shoddy that it might even win a Pulitzer.

That's my call. Welcome to it. In one last appropriation, Travis Magee's bear-pelted pal Meyer says in FREE FALL IN CRIMSON (1981), speaking of a cult director of a couple of motorcycle films (who enjoys the sort of dubious reputation King might conceivably derive from *Maximum Overdrive*):

". . . you have put your finger on the artistic conundrum we all struggle with. How, in these days of intensive communication on all levels, can you tell talent from bullshit? Everybody is as good, and as bad, as anybody wants to think they are."

ABOUT THE AUTHORS

*D*ENNIS ETCHISON is one of the most respected writers in the field of modern horror. His stories have been collected in THE DARK COUNTRY, RED DREAMS, and THE BLOOD KISS, and he authored the paperback novelization from John Carpenter's film *The Fog*. His dramatic adaptation of Stephen King's "The Mist" has been performed on radio. Recently he edited CUTTING EDGE, an anthology of all-new tales of terror. Etchison lives in Los Angeles.

WHOOPI GOLDBERG is a talented actress of stage and screen. Her performance in *The Color Purple* won her an Oscar nomination. More recently she has starred in the action-comedies *Jumping Jack Flash*, *Burglar* and *Fatal Beauty*. Goldberg once said that after romantic comedies of the 1930s, her favorite film *genre* was horror movies of the 1950s.

MARV WOLFMAN has the distinction of having published Stephen King's first story over twenty years ago in a comic book fan magazine. He went on to a career as a professional comic book writer, in time serving on the scripting and editorial staffs for Warren Magazines, Marvel Comics and DC. Among the dozens of titles he has written are *Tomb of Dracula* and *Teen*

Titans, this last one of the most popular comics of the past decade.

FRANK BELKNAP LONG was a frequent contributor to early issues of *Weird Tales* and a prominent member of the literary circle which gravitated around the person of H. P. Lovecraft. Among his many books are the rare poetry volumes A MAN FROM GENOA and THE GOBLIN TOWER, the novel THE HORROR FROM THE HILLS, the story collections THE HOUNDS OF TINDALOS and THE RIM OF THE UNKNOWN, plus dozens of others in the fields of science fiction and gothics. His memoir of his good friend and mentor, HOWARD PHILIPS LOVECRAFT: DREAMER ON THE NIGHTSIDE, is in print from Arkham House.

BURTON HATLEN is a Professor of English at the University of Maine in Orono, where he once taught a student named Stephen King. His poetry has appeared in *The Beloit Poetry Journal* and *The Minnesota Review*, and he has written essays on DRACULA and FRANKENSTEIN for the *Bucknell Review*. An earlier essay, "Beyond the Kittery Bridge," appeared in FEAR ITSELF: *The Horror Fiction of Stephen King*.

CHARLES WILLEFORD is the author of sixteen novels, including COCKFIGHTER, PICKUP, THE BURNT ORANGE HERESY, and the series of crime novels about Inspector Hoke Moseley of the Miami police department: MIAMI BLUES, NEW HOPE FOR THE DEAD, SIDESWIPE and THE WAY WE DIE NOW. His volumes of autobiography include A GUIDE FOR THE UNDEHE-MORRHOIDED and SOMETHING ABOUT A SOLDIER. For many years he has been the mystery and suspense reviewer for the *Miami Herald*.

J. N. WILLIAMSON is one of the most prolific authors of modern horror, with almost forty novels—GHOST, THE EVIL ONE, HORROR HOUSE, THE EVIL OFFSPRING and anthologies—MASQUES I and II, and nearly one hundred stories to his credit. One of the original sixty founding members of the Baker

Street Irregulars, the international Sherlock Holmes fan club, Williamson recently helped inaugurate another organization by serving as first term secretary-treasurer of the new Horror Writers of America. Among recent titles is how-to book edited for Writer's Digest, HOW TO WRITE TALES OF HORROR, FANTASY AND SCIENCE FICTION.

L. SPRAGUE DE CAMP is a Grand Master of American fantasy, having written and edited well over one hundred books in a career that now spans half a century. Titles which de Camp has authored or co-authored include TALES FROM GAVAGAN'S BAR, THE INCOMPLETE ENCHANTER, WALL OF SERPENTS, and THE TRITONIAN RING. He has edited and added to Robert E. Howard's series of stories about Conan the barbarian and served as a consultant on the films. Among his non-fiction titles are THE SCIENCE FICTION HANDBOOK and biographies of H. P. Lovecraft and Robert E. Howard.

THOMAS TESSIER is the author of what many people consider to be *the* classic modern werewolf novel, THE NIGHTWALKER. His other novels include THE FATES, SHOCKWAVES, and PHANTOM. FINISHING TOUCHES is thought to be one of the most frightening horror novels of the last five years. Tessier lives in Watertown, Connecticut.

THOMAS M. DISCH is a wide-ranging author whose work includes poetry, the children's book THE BRAVE LITTLE TOASTER, the modern horror novel THE BUSINESSMAN, and such books of speculative fiction as CAMP CONCENTRATION, THE GENOCIDES, and FUN WITH YOUR NEW HEAD, among many other titles. He lives in New York, where he served for almost two years as book critic for *Twilight Zone* magazine.

GUY N. SMITH of England is another of the most prolific writers of modern horror, beginning with WEREWOLF BY MOONLIGHT in 1974, continuing with NIGHT OF THE CRABS, WOLFCURSE, WARHEAD, ACCURSED, MANIA, CANNIBALS, ABOMINATION, BLOODSHOW, ALLIGATORS and many other novels. In DANSE MACABRE Stephen King singled out the *title* of one of Smith's novels as his "nominee for all-time pulp horror classic: THE SUCKING PIT."

PETER TREMAYNE is the author of nearly twenty-five books, most in the horror-fantasy genre. Recent titles include RAVEN OF DESTINY, MY LADY OF HY-BRASIL, ZOMBIE! and BLOOD-MIST! His books have been translated into many European languages and he has the unique distinction of being the only modern fantasy writer to have been published in all six Celtic languages. Several of his stories have seen print in Irish before their English appearances.

STANLEY WIATER is a critic, short story writer and cineteratologist whose articles and fiction have appeared in *Twilight Zone*, *Fangoria*, *Prevue*, and *Horrorstruck*. Some of his interviews with Stephen King appeared recently in Underwood-Miller's BARE BONES. His first published story was the winner of a competition judged by King in 1980. Wiater and his wife Iris live in Massachusetts.

BILL WARREN is a film archivist and reviewer, author of KEEP WATCHING THE SKIES, a book on 1950s science fiction movies. He has worked on *Famous Monsters of Filmland* and acted as Walt Lee's main assistant on his REFERENCE GUIDE TO FANTASTIC FILM. Part one of his study of "The Movies and Mr. King" appeared in FEAR ITSELF in 1982.

BEN P. INDICK is a familiar name as a commentator on writers of fantasy, horror, and science fiction. He has essayed the writings of Ray Bradbury, L. Frank Baum, Robert Nathan, J.R.R. Tolkien, and many others, including several articles about the work of Stephen King. Indick is a founder and still active member of the Lovecraftian amateur press association the Esoteric Order of Dagon. In his spare time for the past thirty-five years he has worked as a professional pharmacist, for himself and for others.

DENNIS RICKARD is a longtime student of horror literature. He acted as a chairman for the 3rd World Fantasy Convention held in Los Angeles in 1977. His book THE FANTASTIC ART OF CLARK ASHTON SMITH is a photographic survey of the weird paintings and grotesque carvings in stone of this prominent member of the Lovecraft Circle. Rickard has written essays for NYCTALOPS, and did a definitive study of the horror fiction of Robert E. Howard for the critical volume THE DARK BARBARIAN.

DARRELL SCHWEITZER, author of THE SHATTERED GODDESS, WE ARE ALL LEGENDS, TOM O'BEDLAM'S NIGHT OUT, and other books, is a reviewer, interviewer, and critic. His short fiction has appeared in NIGHT CRY and THE YEAR'S BEST HORROR STORIES. For Starmont Books he is editing a "discovery" series, which includes DISCOVERING H. P. LOVECRAFT, DISCOVERING STEPHEN KING, DISCOVERING MODERN HORROR, *etc*. Schweitzer has worked on the editorial staff of *Isaac Asimov's Science Fiction Magazine*, *Amazing Science Fiction*, and the newly revived *Weird Tales*, and is a co-author of ON WRITING SCIENCE FICTION: THE EDITORS STRIKE BACK.

DON HERRON has written on the work of Stephen King for FEAR ITSELF, DISCOVERING STEPHEN KING, KINGDOM OF FEAR, THE PENGUIN ENCYCLOPEDIA OF HORROR AND THE SUPERNATURAL and *Newsday*. He has also edited a critical study on Robert E. Howard, THE DARK BARBARIAN, and written a guide book to literary sites in northern California, THE LITERARY WORLD OF SAN FRANCISCO AND ITS ENVIRONS. For over a decade he has led the Dashiell Hammett Tour in San Francisco. Herron is a frequent contributor to books and periodicals about fantasy, horror and mystery fiction.

TIM UNDERWOOD and CHUCK MILLER are publishers, editors, book packagers and co-founders of Underwood-Miller, an independent press specializing in genre literature and contemporary American culture. Their highly acclaimed limited editions have received the Innovative Publishing Award and a design award from *The American Society of Illustrators*. Their editorial work has received both Hugo and Howard nominations.